American Society for Training

G000024938

I N   A C T

Implementing Evaluation Systems and Processes

EIGHTEEN

CASE STUDIES

FROM THE

REAL WORLD

OF TRAINING

ASTD

JACK J. PHILLIPS

SERIES EDITOR

Ordering information: Books published by the American Society for Training & Development can be ordered by calling 800.628.2783 or 703.683.8100.

Library of Congress Catalog Card Number: 98-74118
ISBN: 1-56286-101-8

Table of Contents

Introduction to the *In Action* Series vii

Preface ix

How to Use This Casebook..xv

Systematic Evaluation: Trends and Practices..1
Jack J. Phillips

Part I: Implementing Evaluation Systems

Integrating Evaluation Into the Training Process: Iterative
Development Testing and Monitoring Training Impact 15
Andersen Consulting
Daniel J. McLinden, Bradley Kolar, Mark McDowell, and Matthew Tobias

Implementing an Evaluation Strategy 37
Nortel (Northern Telecom)
Debi Harrell, Rick Pharris, and Ron Stone

Measuring Training Throughout the Bell Atlantic Organization 45
Bell Atlantic Network Services, Inc.
Toni Hodges

The Role of ROI in a High-Performance Learning Organization ...55
Guthrie Healthcare System
*Pauline Stamp, Michele Sisto, Roberta Sabitus, Christine Burt,
Richard Rava, William Muth, Susan Hall, and Bonnie Onofre*

The Results-Based Approach of Evaluating Learning........................81
First Union's Commercial College
Debra Wallace

Building Accountability Into a Start-up University..............................99
Illinova/Illinois Power Company
Connie J. Schmidt and Jack J. Phillips

Building Evaluation Into External Education Services.....................117
Medical Assurance
Patricia D. Davis

An Evolution of Evaluation of Training and Education 129
Duke Energy Corporation
Derrick Allman

Part II: Specific Evaluation Techniques

Implementing ROI: Creating a Strategic Framework to
   Link Training to Business Results...141
Toronto-Dominion Bank
*Brian Howard, Connie Karlsson, Brenda Chong, and
Kim Japp-Delaney*

Measuring and Evaluating Training at the Technical
   Education Centers...155
Nortel (Northern Telecom)
Salvatore V. Falletta and Jill Murphy Lamb

Implementing an ROI Measurement Process.......................................179
Dell Computer
Ferdinand Tesoro

Lessons Learned With Application Evaluation 193
Exxon
John H. Reed

Assessing the Business Results of Management
   Development Using the Critical Outcome Technique 211
CIGNA Corporation
Brent W. Mattson, Lawrence J. Quartana, and Richard A. Swanson

Using Instrumentation to Manage the Business..................................229
Amoco Corporation
Dian K. Castle

Transfer of Training 243
Nordisk Kellog
Nils Asmussen

Nova Means New: One University's Evaluation for Reinvention 255
Nova State University
Heidi Henson

A Survey of Supervisors' and Managers' Perceptions of HRD
    Training Effectiveness 271
Texas Instruments' Defense System and Electronics Group
Monica Luketich

From Puzzles to Problems: Assessing the Value of Education
    in a Business Context With Concept Mapping
    and Pattern Matching...285
Andersen Consulting
Daniel J. McLinden and William M.K. Trochim

About the Series Editor 305

Introduction to the
In Action Series

As are most professionals, the people involved in human resource development (HRD) are eager to see practical applications of the models, techniques, theories, strategies, and issues the field comprises. In recent years, practitioners have developed an intense desire to learn about the success of other organizations when they implement HRD programs. The Publishing Review Committee of the American Society for Training & Development has established this series of casebooks to fill this need. Covering a variety of topics in HRD, the series should add significantly to the current literature in the field.

This series has the following objectives:

- *To provide real-world examples of HRD program application and implementation.* Each case will describe significant issues, events, actions, and activities. When possible, the actual names of the organizations and individuals involved will be used. In other cases, the names will be disguised, but the events are factual.

- *To focus on challenging and difficult issues confronting the HRD field.* These cases will explore areas where it is difficult to find information or where the processes or techniques are not standardized or fully developed. Also, emerging issues critical to success in the field will be covered in the series.

- *To recognize the work of professionals in the HRD field by presenting best practices.* Each book in the series will attempt to represent the most effective examples in the field. The most respected organizations, practitioners, authors, researchers, and consultants will be asked to provide cases.

- *To serve as a self-teaching tool for people learning about the HRD field.* As a stand-alone reference, each volume should be a very useful learning tool. Each case will contain many issues and fully explore several topics.

- *To present a medium for teaching groups about the practical aspects of HRD.* Each book should serve as a discussion guide to enhance learning in formal and informal settings. Each case will have questions for discussion. And each book will be useful as a supplement to general and specialized textbooks in HRD.

The topics for the volumes will be carefully selected to ensure that they represent important and timely issues in the HRD field. The editors for the individual volumes are experienced professionals in the field. The series will provide a high-quality product to fill a critical void in the literature. An ambitious schedule is planned.

If you have suggestions of ways to improve this series or an individual volume in the series, please respond directly to me. Your input is welcome.

Jack J. Phillips, Ph.D.
Series Editor
Performance Resources Organization
Box 380637
Birmingham, AL 35238-0637

Preface

Evaluation of human resource development continues to be a critical and demanding topic. Most organizations are struggling to solve the evaluation puzzle and tackle the issue in a systematic, logical way. Sometimes there is confusion about the degree of emphasis on evaluation and the mechanisms for the evaluation to be successfully implemented.

We hope to contribute to the understanding of the evaluation issue by offering a variety of systems, processes, and models through the case studies presented in this book. The authors, reflecting several viewpoints from varied backgrounds, are diligently pursuing evaluation of training, human resource development, and performance improvement programs. The cases cover a variety of programs from a diverse group of organizations. Collectively, they should add to the growing database of evaluation studies and make an important contribution to the literature.

Target Audience

This book should interest anyone involved in training, human resource development (HRD), human resources (HR), and performance improvement. The primary audience is practitioners who are struggling to determine the value of programs and to show how the programs contribute to an organization's goals. They are the ones who request more examples from what they often label the real world. This same group also complains that there are too many models, methods, strategies, and theories, and too few examples to show if any process really makes a difference. This publication should satisfy this need by providing successful evaluation systems, processes, and models. Also, this book should encourage more practitioners to tackle this important topic and help them avoid some of the problems that are inherent in the measurement and evaluation process.

The second audience is instructors and professors. Whether in university classes with students who are pursuing courses in HRD, internal workshops for professional HRD staff members, or public seminars on HRD implementation, this casebook will be a valuable reference. It can be used as a supplement to a standard HRD textbook or as a complement to a textbook on measurement and evaluation. As a supplemental text, this casebook will bring practical significance to training and performance improvement, convincing students that there are systematic processes, methods, and models that can evaluate programs.

A third audience is the researchers and consultants who are seeking ways to document evaluation systems and processes. This book shows the application of a wide range of processes, models, and techniques, most of which have their bases in sound theory and logical assumptions. Unfortunately, the HRD measurement and evaluation process does not have a prescribed set of standards and techniques.

The last audience, but certainly not least, is the managers who must work with HRD on a peripheral basis—managers who are participants in HRD programs to develop their own management skills, send other employees to participate in HRD programs, and who occasionally lead or conduct sessions of HRD programs. In these roles, managers must understand evaluation systems and processes and appreciate the value of HRD. This casebook should provide evidence of this value.

Each audience should find the casebook entertaining and engaging reading. Questions are placed at the end of each case to stimulate additional thought and discussion. One of the most effective ways to maximize the usefulness of this book is through group discussions, using the questions to develop and dissect the issues, techniques, systems, and processes.

The Cases

The most difficult part of developing this book was to identify case authors to contribute systematic processes and models that provide a methodical approach to the evaluation of training and performance improvement programs. Where the processes do exist, HRD staffers are not always willing to discuss them. In the search, letters were sent to more than 10,000 individuals who have an interest in evaluation. In order to tap the global market, 1,000 of the individuals contacted were outside the United States. We are pleased that more than 100 individuals requested copies of detailed case guidelines and approximately half made the commitment to develop a case. In the end, 18 case studies have been accepted for publication.

Cases for this publication have been divided into two categories. The first group, part 1, focuses on systematic and methodical evaluation practices. Too often evaluation is a sporadic or haphazard process with no integration between the different levels of evaluation. A more appropriate approach is to view evaluation as a process that must be fully integrated into the design, development, and delivery of a variety of programs. All cases in the first part take this systematic view.

In the second group, part 2, cases present specific techniques to evaluate one or more programs at one or more evaluation levels. These cases add to the richness of this volume making it a valuable reference for many issues in evaluation.

Although there was some attempt to structure cases similarly, they are not identical in style and content. It is important for the reader to experience the programs as they were developed and identify the issues pertinent to each particular setting and situation. The result is a variety of presentations with a variety of styles. Some cases are brief and to the point, outlining precisely what happened and what was achieved. Others provide more detailed background information, including how the people involved determined the need for the process, the personalities involved, and how the backgrounds and biases of the people involved create a unique situation.

There was no attempt to restrict cases to a particular methodology, technique, or process. It is helpful to show a wide range of approaches. We have resisted the temptation to pass judgment on various approaches, preferring to let the reader evaluate the different techniques and their appropriateness in their particular settings. Some of the assumptions, methodologies, and strategies might not be as comprehensive and sound as others.

Case Authors

It would be difficult to find a more impressive group of contributors to an HRD publication than those for this casebook. For such a difficult topic, we expected to find the best, and we have not been disappointed. If we had to describe the group, we would say they are experienced, professional, knowledgeable, and on the leading edge of HRD. Collectively, they represent practitioners, consultants, researchers, and professors. Individually, they represent a cross section of HRD. Most are experts, and some are well known in the field. A few are high-profile authors who have made a tremendous contribution in the HRD field and have taken the opportunity to provide an example of their top-quality work. Others have made their mark quietly and have achieved success for their organizations.

Best Practices?

In our search for cases, we contacted the most respected and well-known organizations in the world, leading experts in the field, key executives in HRD, and well-known authors and researchers. We were seeking examples that represent best practices in measurement and evaluation. Whether they have been delivered, we will never know. What we do know is that if these are not best practices, no other publication can claim to have them either. Many of the experts producing these cases characterize them as the best examples of measurement and evaluation in the field.

Suggestions

As with any new publication, we welcome your input. If you have ideas or recommendations regarding presentation, case selection, or case quality, please send them to Performance Resources Organization, P.O. Box 380637, Birmingham, AL 35238-0637; phone: 205.678.9700; e-mail: roipro@wwisp.com. The letters received will not only be appreciated, but also acknowledged. Your opinions about this book will help improve future volumes.

Acknowledgments

Although this casebook is a collective work of many individuals, the first acknowledgment must go to the case authors. We are grateful for their professional contribution. We also want to acknowledge the organizations that have allowed us to use their names and programs for publication. We realize this action may carry some risk. We trust the final product has portrayed them as progressive organizations interested in results and willing to try new processes and techniques.

At Performance Resources Organization, we would like to thank Vicki Wear for her contribution in the initial organization of this publication. Wear is a truly dedicated member of the team. We would also like to thank Tammy Bush, who has supported us for many years. Her untiring efforts and willingness to see this project through completion is greatly appreciated. Finally, we would like to thank Patti Pulliam who provided coordination and leadership with this and other casebooks. Her professionalism and customer sensitivity are excellent. Thank you for a job well done.

As always, the staff at the American Society for Training & Development are a joy to work with. Nancy Olson, vice president of publications, and Ruth Stadius, development and acquisitions editor, publications, are always supportive and willing to help ensure the success of each publication. Thank you.

Jack J. Phillips
Birmingham, Alabama
November 1998

How to Use This Casebook

These cases present a variety of evaluation strategies, processes, and models that have been systematically integrated into the design, development, and delivery of a variety of human resource development (HRD) programs. Collectively, the cases offer a wide range of settings, methods, techniques, strategies, and approaches representing service, technology, and educational organizations. Target groups for the programs vary from all employees to managers to technical specialists. Programs focus on training and development, organization development, and performance improvement. As a group, these cases represent a rich source of information about the strategies of some of the best practitioners, consultants, and researchers in the field.

Each case does not necessarily represent the ideal approach for the specific situation. In every case it is possible to identify areas that could benefit from refinement and improvement. That is part of the learning process, to build on the work of other people. Although the evaluation processes are contextual, the methods and techniques can be used in other organizations.

Table 1 presents basic descriptions of the cases in the order in which they appear in the book. This table can serve as a quick reference for readers who want to examine the evaluation approach for a particular type of program, audience, or industry.

Using the Cases

There are several ways to use this book. It will be helpful to anyone who wants to see real-life examples of the business results of training and performance improvement programs. Specifically, this book will:

- be useful to HRD professionals as a basic reference of practical applications of systematic evaluation processes. A reader can analyze and dissect each of the cases to develop an understanding

Table 1. Overview of case studies by industry, program, and target audience.

Case	Industry	Program	Target Audience
Andersen Consulting	Consulting	Goal-based learning organization wide	Program developers, sponsors, content experts, and managers
Nortel (Northern Telecom)	Telecommunications	All programs in the Nortel Learning Institute	Management and professional employees
Bell Atlantic Network Services, Inc.	Telecommunications	All programs in network services	All employees
Guthrie Healthcare System	Health care	Personal, professional, and management development programs	Senior executives, managers, professional employees
Illinova/Illinois Power Company	Electric and gas utility	Corporate university programs	Senior managers, managers, staff
First Union's Commercial College	Banking	Wholesale banking college programs	Senior management, managers, employees
Medical Assurance	Health care	Education services	Senior managers, physicians, physician office staff, clinics, hospitals
Duke Energy Corporation	Energy services	Shared-services programs	Managers, technical specialists
Toronto-Dominion Bank	Banking	Corporate education center programs	Senior managers, managers, employees
Nortel (Northern Telecom)	Telecommunications	Technical training solutions	Senior managers, managers, technical specialists, employees

Company	Industry	Training	Audience
Dell Computer	Computer technology	Sales negotiation training	Sales representatives, managers, directors
Exxon	Petroleum	Personal computer training	Managers, instructors, training suppliers
CIGNA Corporation	Insurance	Management development	Senior managers, training team members, HR professionals
Amoco Corporation	Petroleum	Business management	Executives, HR managers, performance consultants
Nordisk Kellog	Food production	Maintenance training	Managers, employees
Nova State University	Education	Diversity training	Managers, facilitators, employees
Texas Instruments	Electronics	Industrial training	Managers, supervisors
Andersen Consulting	Consulting	Concept mapping and pattern matching	Executives, development team, employees

of the issues, approaches, and, most of all, possible refinements or improvements.

- be useful in group discussions where interested individuals can react to the material, offer different perspectives, and draw conclusions about approaches and techniques. The questions at the end of each case can serve as a beginning point for lively and entertaining discussions.

- serve as an excellent supplement to other training and development or evaluation textbooks. It provides the extra dimensions of real-life cases that show the milestones, targets, and goals that have been or will be achieved with evaluation processes.

- be extremely valuable for managers who do not have primary training and performance improvement responsibility. These managers provide support and assistance to the HRD staff, and it is helpful for them to understand the processes used to evaluate HRD programs.

Follow Up

Space limitations have required that some cases be shorter than the author and editor would have liked. Some information concerning background, assumptions, strategies, and results had to be omitted. If additional information on a case is needed, the authors can be contacted directly. The authors' addresses are listed at the end of each case.

Systematic Evaluation: Trends and Practices

Jack J. Phillips

Although organizations have focused much attention on evaluation in the past 40 years, only recently have organizations taken a systematic and comprehensive approach to evaluating training and development, human resource development, and performance improvement initiatives. The outdated, traditional approach to evaluation had the following characteristics:

• Evaluation was considered an "add-on" process after a program had been conducted.
• Evaluation projects were often reactive in nature, conducted only after an influential executive or administrator questioned the value of a specific program.
• Most evaluation data collection consisted of end-of-program questionnaires.
• There was a lack of consistent approaches and successful examples of a comprehensive evaluation process.

Now the situation has dramatically changed. Most organizations are taking a systematic approach to evaluation as they implement a comprehensive process for accountability of human resource development expenditures. This approach involves five key elements, including:

• developing a framework for evaluation appropriate for the organization
• designing evaluation into new programs and processes
• using a systematic process to measure the impact of specific programs
• defining roles and responsibilities for evaluation and accountability
• implementing and communicating the evaluation process and progress.

A description of each element appears in this chapter, which introduces case studies that illustrate a systematic approach.

Needed: A Framework

A systematic evaluation process begins with development of an overall framework to collect evaluation data. Although there have been dozens of approaches, models, and frameworks in recent years, no framework has been as useful and accepted as the concept of the levels of evaluation conceived by Kirkpatrick at the University of Wisconsin in 1959 (Kirkpatrick, 1975). The original work contained four levels of evaluation, which the author has updated to include five levels (Phillips, 1995). As table 1 shows, the five levels focus on diverse types of data collected at different times.

At Level 1, companies collect reaction data directly from participants, usually at the end of a program, to determine the degree to which the program met their specific needs and how effective and successful they perceived it to be. In practice, organizations capture reaction data for most of their programs, usually in the 90 percent to 100 percent range. Some organizations have added an extra dimension at this level, planned actions. Here, they ask participants to outline specific actions they plan as a result of their participation in the program.

At Level 2, companies use various formal and informal methods to measure learning. Because there is no guarantee that a positive reaction to the program will ensure that learning has occurred, it is important to determine the extent to which participants have learned. In practice, most organizations measure learning in about 50 percent to 70 percent of their programs.

Table 1. Evaluation levels.

Level	Description
Reaction and planned action	Measures participant's reaction to the program and outlines specific plans for implementation.
Learning	Measures skills, knowledge, or attitude changes.
Application	Measures changes in on-the-job behavior and specific applications of the training material.
Business impact	Measures business impact of the program.
Return-on-investment	Compares the monetary value of the results with the costs for the program, usually expressed as a percentage.

At Level 3, participants use a variety of follow-up processes to measure on-the-job application. A follow-up evaluation is needed to ensure that learners have transferred what they learned and utilized it on the job. In practice, 20 percent to 30 percent of programs are usually evaluated at this level.

At Level 4, business impact of the application of skills and knowledge is measured in a variety of ways. Some stakeholders are more interested in the bottom-line impact of training. Consequently, business measures become critically important. In practice, companies evaluate about 10 percent to 20 percent of programs at this level.

Finally, at Level 5, the return-on-investment (ROI) is calculated. In this process, companies determine the payoff of the investment in training by comparing the monetary benefits of training's impact on the business with the costs of the program. The ROI has been a recent addition to the evaluation process, and approximately 5 percent to 10 percent of programs are evaluated at this level.

These levels of evaluation are common within organizations and provide a practical overall framework for evaluation. Most of the cases in this casebook use this concept.

Needed: Built-in Evaluation With the New Program Rollout

To avoid the problems associated with the perception that evaluation is an "add-on" process, many organizations are building evaluation into programs, beginning with the needs assessment. As shown in figure 1, a built-in process addresses evaluation early and integrates it throughout the design, development, and delivery stages.

The initial steps of evaluation take place during the needs assessment and analysis process. The training organization, a department, a consultant, or a team of consultants may have responsibility for the process. One or more of the people responsible take charge of the following steps. They identify specific business measures, job performance needs, and skills and knowledge deficiencies, and they develop solutions that may include the need for learning. Armed with all of the data, they can formulate an evaluation strategy and develop specific measurable objectives for learning, application, and impact. This process provides direction for the other traditional steps, with a focus on specific results. With detailed objectives, the design and development stage of the program focuses on the specific outcomes using relevant examples, cases, exercises, and activities. Implementation and delivery will emphasize the desired outcomes of learning, application, and impact. The people responsible tabulate all direct and indirect costs of the program and collect various out-

Figure 1. Program process with evaluation built in.

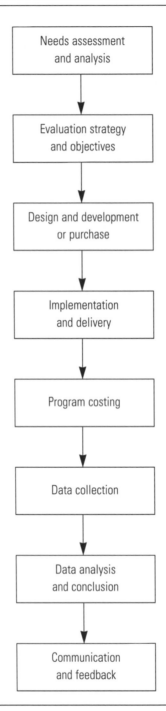

put data representing application and impact. They analyze data, draw conclusions, and communicate the results to the appropriate target groups. This approach to new program design and implementation brings additional focus on results, ensuring that the program not only meets the desired needs but also provides evidence of success. Some models are more comprehensive than the one in figure 1. One very popular model has 18 steps, with no less than 11 devoted to measurement and evaluation (Phillips, 1997a).

Needed: A Process to Measure Postprogram Success

As more organizations place additional emphasis on Level 3, 4, and 5 evaluation, a process is needed to develop specific impact. This process must meet very rigid criteria and account for the influences of other factors or provide an option to collect data at Levels 3 and 4 and develop the Level 5 evaluation. Hundreds of organizations have adopted the model in figure 2 to measure postprogram impact (Phillips, 1997b).

Defining Roles and Responsibilities

Defining specific responsibilities of all stakeholders is critical to the success of a systematic evaluation process. The primary respon-

Figure 2. ROI model.

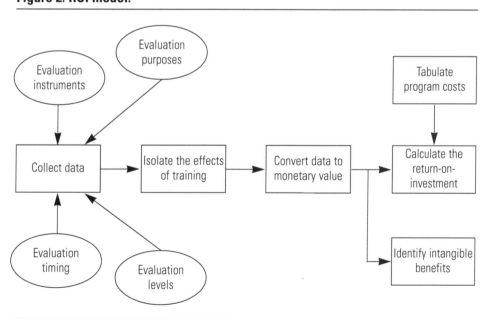

sibilities rest with the training and development staff and are typically divided into two broad areas. The first, and often overlooked area, is the evaluation responsibility for the entire training and development staff, particularly those who are involved in developing and delivering programs and solutions. The typical responsibilities that illustrate the integration of evaluation throughout the training and development cycle include the following:

- ensuring that the needs assessment includes specific business impact measures
- developing specific application objectives (Level 3) and business impact objectives (Level 4) for each program
- focusing the content of the program on performance improvement, ensuring that exercises, case studies, and skill practices relate to the desired objectives
- keeping participants focused on application and impact objectives
- communicating rationale and reasons for evaluation
- assisting in follow-up activities to capture application and business impact data
- providing technical assistance for data collection, data analysis, and reporting
- designing instruments and plans for data collection and analysis
- presenting evaluation data to a variety of groups.

The second area is the technical support to evaluation. Depending on the size and scope of the training and development effort, this responsibility could range from a part-time duty for one person to a full-time responsibility for a whole support team. When the technical support group is established, it must be understood that the experts are not there to relieve others of evaluation responsibility, but to supplement technical expertise. When this type of support is developed, responsibilities revolve around six key areas:

- designing data collection instruments
- providing assistance for developing an evaluation strategy
- analyzing data including specialized statistical analysis
- interpreting results and making specific recommendations
- developing an evaluation report or case study to communicate results
- providing technical support in any part of the evaluation process.

It is also necessary to define responsibilities for the participants and their immediate managers. Too often participants are unaware of their responsibilities to apply or utilize what they have learned and report the results. Their input is critical to the success of the evaluation. In addition, the participant's manager is important to the effectiveness of the program and is sometimes involved in collecting critical evaluation data. The manager exerts a tremendous influence over evaluation. Consequently, some organizations specifically detail responsibilities for both participants and their managers. Following are the typical responsibilities for these two groups, taken from a large multinational organization:

- **Participants** in learning solutions have important responsibilities. They must:
  - participate fully in learning solutions to learn as much as possible.
  - explore ways in which learning can be applied on the job.
  - partner with their manager to choose learning solutions that can best improve business performance.
  - enter into the learning solution with an open mind and be willing to learn new concepts and develop new skills.
  - take responsibility for success of the application of the learning solution.
  - when requested, provide information and feedback on the success of the learning solution and the barriers to implementation.
  - partner with their manager to identify and remove barriers to the application of the learning solution.
  - have the determination to achieve success with the learning solution in the face of many obstacles to application and improvement.
- The **participant's managers** have the responsibility to:
  - partner with their employees in enrolling in learning solutions intended to improve business performance.
  - when appropriate, discuss the learning solution with the participant prior to attendance or involvement to determine expected outcomes.
  - conduct a personal follow-up for the solution results.
  - reinforce behavior after the solution has been implemented and provide positive feedback and rewards for successful application of the learning solution.
  - assist in the planned formal follow-up activities of the learning solution.
  - be proactive in identifying and removing barriers to the application of learning solutions.

Finally, in some situations, the senior executive group may have specific responsibilities for achieving results with training and development. These revolve around issues of providing direction, allocating funds, supporting the process, and allocating time to ensure that the process is successful. Ensuring that responsibilities are clearly defined and communicated will help make the training and development process successful and guarantee that evaluation is systematic, comprehensive, and timely.

Implementing and Communicating the Evaluation Process

Making the transition from the traditional approach of a reactive evaluation process to a more comprehensive and systematic effort will require planning and monitoring as well as reviewing the progress. Several key elements are involved. First, the appropriate person or team establishes targets and goals to provide direction and focus. Typically, the team sets targets for each level of evaluation. These targets enable the staff to focus on improvements at different levels of evaluation. Following this approach, the team members develop the percent of programs planned for evaluation at each level after an assessment of the present situation. They tabulate the number of all programs, including repeated sections of a program, along with the corresponding levels of evaluation presently conducted for each program. They calculate the percent of programs using Level 1 reaction questionnaires. The same percentage is calculated for each level. After detailing the current situation, the team establishes realistic targets for improvement, which may be within a particular time frame. Many organizations set annual targets for planned improvements. Table 2 shows the targets for Nortel Learning Institute, a part of Nortel, a large global telecommunications company. This target-setting process should involve the input of the entire training and development staff to ensure that targets are realistic and the staff is committed to the process.

Another important part of the implementation is project planning for the transition. A transition plan helps the organization manage change in a more systematic way. Items on the schedule include,

Table 2. Evaluation targets for a large telecommunications company.

Level		Percent of Courses
Level 1	Participant satisfaction	100%
Level 2	Learning	50%
Level 3	On-the-job application (behavior)	30%
Level 4	Results	20%
Level 5	Return-on-investment	10%

but are not limited to, developing specific impact studies, building staff skills in measurement and evaluation, developing evaluation policy and procedures, teaching managers the accountability process, and communicating the results at different levels of evaluation. The more detailed the plan, the more useful it will become. The project plan is a living, long-term document that is reviewed frequently and adjusted as necessary. Table 3 shows the transition plan for a large petroleum company.

Another important part of implementing an evaluation plan and communicating the steps and process is to develop or revise the policies, procedures, and guidelines concerning measurement and evaluation. The policy statement, often a part of the overall policy for developing and implementing training and development programs, contains information specific to measurement and evaluation, and its development usually has input from the training and human resource development staff and sometimes from key managers or clients. The policy statement addresses critical issues that will influence the effectiveness of measurement and evaluation. Typical topics include the evaluation framework, the use of objectives, responsibilities for evaluation, types of instruments used, and the communication of results. Policy statements provide guidance and direction to the staff and others who work closely with evaluation. Most organizations also develop detailed procedures and guidelines for the measurement and evaluation process. These guidelines show how to utilize the tools and techniques to guide the design process and ensure consistency with evaluation throughout the organization. The guidelines are more technical than policy statements and often contain detailed steps showing how the process is actually developed and utilized for a particular program. Table 4 shows the table of contents of the evaluation guidelines for a large multinational organization.

Another part of implementation is to develop specific plans for the communication process. These plans define precisely the type of data that will be communicated to specific target audiences. Also, as impact studies are conducted, the results must be communicated to different audiences, and these special event communications must be carefully planned and orchestrated. A part of the communication is to conduct an annual training or HRD review with the senior executive team. This review provides an opportunity to present the success of training and development and obtain executive commitment and support. It is also an appropriate opportunity to address concerns that may have developed from the evaluation processes.

Table 3. Transition plan (by month) for a large petroleum company.

	J	F	M	A	M	J	J	A	S	O	N	D	J	F	M	A	M	J	J	A	S	O	N
Team formed	▓																						
Policy developed		▓	▓																				
Targets set			▓																				
Workshops developed			▓	▓	▓	▓																	
ROI project (A)						▓	▓	▓	▓														
ROI project (B)									▓	▓	▓	▓											
ROI project (C)											▓	▓	▓	▓									
ROI project (D)												▓	▓	▓	▓	▓							
HRD staff trained								▓	▓							▓	▓						
Vendors trained																							
Managers trained																		▓	▓	▓	▓		
Support tools developed		▓	▓	▓																			
Evaluation guidelines developed			▓	▓	▓																		

Table 4. Table of contents for the evaluation guidelines of a multinational company.

Section 1: Policy
1.1 The Need for Accountability
1.2 The Bottom Line: Linking Training With Business Needs
1.3 Results-Based Approach
1.4 Implications
1.5 Communication
1.6 Payoff

Section 2: Responsibilities
2.1 Training Group Responsibilities: Overall
2.2 Training Group Responsibilities: Specifics for Selected Groups
2.3 The Business Unit Responsibilities
2.4 Participant Manager Responsibilities
2.5 Participants Responsibilities

Section 3: Evaluation Framework
3.1 Purpose of Evaluation
3.2 Levels of Evaluation
3.3 Process Steps for Training Implementation
3.4 Evaluation Model

Section 4: Level 1 Guidelines
4.1 Purpose and Scope
4.2 Areas of Coverage—Standard Form
4.3 Optional Areas of Coverage
4.4 Administrative Issues
4.5 How to Use Level 1 Data

Section 5: Level 2 Guidelines
5.1 Purpose and Scope
5.2 Learning Measurement Issues
5.3 Techniques for Measuring Learning
5.4 Administration
5.5 Using Level 2 Data

Section 6: Level 3 Guidelines
6.1 Purpose and Scope
6.2 Follow-Up Issues
6.3 Types of Follow-Up Techniques
6.4 Administrative Issues
6.5 Using Level 3 Evaluation

Section 7: Level 4 and 5 Guidelines
7.1 Purpose and Scope
7.2 Business Results and ROI Issues
7.3 Monitoring Performance Data
7.4 Extracting Data from Follow-Up Evaluation
7.5 Isolating the Effects of the Learning Solution
7.6 Converting Data to Monetary Values
7.7 Developing Costs
7.8 Calculating the ROI
7.9 Identifying Intangible Benefits
7.10 Administrative Issues
7.11 Using Business Impact and ROI Data

The Systematic Process Continues

This brief introduction has attempted to illustrate how organizations are taking a more comprehensive and systematic approach to evaluate the investment in training and human resource development. The cases in this book highlight different approaches and underscore the successes and rewards for taking the systematic and planned approach to evaluation.

References

Kirkpatrick, D.L. (1975). "Techniques for Evaluating Training Programs." *Evaluating Training Programs*. Alexandria, VA: American Society for Training & Development, pp. 1–17.

Phillips, J.J. (1995). "Return on Investment—Beyond the Four Levels." In E. Holton (editor), *Academy of HRD 1995 Conference Proceedings*. Baton Rouge, LA: Academy of HRD.

Phillips, J.J. (1997a). *Handbook of Training Evaluation and Measurement Methods* (3d edition). Houston: Gulf.

Phillips, J.J. (1997b). *Return on Investment in Training and Performance Improvement Programs*. Houston: Gulf.

Part I

Implementing Evaluation Systems

Integrating Evaluation Into the Training Process: Iterative Development Testing and Monitoring Training Impact

Andersen Consulting

Daniel J. McLinden, Bradley Kolar, Mark McDowell,
and Matthew Tobias

Pilot testing of training programs prior to completion is a well-accepted procedure in the development of training programs. It is a challenge, however, to integrate the different functions of training design and training evaluation. In an effort to make evaluation more useful to the development process, we integrated evaluation into the design and development process. In addition to moving evaluation activities earlier in the life cycle, we also changed the tasks. Specifically, the evaluation tasks were important for effective development, and effective development was important for the evaluation tasks. Our intent with this model has been to move away from the perspective of evaluation as an isolated measurement event conducted at the conclusion of an educational program. Rather, we attempted to thread evaluation processes throughout training processes. In this way, evaluation encompassed both the testing of educational products in development and assessment of the performance of the training product that has been implemented.

Background

At Andersen Consulting's internal training organization, the testing of educational products prior to finalizing and releasing them to the organization is a well-accepted practice. However, in a recent project, an innovative approach to learning necessitated a corresponding innovation in the evaluation process. In this case, the learning environment did not include topical lectures; instead, this was a simu-

This case was prepared to serve as a basis for discussion rather than to illustrate either effective or ineffective administrative and management practices.

lation of the work environment or a goal-based scenario (GBS), a learning framework predicated on the idea that individuals learn best when presented with information in context and at the point of need. Further, a GBS environment is based on the premise that learning occurs at a point when an individual's prediction of what will occur in a given situation fails. Simply put, there is truth to the adage that we learn from our mistakes. However, although the idea may be stated simply, the development of a powerful learning experience that incorporates GBS principles is a complex undertaking.

A GBS is not organized around a series of individual topics with a centralized leader or teacher who disseminates information. Rather than a teacher focus, a goal-based environment facilitates learning by presenting the learner with a goal to achieve, information necessary to achieve the goal, and the necessary support to build skills and correct mistakes. For example, a goal may be for a team to design a job for a new position in the organization. In attempting to reach this goal, the learner will gather data (for example, the legal aspects of personnel issues in job design), make decisions (for example, to determine the acceptable hiring profile), and take actions (accept or reject candidates) to reach the goal. In the process, learners will often discover their lack of necessary knowledge or skill. At that point, the learner can access reference systems, coaches, process guides, and other support tools that provide information to reach the goal. In choosing to seek help, learners direct their learning on the basis of their need for information or feedback at the point at which they determine they need help. However, because this is a learning environment, mistakes happen. For example, the learner may not recognize or anticipate the need for information or feedback and, as a result, will make a mistake, such as adding an inappropriate hiring criterion. In this environment, coaches or other support personnel let mistakes continue until learners see the results of their actions. Then, at an appropriate point, the coach intervenes to help the learner make sense of the situation and to take corrective actions.

Because goal-based learning environments are quite different from traditional learning environments, these programs present new and complex challenges for training evaluation. In this environment, it was not reasonable to ask trainees for an opinion about a topic (such as a topic on teamwork) or some feature of the program (faculty, for example) and then to infer the quality of learning. Topics or time-limited packages of content did not exist, faculty performed different roles (for example, role-playing a client or acting as a process coach), and individual students focused their time on different learning opportunities. As a result of this atypical learning environment, a unique approach to training evaluation was needed. Consequently, the authors viewed this as an opportunity to make evaluation activities more responsive to the needs of the team developing this program. Implementing this strategy required the development of a structured process that incorporated both quantitative measurement and qualitative methods. In addition to collecting data, we expanded the role of evaluation to articulate detailed expectations for program effects prior to collecting data. In other words, we created our own internal benchmark or theory for the course, which we subsequently tested with the collected data.

The General Evaluation Model

Our general model, shown in figure 1, is characterized by evaluation iterations through the cycles of developing and delivering training. One difference between phases is intensity; development evaluation was much more intense than delivery. Intensive testing during the development ensured the development of a high-quality educational product before release to the organization. Further, we used an iterative approach to development testing to ensure that the correct decisions were being made and implemented long before development was complete. Rather than simply providing a grade on performance at the conclusion of the testing event, evaluation activities were integrated with training activities in a proactive "assurance" manner rather than a reactive "testing" manner.

Lessons from other industries may help to illustrate this perspective. Consider the development of a computer system. The effort required for error correction increases by several degrees of magnitude as a project proceeds further into development. Likewise, in manufacturing, total quality management (TQM) principles have shifted the focus of quality assurance from a quality check at the end of the assembly line to several quality assurance checks throughout the assembly. Learning environments have all of the complexity of computer or manufacturing systems, and it is appropriate to take a lesson from those disciplines. In training development, iterative testing identifies necessary improvements when the cost of rework is at its lowest. At the point when the course is out of development and is of sufficient quality for general release, less inquiry is necessary. In the postdevelopment period, two evaluation goals need to be met. First, conduct sufficient evaluation to monitor the program, and second, conduct sufficient evaluation to ensure that the clear and defensible conclusions can be drawn and communicated to stakeholders.

Figure 1. Iterative evaluation model.

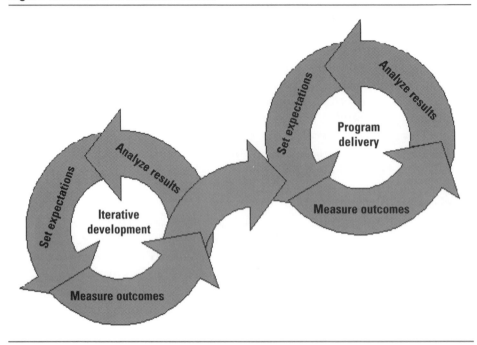

Our intent with this model has been to move away from the perspective of evaluation as an isolated measurement event conducted at the conclusion of an educational program. Rather, we attempted to thread evaluation processes throughout training processes. In this way evaluation encompassed both the iterative testing of educational products in development and the assessing of the performance of the implemented training product. We begin this case with a description of an innovation in evaluation methodology: concept mapping and pattern matching. We then illustrate the application of this methodology, first in the formative evaluation of a training program in development and second in the ongoing evaluation to monitor the effectiveness of the same program.

New Approaches to Measuring Training Effects
Gathering the Evidence—Measurement Methods

Concept mapping is an analytical process that integrates the diverse views of different stakeholder groups about a single domain into a consensus view. Given the fact that training programs are designed to change people and organizations, our view is that these programs are quite complex and that evaluation ought to take that complexity into account. Of particular value is the fact that a concept map can organize the evaluation tasks and represent complexity in a manner that is understandable by the stakeholders in the training effort. In turn, these features allow the process of concept mapping to influence both development and evaluation efforts.[1] We will briefly outline the steps in the process here. For more detail, consult the suggested readings at the end of this chapter.

GENERATE THE OUTCOMES. Each stakeholder in the program contributes to naming the expected outcomes. Stakeholders provide specific statements of what they expect program participants will know or be able to do as a result of the training program. Given that stakeholders include program sponsors, content experts, developers, and management, the resulting outcomes are both diverse and numerous. Our intent in this step is to get all stakeholders to participate actively and articulate their assumptions about the impact of the training program.

STRUCTURE THE OUTCOME DOMAIN. Each stakeholder sorts the entire list of outcomes and groups items according to similarity of meaning. The intent in this step is to determine the smaller number of concepts represented in the ideas generated in the prior step. However, rather than engaging in group effort, often impossible because stakeholders may be distributed around the world, we have used a statistically based process to decide on the final groups.[2] The results of each individual's sorting or structuring of items can be combined and represented as a two-dimensional map. Each outcome is represented as a point on the map, much like a city on the map of a country. Points that are close to each other are considered by the stakeholders as being quite similar, whereas points that are far apart are viewed as being quite dissimilar. Because outcomes can be diverse and numerous, we have found it useful to create groups of outcomes with titles that describe the theme or concept implied by the group items. Using the map metaphor, this would be like creating boundaries around cities and calling these boundaries states. Analytically, we also used a statistical process to cluster points into concepts.[3]

VALUE THE OUTCOMES. In order to ascertain the design assumptions that influence the development of the course, stakeholders responsible for the course individually rated expected levels of achievement. They based their ratings on their view of what training participants could achieve on each outcome. Expectation values were aggregated, and then an average was calculated by item and also for each concept. This value system became the baseline against which we judged performance.

Evaluation in the Development Process

Although concept mapping provided value as an evaluation process, this and other data collection strategies still needed to be integrated into the development process. We designed a four-step process, shown in figure 2, to provide detail for executing evaluation and development tasks.

Plan

COURSE STRUCTURE. First, we defined the course structure—the parameters of the learning experience. For example, will this be a classroom experience? How many days will the training last? Additionally, at a broad level, what outcomes will the course achieve? This step served to provide stakeholders, including evaluators, with a common view of the final product. In this example, the focus was a two-week GBS of a consulting environment for new staff. The program was modularized into three segments. Training participants needed to work in teams as they would be expected to perform on the job. Faculty played the roles of clients and managers, and trainees played the role of staff. In the second module, which is reported in this case, trainees were given the assignment, or goal, to develop the conceptual design for an educational program to improve employee skills in a fictitious company.

DEFINE CONCEPTS. The second activity in the planning process involved identifying the specific skills that lead to the desired performance outcomes. Concept mapping was used to enumerate the specific outcomes for the program (module two in this instance) and the conceptual structure for those outcomes. Managers, developers, and content experts developed the list of outcomes (n=79), sorted the outcomes, and rated the expected achievement on each outcome. The result was a concept map, shown in figure 3, picturing the outcomes that should result from this module.

ESTABLISH VISION FOR RESOURCES. Once the outcomes were identified and clustered, the third step was to determine how best to teach those skills. Examples of teaching resources include instructors, computer-based support, and print materials. Each of these resources is under the control of the developer and can impart information, skills, or knowledge. Because the developer has a limited number of resources, each resource must be used as effectively and efficiently as possible. To do this, developers established a strategy for deploying the resources. For example, a vision for the resources might broadly describe the role of faculty in this course, such as how faculty should play the role

Figure 2. Evaluation in the development cycle.

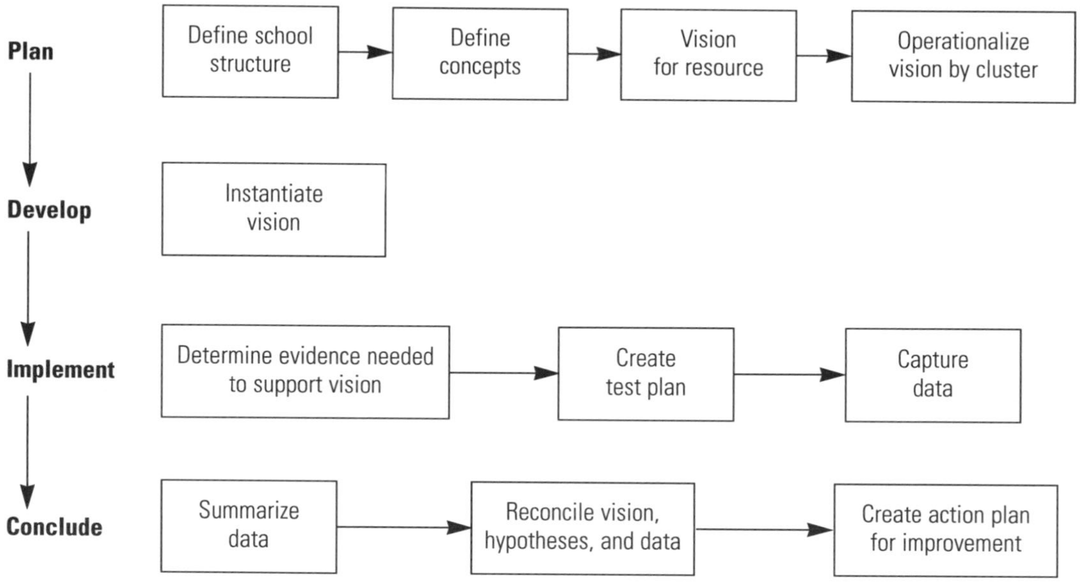

Plan →

Develop →

Implement →

Conclude

Define school structure → Define concepts → Vision for resource → Operationalize vision by cluster

Instantiate vision

Determine evidence needed to support vision → Create test plan → Capture data

Summarize data → Reconcile vision, hypotheses, and data → Create action plan for improvement

Figure 3. Expected outcomes.

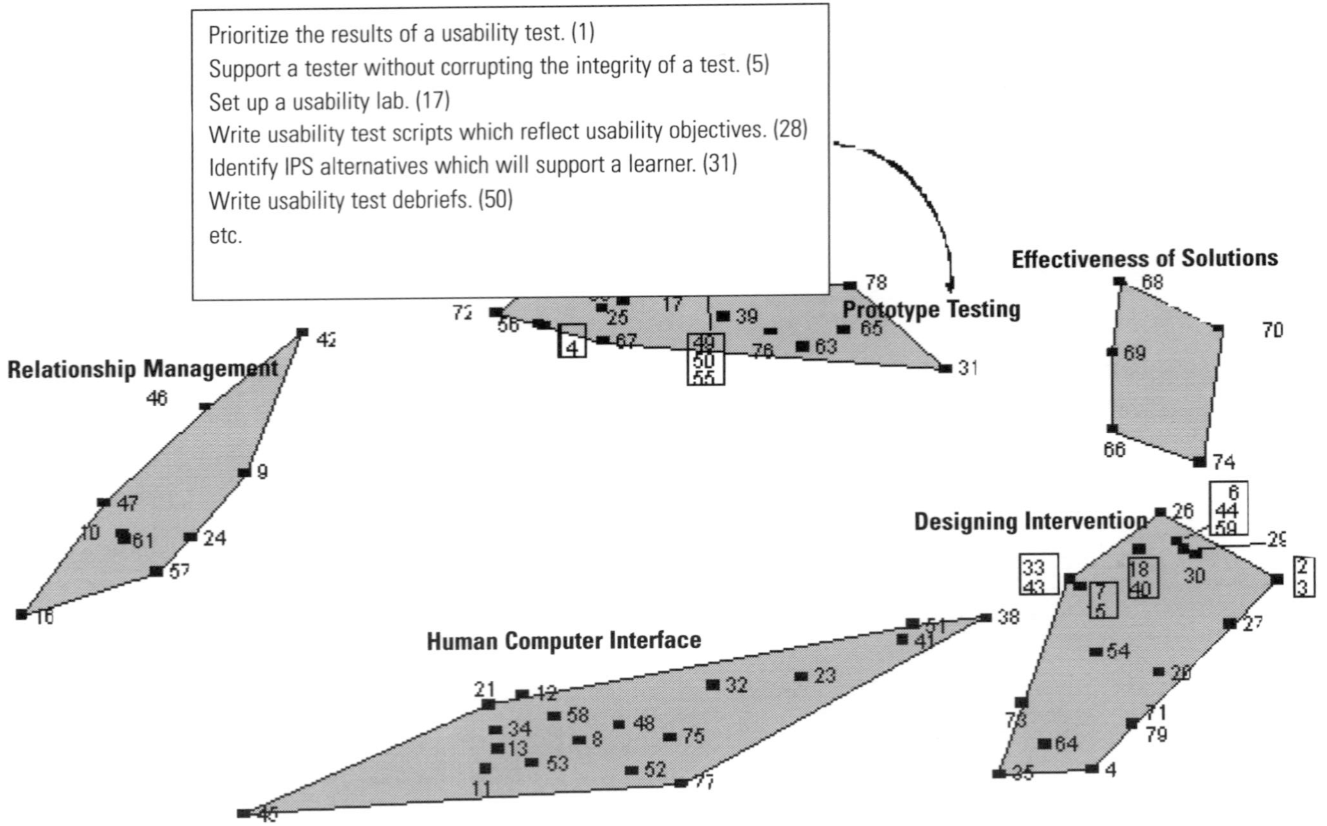
Prioritize the results of a usability test. (1)
Support a tester without corrupting the integrity of a test. (5)
Set up a usability lab. (17)
Write usability test scripts which reflect usability objectives. (28)
Identify IPS alternatives which will support a learner. (31)
Write usability test debriefs. (50)
etc.
Relationship Management
Prototype Testing
Effectiveness of Solutions
Designing Intervention
Human Computer Interface

of a client in the simulation, to what extent faculty acting as managers or clients should challenge staff, how helpful faculty should be, on what points should faculty coaches focus, and so on.

OPERATIONALIZE THE VISION. Once the developers established a strategy for each resource, they assigned the methods by which each resource would support each learning outcome. Basically, cause-and-effect relationships were hypothesized between events designed into the learning environment and the performance outcomes desired for students. A technique for summarizing and portraying the relationship of causes and effects was to array the learning outcomes and resources in a matrix, as shown in figure 4. The developers then determined how each resource supported each learning outcome and what evidence would substantiate a conclusion that the desired effect had occurred. In other words, the theory of the course was articulated in the cells of the matrix. Specifically, how a given instructional resource would cause an outcome was explicitly stated. Further, the designer could look across the rows (expected learning outcomes) to see if each outcome was properly supported. (Higher-priority items should generally have more resources.) Similarly, the designer could look down a column (resource) to see if the resource was being used consistently. With a clear vision of what the performance outcomes are and how to effect them, the designers developed the learning event. Likewise, the evaluators were in a position to develop methods to assess the theory expressed in the cells of the matrix.

Develop

Given the plan, the developers created the performance solution. This involved the development of learner materials, performance aids, and so on. The concept map and vision matrix continued to serve as guiding tools to help designers identify which media to use for the various materials they created. By comparing new materials with the vision matrix, designers ensured that they were making the best possible use of each resource. In other words, development of the product and evaluation of the product shared the same basis.

Test

Testing was done in three iterations. The two initial tests were characterized by draft materials and high support of the learning event, and the final testing was characterized by nearly finalized materials and minimal support. The purpose of iterative testing was to incrementally improve methods and materials used in the program

Figure 4. Linking instructional resources (causes) with outcomes (effects).

	Resources		
Expected Learning Outcomes	**Case Materials**	**Faculty**	**Activities**
1. Partnering			
2. Prototyping	How will case materials CAUSE learning the proto-typing? What evidence will exist that demonstrates that case materials are supporting prototyping?		
3. Etc.			

before the final release of this program to the intended audience. Evaluation involved testing the cause-effect relationships between resources and performance outcomes. For example, the performance support database in the training program was supposed to support the outcome of prototyping. Issues included how this would occur, what students would do, when they would do it, what evidence would be generated, and so on. The performance support database contained examples of testing protocols, information on prototyping, and the like. The hypothesized cause-effect relationship stated that someone from each team of trainees would review the database and extract key points to discuss with colleagues. The theory further stated that not everyone would review the database because this would be redundant effort and not consistent with the way work is performed in the field. If evidence obtained was not consistent with the theory of use for this resource (for example, the database will not support this outcome), the developer was in a position to revise the theory on the basis of new evidence, seek other ways to support the outcome, or revise the instructional design to increase the impact of the database. Obviously, inquiry was required to reach conclusions, and several strategies were required to provide the evidence necessary to reach conclusions.

First, throughout the test of the program, individuals in the role of evaluator observed the training event. Specifically, in this course, evaluators considered the activity of the classroom and recorded their observations (for example, how trainees were interacting with the performance support database, what information they were using, and for what purposes). Evaluators also noted ideas for improving any problems they observed. Observers recorded and coded points by resource and by outcome; in effect, recording was a version of the cause-and-effect matrix.

Second, evaluators and developers debriefed students several times a week. However, rather than being asked for their opinions about the program, students were asked to describe what they did during the day and what they learned as a result of their activities. In effect, this inquiry constituted a task or job analysis for the students' simulated role. In asking students why they made a certain decision, the evaluator could probe for specific criteria or the origination point of the decision, or both. For example, one of the main functions of the support tool was to "suggest" courses of actions that students could take. In some cases students made decisions without using the support tool. In other cases the support tool provided the impetus for the decision. Although the decisions might be the same, training caused the outcome in one case and prior experience caused the outcome in another. When evaluation focuses on "how satisfied" students are with a training program rather than "what occurred," the risk of drawing erroneous conclusions about the effectiveness of training is significant. In this case, if an outcome was achieved, it was not assumed that learning took place as a result of the instructional design unless specific evidence was uncovered to support that claim. For example, if students made appropriate decisions and used the support tool, a reasonable conclusion would be that the support tool contributed to the outcome. This approach avoided the error of concluding that the instructional design caused a particular outcome, when in fact the students already might have known the appropriate action due to other causes, such as prior work experience. Alternatively, in cases where students did not perform as expected—that is, the students' descriptions of their experiences were at odds with the theory—the interviewer was able to pose the theoretical scenario to the students for critical consideration. In turn, students could then explain why they had not seen that scenario as viable, describe obstacles, and so on. The value here is that evaluators obtained facts about an activity, not opinions about student desires. The development team then considered these facts in comparison with the theory of the program.

Third, at the conclusion of the test, students evaluated their own learning on a questionnaire. In addition to asking overarching questions about their attitudes about the program, students were also asked to assess their learning on each of the 79 outcome statements generated during the plan phase. To complete this task, students rated their current level of proficiency on a five-point scale (1=little or no proficiency, 5=able to perform this task independently). These data were then compared with the expected outcomes.

Conclude

The final phase, conclude, provides designers with an opportunity to assess the impact of their product and to set forth an action plan for making improvements. Extensive data obtained from a variety of sources in the pilot resulted in a significant quantity of data. However, because of the effort in the "plan" phase, managing the data was a relatively straightforward task. First, the extensive qualitative data from observations and debriefings were summarized into the original vision matrix to help the developers assess the degree to which the design enabled performance. Second, the degree to which the outcomes were met was reviewed. With the results, the developers drew conclusions, identified next steps, and prioritized their work.

Reviewing evaluation data involves risks of responding reactively to feedback generated from the test and, in an effort to address users' concerns, making the wrong types of changes. For example, during a test, some participants may indicate a need for the coach to provide more facts about the company in the case study. Simultaneously, other participants may want more facts about that company built into the reference system. Without realizing it, designers may address each issue separately, adding content to both coaching materials and the reference system. Over time, as these types of changes are made, the various support vehicles for the learning environment begin to become more homogenous, losing their original purpose. Learners become increasingly confused as they no longer know what to expect from the various resources. Also, each resource loses its original power and purpose.

By starting with a vision for how resources are to be used and how resources should aid in the learning outcomes, designers have an alternative base from which to make decisions. In the previous case, the designer would determine which resource had responsibility for disseminating case materials. The designer would then seek an explanation for why that current resource was not adequately disseminating the case materials. In addition, the designer may revisit the relationship between resources and case material to determine whether a link needs to be made or reinforced. (For example, the designer may have the coach direct learners to the reference system.) In either case, the designer is able to maintain the consistency of each resource and ensure that it maintains its original function. This protects the integrity of the learning environment and the resources, and allows the designer to continue maximizing each resource for its most appropriate use. In this case, the coach can continue to provide interpretations, experience, or techniques, which is the coach's main purpose. The reference system can harbor the facts of the case, a purpose for which it is better suited. The designer is able to modify the original cause-and-effect relationship or clarify it through corrective actions. In either case, the designer stays in control of the environment and maintains the ability to directly link the learning environment to the learning that occurs.

Evaluation in the Delivery Process

Testing ensures that a quality product has been developed; whether that product has an impact is still unanswered. Once the entire two-week course was complete, a new set of expectations encompassing the entire course was generated. In other words, the concept mapping process was repeated with a focus on the entire training program. These new items (n=53) were then sorted and rated to develop a picture of the conceptual structure of the entire course. This resulted in a single concept map representing the completed educational product, as shown in figure 5. As with testing, students were asked to reflect on their educational experience and rate their level of achievement on each of the 53 detailed outcomes. These data were aggregated into concepts and compared to the expectations for the course. We constructed a ladder graph of the results to portray these data, both for development testing and for the delivery phase.

The theoretical basis for ladder graphs is the research theory of pattern matching (see references). In this case, resulting graphs compare the values placed on issues by stakeholder groups with potentially differing perspectives (for example, the expectations for training impact versus participant learning). To construct a ladder graph to compare patterns, values for items are aggregated by con-

Figure 5. Complete course map.

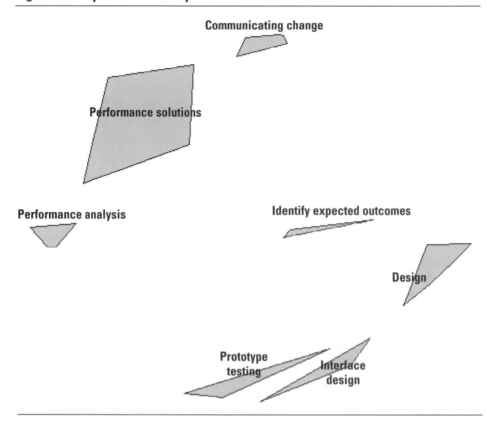

cept, and an average is obtained for each concept. These concept means are arrayed on a demarcated vertical line. By comparing the data obtained in setting expectations with data obtained from students, it is possible to draw the graphic in figure 6. Connecting mean values for concepts between the lines visually portrays the degree of alignment. Although the same goal could be accomplished by comparing numbers, the visual nature of the output in this case displays a considerable amount of data. Furthermore, the graphic provides course stakeholders with a snapshot of performance. Slanted lines indicate a misalignment between expectations and outcomes. A downward slope moving from left to right indicates that the program is not achieving goals at the desired level. Conversely, lines sloping up from left to right may indicate an excess commitment of resources. The desirable outcome is to have a match between what students are expected to achieve as a result of a training program (the development perspective) and the student's assessment of their achievement. In essence, a series of parallel lines similar to a ladder is the desired pattern.

It is also possible to compare the outcomes across sessions, as figure 7 shows. Of particular importance to a large organization that conducts multiple sessions of the same program is the issue of consistency. That is, students in different sessions of the same program need to receive a similar educational experience even though they attend at different times. The results led to the conclusion that the course was performing adequately (that is, outcomes were being achieved) and that the sessions were consistently implemented.

Discussion: What Is the Value of Evaluation?

In a business environment, the goal of training is to deliver a product that has an impact on the business of the organization. The challenge in arriving at this point lies in managing the processes of development, delivery, and communication. Our view is that an investment of resources in formative evaluation contributed to the successful development of an educational program. The testing and evaluation approach used on this project was successful from multiple perspectives. First, the timing and frequency of the testing were critical because they enabled the development team to identify problems and inconsistencies early in the development cycle. For example, faculty materials were based on assumptions about the tasks associated with and success of student activities. Therefore, student activities were tested and refined before constructing detailed faculty support materials. This staged or iterative approach provided an opportunity early in the development process to make significant changes to the design without incurring the significant cost of rework to all other components of the course. Although avoiding unnecessary costs is important, the cost required to achieve that benefit also should be favorable. Our conclusion is that the cost or resources required for evaluation did not substantively differ from the resource requirements of comparable approaches. The basis for this conclusion is that the activities that would typically occur in any development process were reworked in this case. For example, all programs need to set objectives; in this case that activity was reworked using the concept mapping process.

Secondly, development needs to occur. In this case, the process was revised to include the development of a vision for resources, building the cause-effect model, and mapping back to that model as new decisions were made rather than just letting them "evolve." This is

Figure 6. Alignment between expectations and outcomes.

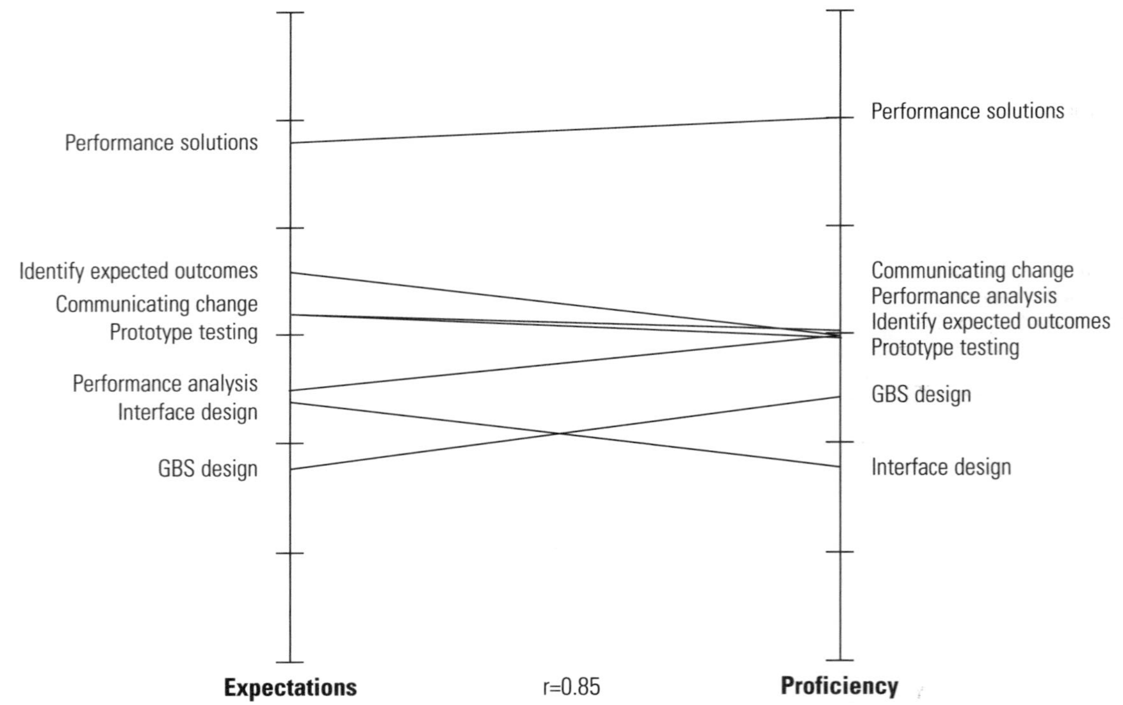

Figure 7. Consistency of outcomes across two sessions.

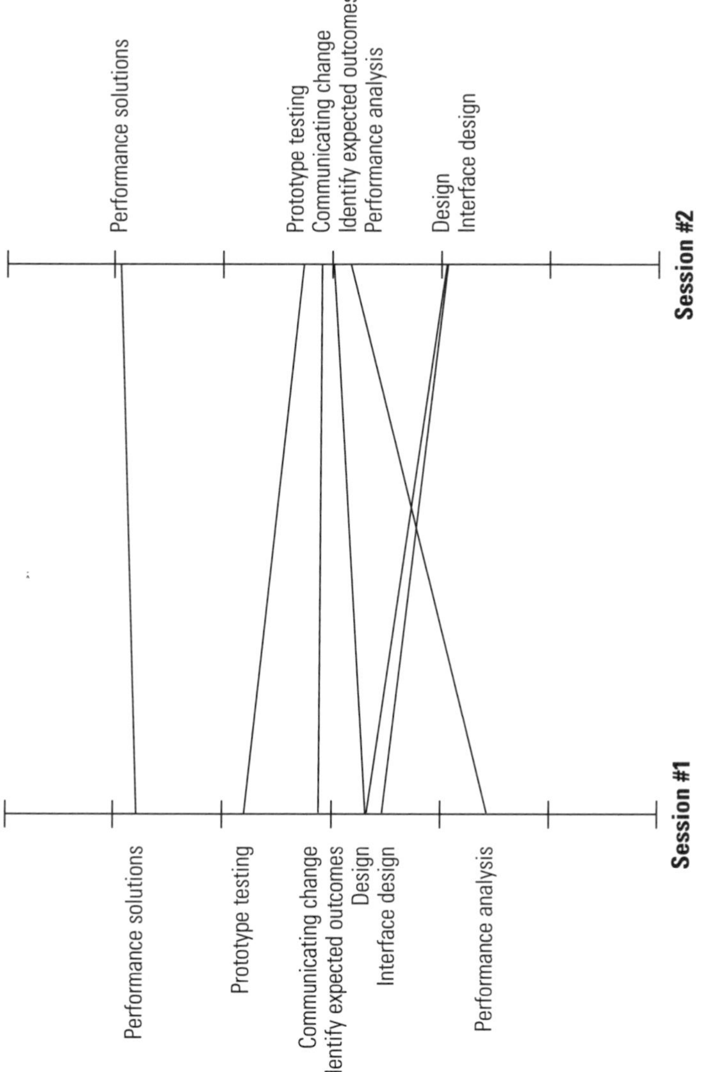

important because there is a tendency to become reactive during testing. For example, students might request more of a certain type of interaction from the coach or support system. Generally, if the change seems "reasonable," the designer may make the enhancement. In simply responding to suggestions, a clear vision for the use of instructional resources gets lost. Using this evaluation approach, the developer could respond to student desires on the basis of the theory of the program and subsequently possibly choose not to add the desired support because it did not fit with the theory of the course. As a result, some development work and the associated costs were avoided, and the quality of the program was maintained.

Thirdly, results of evaluation need to be communicated, and this activity was reworked using the results of pattern matching. The pattern match provided a graphical representation of the course outcomes and the achievement expected for each of those outcomes to stakeholders. Pattern matching was used to test whether the student goals and activities accurately reflected prioritization of skill building and content areas determined during the design. By comparing the correlation between expectations and outcomes, it was possible to quickly and effectively communicate the results of the test. For example, after this first test, the overall correlation with the design of .85 and the degree of alignment for each content area was communicated. This provided a rich description of how well the design met the original goals, more so than data from overarching questions, such as how students liked the course. Following testing and rollout, pattern matching continues to be used to communicate alignment between expectations for trainee proficiency levels and the students' self-assessment of achieved proficiency levels. Again, the degree of alignment between concepts provides a meaningful yet succinct way to describe the ongoing effectiveness of the training program.

In addition to the favorable economics associated with this approach to evaluation, additional benefits emerged. The vision of the course portrayed in the concept maps was used to help coordinate subgroups working on different aspects of the course, design learning support materials, and evaluate the success of the training. During the plan segment, concept maps and skill lists were used to communicate the content areas targeted for the course. Not surprisingly, the results clearly indicated that not everyone agreed on the importance of each specific skill. The valuing of outcomes by individuals on the team provided data useful to discuss content areas where there was significant divergence among the team members. This development project included 12 people who were involved with a variety of aspects of the course. There was division of labor across sections of the course and a division of expertise across people, with different people responsible for technology support, graphics, evaluation, and management. The concept maps with prioritized skill rankings provided a very clear way to communicate program goals across the team. In effect, individuals, regardless of their specific area of expertise or specific responsibility, had a clear vision of how the final completed product needed to affect students. The graphical nature of the quantitative data (that is, concept maps and pattern matches) was particularly useful for communicating with project sponsors. The task of generating outcomes was used to move down from high-level objectives to specific and numerous statements of outcomes like "analyze a performance problem and determine the root cause." The resulting map served as a communication vehicle to provide both a summary and a detailed description of plans for the training program in much the same way as the map used for intrateam discussions and consensus building.

Rigorous evaluation requires more effort than that required for less-structured approaches, such as brief survey questionnaires. If additional cost is warranted, the benefit must be that development is enhanced. Recalling lessons learned from other industries, rework needs to be minimized, problems need to be anticipated, and data need to influence development processes. Our view is that these benefits were realized; iterative testing avoided rework, creating a theory of the program-anticipated problems and the reasonableness of student suggestions, and results from pattern matching, debriefings, and observation-influenced development efforts after a test. Additionally, probably the most important aspect of the evaluation approach used on this project was the integration of evaluation into the development effort. Data collection was not a disparate activity with only minimal influence on development and implementation. Particularly as a result of concept mapping, the line between evaluation process and development process was blurred. The result was that evaluation was not simply a tool used to gather high-level impressions but also an integral part of the development process.

Questions for Discussion

1. Concept mapping techniques were used as a basis for this evaluation approach. As a result of the tasks associated with this evaluation methodology, evaluation tasks were integrated into early phases of development work. What are the advantages and disadvantages of

using this approach even earlier in the process, such as during the needs assessment?

2. The self-assessment by students has been shown to be both valid and reliable. What other approaches to assessing program outcomes could be employed to make the results even more credible?

3. Hypothesizing and anticipating cause-and-effect relationships were considered particularly important in the testing phase of this training program. In other programs with which you are familiar, what are some ways of determining these cause-and-effect relationships between resources deployed (for example, faculty, technology) and program outcomes?

3. In this case, evaluation and instructional development are closely intertwined. Although this has some apparent advantages, what challenges can you see in trying to achieve this integration of functions?

The Authors

Daniel J. McLinden is director of evaluation and performance measurement for Andersen Consulting at the Center for Professional Education in St. Charles, Illinois. Over the course of his career in human resource development in business, his consulting efforts have included program evaluation, needs assessment, testing, and organizational assessment. His current focus is on conceptualizing program impact and the evaluation of investments in the development of human resources. Much of his current work in writing and presentations has focused on the importance of linking program conceptualization and evaluation. McLinden holds a doctorate in educational psychology from Northern Illinois University. He can be contacted at the following address: Andersen Consulting, Center for Professional Education, 1405 North Fifth Avenue, St. Charles, IL 60174-1264.

Bradley Kolar is a manager with the Andersen Consulting Education Capability Assessment Team. Kolar has been with Andersen Consulting for six years. He has developed traditional instructor-led and self-study materials, classroom-based simulations, multimedia knowledge dissemination products, and multimedia simulations. He is currently working on projects to define the process, tool, and training requirements for program management and human resource capabilities. Kolar holds a B.A. in economics and an M.A. in speech communication from the University of Illinois at Urbana-Champaign as well as an M.S. in computer science from Northwestern University.

Mark McDowell works for Andersen Consulting as the director of the Classroom Training Solution Center. In that role, he leads a team of 50 people responsible for the development of all classroom training targeted for Andersen consulting professionals. His responsibilities include project planning, resource scheduling, and the development of solution center processes and metrics. In previous projects, McDowell served as project manager responsible for project planning, design, schedule, budget, and quality management. McDowell joined Andersen Consulting in 1985, after graduating from the University of Nebraska-Lincoln where he majored in industrial engineering.

Matthew Tobias was an evaluation specialist with the Evaluation & Performance Assessment group for Andersen Consulting Education, where he specialized in training evaluation, on-line evaluation systems, and the application of concept mapping methods.

Notes:

[1]The results reported here have used concept mapping software by Concept Systems© Inc.

[2]The data for each stakeholder are aggregated into a similarity matrix and are analyzed using multidimensional scaling (MDS). The resulting MDS analysis produces a two-dimensional map that locates each outcome as a point with an X and Y coordinate. In our analysis, we used Concept Systems Software to conduct this analysis.

[3]Concepts Systems Software uses Ward's method for cluster analysis.

References
Goal-Based Learning

"Goal Based Scenarios: A New Approach to Professional Education." (1994). *Educational Technology, 34*(9), 3–64.

Schank, R. (1997). *Virtual Learning: A Revolutionary Approach to Building a Highly Skilled Workforce.* New York: McGraw-Hill.

Concept Mapping and Pattern Matching

Concept Systems© Inc. 118 Prospect Street, Suite 309, Ithaca, NY.

Trochim, W.M.K. (1989a). "An Introduction to Concept Mapping for Planning and Evaluation." *Evaluation and Program Planning, 12,* 1–16.

Trochim, W.M.K. (1989b). "Outcome Pattern Matching and Program Theory." *Evaluation and Program Planning, 12,* 355–366.

Evaluating the Impact of Training Programs

Kirkpatrick, D.L. (1987). "Evaluation." In R.L. Craig and L.R. Bittell (editors). *Training and Development Handbook* (pp. 301–319). New York: McGraw-Hill.

McLinden, D.J. (1995). "Proof, Evidence, and Complexity: Understanding the Impact of Training and Development in Business." *Performance Improvement Quarterly, 8*(3), 3–18.

McLinden, D.J., M.J. Davis, and D.E. Sheriff. (1993). "Impact on Financial Productivity: A Study of Training Effects on Consulting Services." *Human Resource Development Quarterly, 4*(4), 367–375.

Phillips, J.J. (1994). *Return on Investment in Human Resource Development: Cases on the Economic Benefits of HRD* (volume 1). Alexandria, VA: American Society for Training & Development.

Issues in the Testing of Training Materials

Dupont, D., & H.D. Stoltovich. (1983). "The Effects of a Systematic Revision Model on Revisers in Terms of Student Outcomes." *Performance & Instruction, 22*(2), 33–37.

Stoltovich, H.D. (1978). "The Intermediate Technology of Learner Verification and Revision (LVR)." *Educational Technology, 18*(2), 13–17.

Stoltovich, H.D. (1982). "Applications of the Intermediate Technology of Learner Verification and Revision (LVR) for Adapting International Instructional Resources to Meet Local Needs." *Performance & Instruction, 21*(7), 16–22.

Wedman, J., & M. Tessmer. (1992). "Instructional Designers' Decisions and Priorities: A Survey of Design Practice." *Performance Improvement Quarterly, 6*(2), 42–57.

Zemke, R. (1985). "The Systems Approach: A Nice Theory but..." *Training, 22*(10), 103–108.

Implementing an Evaluation Strategy

Nortel (Northern Telecom)

Debi Harrell, Rick Pharris, and Ron Stone

Nortel (Northern Telecom) has long been recognized for leadership in the telecommunications industry. Nortel's vision is to be a trusted partner, a company that is valued by customers, employees, shareholders, and communities around the world. Nortel, a $13 billion company, has operations and offices in North and South America, Asia-Pacific, Europe, and the United Kingdom. Attracting and retaining exemplary employees is a key factor to Nortel's business success. Learning opportunities are very important to Nortel's 68,000 employees, and the opportunity for development is often cited as a key reason potential employees are drawn to the company.

Background

The Learning Institute (LI), Nortel's training and development organization for leadership development was established in 1991 to serve the training needs of the company's North American employees. Prior to 1991, there were separate training organizations for the United States and Canada. In 1996, LI staff was extended to include South America, Asia, and Europe. The LI provides both classroom-style training and performance consulting to Nortel's four key lines of business across the world. There are account teams assigned to each line of business, program primes who manage the curriculum for leadership development, a design team, and an operations team. The Learning Institute has 57 regular employees and an adjunct staff of 40 or so external facilitators who deliver classes.

This case was prepared to serve as a basis for discussion rather than to illustrate either effective or ineffective administrative and management practices.

Tough Questions

In 1995, the Learning Institute began to face some tough inquiries from Nortel senior management. With an operating budget of $15 million per year, some very legitimate questions began to surface: What is the value-add of this organization? What was the impact of over 45,000 student-days per year? How was the LI helping Nortel achieve its business performance objectives? Could the LI show its impact on the business? How should success in training and development be measured?

The LI was widely recognized for its outstanding learning solutions, both classroom-style training and performance consulting. Although the Learning Institute had been very conscientious about Level 1 evaluations, these questions were unsettling. All students were diligently asked to complete a reaction sheet (also known as smile sheet) at the end of every session. These were sent to a central location and were scanned into a database. For the most part, the feedback indicated that course objectives were met, the facilitators did an outstanding job, the classroom was conducive to learning, the preclass processes such as registration were acceptable, and participants left the session feeling really good about how they had spent their time. Of the 50-odd courses the LI offered, fewer than 10 had Level 2 evaluations. Formal Level 3 evaluations did not exist. Value-add? Well, the LI was very certain that employees liked the programs: The smile sheets said so, participant comments said so, and program enrollment continued to climb year after year. Impact? Level 2 information on the courses that had Level 2 evaluations indicated that learning was taking place in the classroom. Pre- and posttest scores and percent of change were recorded and sent in with Level 1 reaction sheets. Were participants applying their new skills and knowledge on the job? Was training helping Nortel achieve business objectives? Now the questions were getting tough.

The Learning Institute began searching for answers. Of particular interest were the culture-building programs the LI offered around the world. There were five different programs, aimed at new employees, first-time managers, midlevel managers, senior managers, and executives. These flagship programs ranged from three and one-half to five days long, involved participation from executives and senior managers, were usually taught by a team of facilitators or consultants, and tended to be residential (held at hotels to get employees away from the distractions of office, computers, and telephones). Something had to be done to prove what LI staff intuitively knew—that the programs were instrumental in moving the company forward.

An Implementation Strategy
Step 1

The Learning Institute got serious about evaluation. Through the years, there had been several attempts to focus more on evaluation, but beyond Level 1, most efforts floundered. A comprehensive strategy was clearly the best way to answer the toughest questions. The LI researched evaluation theory and practice and discovered some intriguing literature from Performance Resource Organization (PRO), founded by Jack Phillips. No one in the LI had ever tried to measure the actual return-on-investment, but Phillips had developed processes to do this. The idea of showing a monetary return-on-investment was intriguing. The Learning Institute asked Phillips to conduct a two-day, in-house session on evaluation. Although only a few persons attended the initial workshop, that was enough to get renewed interest in evaluation. Following the workshop, Nortel commissioned Phillips to conduct an impact study of the culture-building programs and to assist the LI in creating a comprehensive evaluation strategy.

Step 2

The Learning Institute created an "evaluation prime" management-level position and assigned full-time evaluation responsibilities to one person with guidance to be provided by one of the most senior persons in the entire organization. This represented a big change for the LI. Historically, the organization had assigned evaluation responsibilities to student interns or other persons who typically rotated in and out of the organization after a few months. Small wonder there was little continuity from year to year.

Step 3

Next, the Learning Institute created a framework for its evaluation initiative by establishing guidelines, policies, and procedures for the entire organization. These were published in a white paper that was circulated during the 1996 annual LI Symposium. The philosophy states that:
- The purpose of all learning solutions (training and consulting) is to achieve corporate, business, and individual goals. (Gone are the days of offering training without assessing needs first.)

- Learning solutions should offer tangible and intangible returns to the client and short- and long-term improvement for Nortel.
- Evaluation of programs and services will accomplish measurement of the desired improvement. (All new learning solutions must have clearly stated objectives that are aimed at Level 3 and 4 evaluations.)

The framework was designed to help the Learning Institute:

- improve programs and processes
- discontinue some programs and expand others
- approve projects on the basis of pilots
- inform and educate management about what they are getting for their training investments
- inform and educate target groups
- build skills with the LI staff.

The Learning Institute adopted a results-based approach. It states:

- Learning solutions will be initiated, developed, and delivered with the end result in mind.
- An evaluation plan will be written by program managers or primes for all products and services.
- Responsibility for achieving results will be shared.
- All new learning solutions are to be designed to have the capability of measuring business impact, cost-effectiveness, and return-on-investment (ROI).

Communication is also a key aspect of the framework.

- Regular reports are made to management regarding evaluation plans, strategies, results, costs, priorities, and concerns.
- Major evaluation findings would be reported to key stakeholders in a manner that would enable them to see the contribution of learning solutions to business performance improvement.

Step 4

A two-day workshop, based on a public workshop from Performance Resource Organization, was customized for Nortel and taught to all Learning Institute staff. All staff members were expected to attend, from the vice president to support staff. Adjunct staff members were also asked to attend the workshop because they would be instrumental in implementing the strategy in the classroom. Several LI staff members, including course designers, were sent to intensive evaluation and return-on-investment training provided by PRO. LI published a comprehensive reference document for all its staff. This guide includes step-by-step instructions for conducting Levels 1 through 5 evaluations. A brochure for marketing and socializing the LI's commitment to accountability was designed for nontraining employees and managers. The brochure's message stresses the importance of part-nering with the business to measure results.

Step 5

All Learning Institute courses are now targeted for specific lev-els of evaluation based on a set of criteria. The criteria include visi-bility, monetary investment, training that crosses functions within the company, and special requests or interest from senior management.

The following targets were established and communicated through-out the organization: By December 1998

- 100 percent of all learning solutions will be evaluated at Level 1 (re-action). The standard Level 1 form was revised to include a section for specific actions planned as a result of attending the training, and a section was added for self-assessment of readiness for training.
- 50 percent of all learning solutions will be evaluated at Level 2 (learning).
- 30 percent of all learning solutions will be evaluated at Level 3 (ap-plication on the job).
- 20 percent of all learning solutions will be evaluated at Level 4 (busi-ness impact).
- 10 percent of all learning solutions will be evaluated at Level 5 (re-turn-on-investment).

For Levels 3 and 4, the plan is to collect postprogram data and to isolate the effects of training. Level 5 evaluations also use a plan to convert data to monetary value, tabulate program costs, calculate ROI, and report intangible benefits, all on the basis of Phillips's mod-el. The LI finance and budget reporting system was revised to include data fields for capturing and reporting course-related costs.

Initial Results

The Learning Institute and PRO completed the impact study of the five culture-building programs and presented the findings to Nor-tel senior management in early 1996. Four of the five courses showed positive ROIs, ranging from 100 percent to over 800 percent. The on-ly program that had a negative ROI (–58 percent) was an orientation class for all new Nortel employees. The LI gathered some very valu-able information from the evaluation, and the program was re-designed and shortened by one and one-half days. New employees are now given a CD-ROM to view after attending class. This seems to be working well.

A meeting effectiveness class was also evaluated at Level 5. This was a special program that was customized for a lab located in Germany. The results indicate an ROI of over 600 percent on the basis of the changes the lab employees were able to make in how they managed meeting time, meeting frequency, and meeting outcomes.

Another result of the implementation of the evaluation initiative was the redesign of the Level 1 form. The new form asks participants to indicate planned actions they will take as a result of participating in the learning solution. It also asks participants to assess their motivation to attend the class, their preparedness to learn, their participation in the learning solution, and their sense of responsibility for their own learning.

Issues and Barriers to Implementation

This would not be a complete picture of the Learning Institute's implementation strategy without a few words about barriers that had to be overcome and issues that still loom on the horizon.

Resources

The LI's goals are aggressive. Finding time and resources to write evaluation plans and implement them remain key barriers. Creating strategies to measure learning, isolate the effects of training, collect postprogram data, and calculate cost-benefit ratios requires knowledge, commitment, and support across the organization.

Interest in Evaluation

The customized two-day training program was quite well received throughout the Learning Institute. A couple of key program managers took early action to initiate Level 3 to 5 evaluations in a few courses. For the most part, LI staff believed a solid evaluation program would be helpful, but enthusiasm seemed to disappear shortly after the realities of their normal workloads set in.

Buy-in From Business Units

Educating learning partners and changing the culture of a company as large as Nortel will not be accomplished overnight. The LI must continue to educate the corporation that a multipronged approach to development is the surest way to move the business forward. Managers must be encouraged to discuss training outcomes with employees prior to attending classes. Postcourse follow-up and reinforcement of new knowledge and skills help ensure application of the training. Although there is some evidence of change, there is much work to be done.

Connectivity to Other Processes

Implementing a comprehensive evaluation strategy into Learning Institute processes has been an evolutionary endeavor. In the past, evaluation was relegated to an individual who then had the monumental task of evaluating all LI products and services. Now the design team, business account teams, and curriculum primes have been asked to integrate evaluation processes into their products and services. The LI design staff plans to include evaluation plans as an integral step of course design and development. Some account teams are including evaluation plans in their work with lines of business. If training programs are purchased from external vendors, high consideration is given to programs that can be readily integrated into the LI's evaluation processes.

Data Tracking and Reporting

Tracking relevant data and reporting through a common system will be a crucial component of the Learning Institute's success. Shared learning and speed through application of consistent tools reflected in the database will allow greater transfer and integration with other training functions. Building and maintaining the system will be an evolutionary journey.

The Future

The implementation of a comprehensive evaluation strategy in Nortel is still a work in progress. Through steadfast effort and commitment to moving the business into the next millennium, the Learning Institute is continuing to evolve to an organization that can measure the impact of training and development.

Questions for Discussion

1. What kinds of information can a training and development organization learn from evaluating training programs?
2. Why did the Learning Institute require that learning solutions be developed with the end in mind? How does this have an impact on design, delivery, and follow-up?
3. What criteria were established in targeting Learning Institute programs for different levels of evaluation? What additional criteria could be used?
4. Is it realistic to expect a positive ROI on a new-employee orientation program? What should be done when a program has a negative ROI?

5. What are the key steps in implementing a comprehensive evaluation and assessment strategy?
6. Who should be involved in the creation and implementation of an evaluation initiative and when?
7. What steps would you follow in developing an evaluation strategy in your organization?

The Authors

Debi Harrell is a training advisor in Nortel's Learning Institute, where she has worked since 1987. Harrell has held a variety of responsibilities in the LI including classroom instruction, curriculum management, learning architecture design, budget management, and operations management. Prior to Nortel, she worked as a training manager for the state of Tennessee for six years. She earned her bachelor's degree in psychology and her master's in education and counseling from the University of Tennessee. She can be contacted at Nortel Learning Institute, 200 Athens Way, Nashville, TN 37228.

Rick Pharris is director of learning operations in Nortel's Learning Institute, where he has worked since 1988 in a number of responsibilities including program facilitation, instructional design, curriculum and program management, strategic development and implementation, and management of Learning Institute operations. Prior to Nortel, Pharris was a training officer for the state of Tennessee with responsibility for management and computer-assisted training. He received a B.S. degree from Louisiana State University.

Ron Stone directs the international consulting practice of Performance Resources Organization. He has worked with a diverse group of clients to develop evaluation policies and strategies and to implement the ROI process. Before joining PRO, he had 27 years of experience in human resource development in the aerospace and electric utility industries. He served 18 years in a managerial capacity with working for two subsidiaries of the Southern Company. Stone currently serves on the steering committee and faculty for the University of Alabama Human Resource Development program. He is a member of the Society for Human Resource Management and the American Society for Training & Development. Stone received his B.B.A. from Georgia State University and is certified in the ROI process.

Measuring Training Throughout the Bell Atlantic Organization

Bell Atlantic Network Services, Inc.

Toni Hodges

Bell Atlantic Training, Education and Development has developed a process for evaluating and tracking the progress and success of its intervention programs. The process involves formative and summative evaluation techniques and corporate-level reporting. Correlations are made between the different levels of evaluation, and management is informed of progress on a continual basis.

Background

Bell Atlantic's operating telephone companies serve a region rich with the most valuable customers in the world—25 million households, 34 percent of *Fortune* 500 companies, the federal government, Wall Street, and the headquarters for television publishing, newspaper, and advertising industries. Our 38 million access lines reach homes and businesses from Maine to Virginia. Our telephone company employees have more than 100 million customer contacts a year. Thirty million customers see our name on their phone bill every month. And our wireless company is the largest on the East Coast with over 4.6 million customers. Bell Atlantic has a market presence in 21 countries and is also the world's largest provider of directory information.

Bell Atlantic has approximately 120,000 employees whose jobs represent varying functions within the telecommunications industry. All Bell Atlantic employees develop a training plan for themselves each year to ensure the company has a workforce well prepared to meet

This case was prepared to serve as a basis for discussion rather than to illustrate either effective or ineffective administrative and management practices.

the challenges required in a competitive communication and information services environment. Bell Atlantic spends millions of dollars each year to implement those training plans. Following is a description of the process, methodologies, and tools the company uses to ensure our training and other intervention programs meet the standards necessary to face our workforce challenges.

Purposes for Measurement and Tracking

Our goal for measuring and tracking our training and other intervention programs is to have a clear picture at any given point of how much training we are providing and how well we are accomplishing the program objectives. Specifically, we measure and track to:
- determine whether a program is accomplishing its objectives
- identify the strengths and weaknesses in the intervention process
- determine the cost-benefit ratio of an intervention program
- decide who should participate in future programs
- test the clarity and validity of the test, questions, and exercises
- identify which participants benefited the most or the least from the program
- reinforce major points made to the participant
- track who and how many are participating in interventions
- gather data to assist in marketing future programs.

The Measurement and Tracking Process

The measurement and evaluation (M&E) group within the Training, Education and Development Directorate is responsible for ensuring that Bell Atlantic intervention programs are evaluated appropriately with valid and current methodologies. The measurement and tracking process employed at Bell Atlantic is systematic and standardized to avoid dependence on any single group of measurement and evaluation experts. Figure 1 depicts the process to which we ascribe.

Formative Evaluations

Formative evaluations include needs assessments, usability testing, quality assurance testing, and pilot testing. Traditionally, needs assessments are not considered part of measurement and evaluation. However, during the needs assessment, tentative program intervention objectives are negotiated with the client and, thus, evaluation considerations are important. At this time, it is important to ask questions such as the following: "Are the objectives stated in measurable per-

Figure 1. A systematic, standardized measurement tracking process.

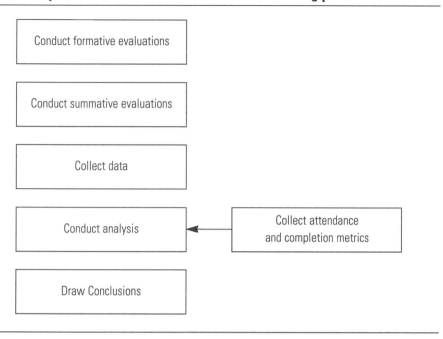

formance and business impact language?" and "Can evaluation techniques be determined initially so that they can be put into place at the appropriate time?" When you determine the answers to these questions, an evaluation strategy can be formulated. For example, at this early stage, you could designate a control group that would not take part in the program. Bell Atlantic has performance consultants within each line of business who conduct the needs assessments and work with the M&E group to develop evaluation plans.

Bell Atlantic has a usability laboratory and a usability testing manager assigned to conduct testing and evaluate the results. The manager conducts most of the company's usability testing for computer-based training (CBT), multimedia, and Web-based training programs. The quality assurance testing is conducted, again, mainly for our CBT, multimedia, and Web-based programs. Pilot testing is a critical component for M&E in that it is the last opportunity to make changes on a program before it is implemented. Once implemented, changes are costly and often not made. Bell Atlantic has a systematic process for pilot testing that either the M&E group or the program's project manager accomplishes.

Summative Evaluations

Summative evaluations include the following:

- attendance or completion metrics
- reaction measurement
- knowledge/proficiency measurement
- job application performance measurement
- business results measurement
- client satisfaction or return on expectation (ROE) measurement[1]
- return-on-investment (ROI) measurement[2]
- measurement tracking

Attendance or completion metrics are gathered on a continuous basis and reported to management monthly. These data include the following:

- hours and number of employees enrolled by delivery mode
- hours and number enrolled by discipline
- hours and number enrolled by class type
- hours and number enrolled by line of business
- percent or number of employees trained to standard performance
- percent or number of employees trained monthly
- year-to-date number of curriculums developed by job title
- end-of-year training expense per employee
- end-of-year training expense per employee by line of business

Reaction measurement is conducted by the use of standardized post-course questionnaires for leader-led, multimedia, mixed media, self-paced, and Web-based programs. Questions have been carefully designed to provide data for internal continuous improvement and for benchmarking with other corporations.[3] The data are provided either in a scannable answer sheet or online as part of online programs. Reaction data is housed in the Bell Atlantic Course Evaluation Database System (CEDS). CEDS provides data compilation and charts for monthly and quarterly management reports, and customized reports for field and management personnel.

Knowledge/proficiency measurement is conducted by gathering post-course performance data. Participants complete testing to determine if knowledge has been gained or proficiency acquired in accordance with the program objectives. Testing consists of pretests, posttests, or proficiency tests, or a combination of these tests. We call these data Student Measurement Analysis and Results of Training (SMART) data. SMART data are also recorded in CEDS and reported monthly and quarterly.

We strive to track and analyze completion, reaction, and SMART data on 100 percent of our courses.

Job application performance data, however, are gathered selectively. Programs chosen to be analyzed to determine if knowledge and skills have been transferred to the job are based upon the following:

- Course objectives: Are they performance based and measurable?
- Client expectations: Are they tied to the program only, and are they realistic?
- Opportunities for future course improvements: Are there any?
- Cost of the program: Is it worth the evaluation effort and costs?
- Importance to the organization: Is it a visible program?
- Cost of the evaluation: Will it be too expensive to evaluate?

Business results and ROE data are also gathered selectively, based upon the following:

- Needs assessment: Does it provide a business need?
- Cost of the program: Is it significant from a business perspective?
- Client expectations: Are they committed?
- Importance to the organization: What does impact and ROE success mean to the organization?
- Cost of the evaluation: Will it be too expensive to evaluate?

Return-on-investment (ROI) data are also gathered selectively, based upon the following:

- Length of time the program is expected to be viable: Is it a one-shot program?
- Visibility of the program: Is it important to management?
- Size of the target audience: Will it have an impact on a fair number of employees?
- Feasibility for measurement: Can it be measured validly?
- Cost of the program: Is it significant from a business perspective?
- Importance to the organization: What does ROI success mean to the organization?
- Cost of the evaluation: Will it be too expensive to evaluate?

Analysis Measurement and Tracking Results

At this point in the M&E process, we have data. We know how much training has taken place and how often and how effective the programs have been based upon the reaction and testing data of the participants. We also know, in some cases, the impact that the programs have had. These data are reported on a monthly basis. Quarterly and as needed, the M&E group conducts correlation analyses

Figure 2. Correlation pyramid.

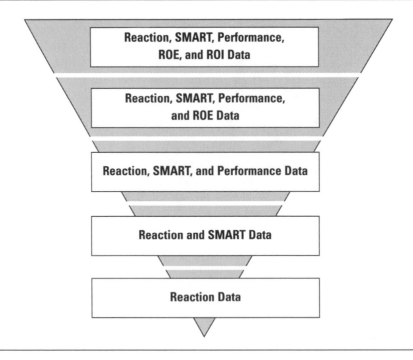

to explore potential reasons for data results. Figure 2 depicts the philosophy to which the M&E group ascribes to conduct such analyses.

Attendance completion metrics are raw data that Bell Atlantic has historically collected to determine how much, how many, and how often. At this point, these data are not used for correlation analysis. Reaction data are used to give us the first picture of how well we are doing with our programs. We then look at our SMART data combined with our reaction data to find correlation, and so on, further up the pyramid for which we have data.

Tables 1 to 5 explain the questions that we ask at each level of evaluation. They also provide possible solutions for us to consider as we ask those questions.

We recognize that there are many more questions and solutions that can be considered than those listed. Every program has its unique issues, and every program has political and other business considerations that may be relevant to final decisions. However, this type of careful and comprehensive analysis and reporting provides Bell Atlantic management with data and M&E assessments of what the data

Table 1. Correlations for reaction data.

IF	Question	Solution
Scores are high.	None	
Scores are low.	In what area? How low?	• Course material revision. • Reassess student requirements. • Coach instructor.

Table 2. Correlations for reaction and SMART data.

IF	Question	Possible Solution(s)
Reaction scores are high, and SMART scores are high.	None	
Reaction scores are high, but SMART scores are low.	Which scores are low?	• Revise course objectives. • Revise course material. • Coach instructor.
Reaction scores are low, and SMART scores are low.	Which questions are low? Which scores are low?	• Revise objectives. • Revise course material. • Coach instructor.

mean to ensure that decisions are made with the full realization of the impact the program.

Questions for Discussion

1. Would this process work for most companies?
2. Does this process require support from people outside the evaluation group?
3. Which part of this process is the most meaningful?

Table 3. Correlations for SMART and performance data.

IF	Question	Possible Solution(s)
Scores are high.	None	
Scores are high, but performance data is low.	Is testing valid? Are objectives too low? Are environmental impacts contributing?	• Revise testing. • Revise objectives. • Investigate.
Scores are low.	Is training meeting the objectives? Are objectives unrealistic for user?	• Revise training. • Revise objectives. • Investigate recruitment requirements.
Scores are low, but performance data is high.	Are objectives too low? Is testing valid?	• Revise objectives. • Revise training.

Table 4. Correlations for performance and ROE data.

IF	Question	Possible Solution(s)
Performance data is high, and ROE data is high.	None	
Performance data is high, but ROE data is low.	Were expectations understood?	Revise expectations.
Performance data is low, but ROE data is high.	Were expectations too low?	Revise expectations.
Performance data is low, and ROE is low.	Were expectations realistic? Is training meeting the objectives? Are environmental impacts contributing?	• Revise objectives. • Revise training. • Investigate. • Eliminate course.

Table 5. Correlations for ROE and ROI data.

IF	Question	Possible Solution(s)
ROE is high, and ROI is high.	None	
ROE is high, but ROI is low.	Is that good enough? How low is ROI?	• Eliminate course. • Future intervention decisions. • Influence enrollments.
ROE is low, but ROI is high.	Is that good enough?	• Revise course. • Revise expectations. • Influence enrollments.
ROE is low, and ROI is low.	Is course beneficial?	• Eliminate course. • Influence enrollments. • Revise course. • Revise expectations • Future intervention decisions.

Notes:

[1] Bell Atlantic has a structured approach to gathering ROE data. The approach is available from the author upon request.

[2] Bell Atlantic M&E personnel received certification to conduct ROI analyses from the Performance Resources Organization, March 1996 and May 1997, and are founding members of the ROI Network.

[3] Many of the questions in the postcourse questionnaire were developed in 1997 by the author and other corporate representatives from the American Society for Training & Development (ASTD) Benchmarking Forum, Performance Metrics Working Group.

The Author

Toni Hodges has 15 years' experience working in the behavioral analysis, systems engineering, and communication environment. Her work has included designing corporate process flows for behavioral programs; designing functional requirements for database designs; conducting needs analyses that have defined training, operational, and system design requirements for the United States Department of Defense (DoD), the British Military of Defence (MoD) equipment and systems, and the Federal Aviation Administration (FAA) communication equipment and systems; conducting seminars for integrating safety, human factors, personnel, and training requirements into system design processes both in the United States and Europe; conducting operational evaluations and assessments of air traffic control personnel and commercial airline personnel operations; conducting pilot program evaluations, performance assessments, and ROI analyses; and developing measurement and evaluation guidance, standards, and policies. Hodges currently manages measurements, evaluations, and benchmarking for the Bell Atlantic Training, Education and Development group and has established corporate standards and policies for training, education, and development program evaluations. She has published articles on ROI analysis and is a founding member of the ROI Network. She can be contacted at the following address: Bell Atlantic Network Services, Inc., 1 East Pratt Street, 2E, Baltimore, MD 21202.

The Role of ROI in a High-Performance Learning Organization

Guthrie Healthcare System

Pauline L. Stamp, Michele Sisto, Roberta Sabitus, Christine Burt, Richard Rava, William Muth, Susan Hall, and Bonnie Onofre

This case study examines the Guthrie Healthcare System's journey from a traditional, hierarchical organization to one of collaborative leadership. The recognition that competitive advantage can be directly related to an organization's ability to innovate and learn led to Guthrie's commitment to become a learning organization.

The commitment to high performance, to learning, to responsibility, and to accountability led to this organization's investigation into, and investment in, return-on-investment (ROI). This case documents Guthrie's experience in crafting a multidisciplinary approach in adopting the ROI process. It demonstrates the challenges, the learning, and the benefits of incorporating ROI into the larger context of creating a high-performance learning organization.

Background

Nestled between two rivers in the small rural community of Sayre, Pennsylvania (population about 70,000), the Guthrie Healthcare System (GHS) serves as a regional center for this sparsely populated area of Pennsylvania and New York. This 501(c)(3) tax-exempt charitable health-care organization was founded in the 1800s. The multispecialty system consists of four divisions: acute care, long-term care, education and research, and for profit. Over 450,000 patients come from a 130-mile span east and west and a 60-mile span north and south to seek treatment for their health-care needs. The spectrum of medical

This case was prepared to serve as a basis for discussion rather than to illustrate either effective or ineffective administrative and management practices.

services and specialties offers a range from preventive to therapeutic medicine, for the newborn to the elderly, through outpatient, inpatient, and home care settings. The key ingredients of the system are patient care, community service, quality, affordability, education, and research. The parent corporation establishes overall policy for the system and monitors activities of the corporate divisions and subsidiary organizations. In addition, the parent is the gatekeeper for charitable gifts, endowments, and investments for the entire corporate system. GHS has over 2,300 employees within 200 job categories. The CEO works with a senior executive team of seven. There are approximately 220 managers and supervisors in the system.

The Learning Organization Journey

Like other health-care systems throughout the country, GHS was experiencing an environment of constant change, rapidly shifting markets, continuous technological evolution, and organizational restructuring. Our competitive environment was in constant flux and was becoming more challenging. Technological innovation was occurring faster than most of us could comprehend, and our customers and business partners were becoming more demanding.

To respond effectively to these demands, GHS began to rethink its priorities and behavior. As stated by Senge (1990), competitive supremacy will be a result not only of increased profits and performance, but also of an organization's capacity to innovate, learn, respond quickly, design the appropriate infrastructure to meet demands, and have maximum control over its destiny. A review of current organizational strategy, leadership, scientific management, organizational learning, and learning organization literature (Argyris, 1993; Bennis & Nanus, 1985; Burgoyne, 1992; Pedler, Burgoyne, & Boydell, 1991; Senge, 1990; Watkins & Marsick, 1993) led GHS to the conclusion that learning was the single most important key to organizational success. As stated by Schein (1993, Winter), current circumstances in organizations and the world tell us that learning is no longer a choice but a necessity, and that the most urgent priority is learning how to learn, and how to learn at a faster pace.

For a number of years GHS implemented a variety of improvement programs as the organization strived to better itself and gain a competitive edge. The list of topics was long and varied, and sometimes it seemed as though one program per month was needed to keep pace with the changing environment. Unfortunately, failed programs far outnumbered successful ones, and improvement rates remained distressingly low because GHS, like most companies, failed to grasp a basic truth—continuous improvement requires a commitment to results and clear focus on them.

President and CEO Ralph Meyer observed that Guthrie's previously successful business practices were becoming quickly outmoded, as table 1 shows. In 1994, Meyer created a new vision for GHS: "to become a high performance system, within the cultural context of a learning organization, in which patient care divisions are integrated with the goal of providing a seamless system of care." Realization of this vision required a transformation of organizational culture, from one saturated with rigid, hierarchical structure and entrenched patterns of thought processes to one that fostered an environment of collaborative leadership, creativity, and learning. In 1997, GHS could be described as an organization of team players and thinkers, and people who are beginning to learn, recognize, and understand the system in which they operate and how they can contribute to its betterment.

To lay the groundwork for the organization, the GHS board of directors agreed, as one of its fiscal year 1995–1996 goals and objectives, "to provide leadership and direction in transitioning the system into a learning organization." In addition, the organization's senior executive team adopted the following set of values and corresponding operating principles to lay the foundation of its interaction and pursuits:

- Display a willingness to change.
- Learn about the process of outcomes of change.
- Initiate and display personal commitment to change.
- Evaluate the consistency of messages and actions.
- Form task forces and invite change at grassroots levels.
- Results focused.

Table 1. Business strategy.

Old	New
"Holding company"	"Operating company"
Maximize independent value of entities	Maximize systemwide synergies
Focus on internal affairs	Facilitate strategic investments
Focus on profitability	Create a seamless system of care
Support fee for service	Support managed-care environment
Activity driven	Results driven

GHS developed a picture of its desired outcome and evaluated the resources that were available to provide a pathway to change before journeying down the path to transformation, as figure 1 shows. GHS was committed to challenging traditional thinking, removing hindrances to creativity and risk taking, and changing the leadership perspective to include employees as partners. As a result of this process, the shift in culture from a traditional health-care system to a high-performance learning organization accomplished the following: increased the satisfaction of employees by allowing them to flourish as individuals in the context of teams; fostered an effective and efficient workforce by inviting the workforce to make a practical, measurable impact on a problem or challenge facing its team or service line; encouraged personnel to assume more ownership of their positions by giving them responsibilities and inviting them to participate creatively in their work; and prepared the workforce for change in a dynamic and competitive health-care environment by propelling people to innovation.

GHS began to forge systemwide partnerships with a common goal of implementing change, and expanded the CEO's administrative team of seven individuals to include 22 key administrators across the system. The concept of teamwork, new to many of the administrators on the team, was introduced at a first-ever leadership retreat in May 1995. Several tools were used to facilitate teamwork, including the Myers Briggs Personality Assessment and the Leadership Behavior Questionnaire. In an unprecedented activity, the senior executive team—all 22 members—assessed the CEO's leadership abilities. In turn, the CEO presented the overall results, both good and bad, to the group. The willingness of the CEO to demonstrate vulnerability in an open

Figure 1. GHS learning organization practice model.

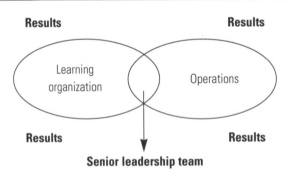

and honest way with those subordinate to him on the organizational chart helped make learning organization principles real to the team.

In 1990, Guthrie was structured in operating divisions, each with its own senior vice president, board of directors, individualized goals, objectives, and strategic plans. Structural barriers to collaborative leadership had to be eliminated. In 1995, the CEO introduced a new alignment, creating a new level of interdependency and replacing the organizational silos with a functional structure, as figure 2 shows.

To further create homogeneity in the historically disparate system, the leadership created six systemwide, cross-functional task forces. Each task force would provide a systemwide voice and cross-functional counsel on a given issue, replacing the formerly isolated approaches to solving problems and implementing change. In addition, because the task forces were systemwide, their visibility would raise awareness concerning the reality and pervasiveness of change within the organization.

The CEO and senior executive team wanted to increase their visibility within the organization, introduce high-performance concepts to the employees at large, and catapult the organization into widespread implementation of the new culture. The system began by adopting and implementing new communication practices, as shown in table 2, and the following new communication plan:

- Align messages.
- Identify corporate voice.
- Tie to goals, vision, mission, values, and results.
- Increase consistency.
- Hold CEO and employee meetings.
- Hold CEO and manager get-togethers.

In 1995, the CEO began to travel to each GHS regional site, often visiting a given site multiple times to conduct employee meetings. Within a four-week period, he had held approximately 20 meetings with roughly 900 employees. These meetings continue to foster an environment where employees throughout the system can conduct open, honest dialogue in which they address their concerns directly with the CEO.

Human and Organizational Development—More Than a Department

A major steppingstone in GHS's journey to become a high-performance learning organization was the creation of a new department, Human and Organizational Development Department. In November 1995, the CEO formed a committee to develop a strategic plan for

Figure 2. GHS functional organization plan.

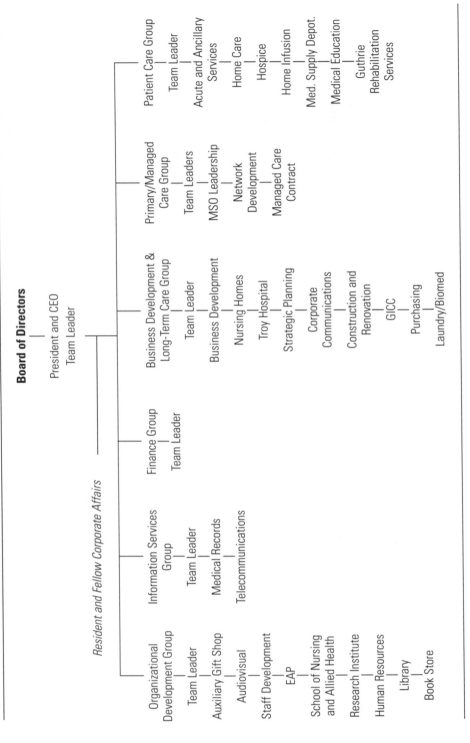

Table 2. Communication practices.

Old	New
One-way: top-down communication	Two-way: originates at any level
Driven by senior management	Driven by service line or product
Delivered by senior management	Delivered by appropriate messenger
Organization-wide message (TEAM)	Targeted to appropriate audience
Situation specific	Integrated with all messages
Memo and policy statements	First line, face to face, or newspaper
Delayed feedback	Immediate feedback
?	Results focused

staff development. The committee proposed the following strategy to accomplish this task:

- Develop a learning perspective that would:
  — Link development, training, and communication to organizational goals.
  — Maintain a strong patient and customer focus.
  — Use measurement and feedback to improve the process of learning and change.
- Assess the present infrastructure and delivery system to maximize human capital investment through improved training, education, and communication.
- Identify gaps in current training and development programs.
- Develop innovative ways to link the resources, skills, and expertise of staff development, nursing education, human resources, finance, information services, corporate communications, the employee assistance program, and audiovisual to maximize the effectiveness for Guthrie Healthcare System.

The committee met actively and often for six months and identified the following gaps:

- insufficient performance data
- no focus or integration of messages between departments
- no method to assess bottom-line impact of training and education
- "event"- versus "results"-based training
- no alignment with management or core business strategies
- little or no integration of resources
- departmental independence

- lack of "systemness"
- minimal programs and initiatives targeted for managers and supervisors.

During this period, human resources realized it was spending about 90 percent of its time performing routine administrative tasks and only 10 percent on organizational changes necessary to meet the system's business strategy. As a result, three departments, human resources, staff development, and audiovisual services, decided to merge and align their strategies to maximize the potential and positive effect on the system and to actively engage in strategies to bridge the gaps between nursing education, information services, corporate communications, finance, and employee assistance, as figure 3 depicts. In essence, the Human and Organizational Development (HOD) Department emerged in March 1996, with a strategic plan designed to address all the gaps the original committee identified.

Once viewed as maintainers, these three departments function today as change facilitators and strategic business partners within Guthrie Healthcare System. Included in the new department's first-year goals was a commitment to develop a plan to maximize return-on-investment (ROI) in training and development.

ROI: An Integrated System Approach

The journey to understanding ROI actually began in March 1996 (prior to an ROI workshop at Guthrie Healthcare System that December), when Susan Hall, HOD staff development, and Roberta Sabitus, HOD

Figure 3. Bridging of islands.

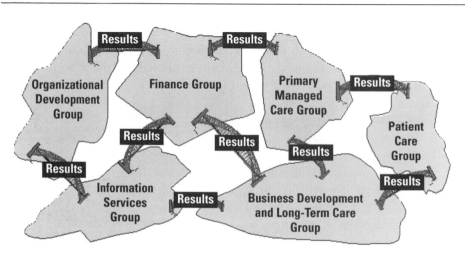

human resources, attended a three-day conference titled "Measuring the Performance and Profit of Workforce Education Programs." Of the many presenters, two were of particular value in demonstrating the potential of ROI. Jack Phillips, president of Performance Resources Organization, conducted a seminar, Measuring Return on Investment: A Search of Best Practices. He addressed identifying trends of measuring ROI, understanding the approaches for isolating the effects of training and converting data to monetary values, and recognizing the basic issues and challenges of measuring ROI. Overall, his presentation illustrated the value and need for ROI. In the other presentation, Edward Gordon focused on determining the economic value of management development, and skills training and forecasting ROI before offering training.

The original purpose in attending the 1996 conference was to gain an understanding of ROI concepts and then present the information to the HOD management team. By the end of the conference, however, Hall and Sabitus realized that the concepts of ROI were far too complex. Not only were they unable to present the concept to others but also they needed further, more specific, ROI training. On the basis of extensive feedback from Hall and Sabitus regarding embracing the ROI process and learning organization principles, Pauline Stamp, senior vice president of human and organizational development, crafted a systemwide interdisciplinary ROI task force with the chief financial officer as co-chair. The task force contracted with Performance Resources Organization for an on-site, five-day ROI certification program. The task force was interdisciplinary in nature with representatives from finance, human and organizational development, nursing administration, and information services.

A by-product of the certification workshop was the organization's commitment to demonstrate ROI on identified projects as well as to create a network of supporters throughout the system to make it happen. Each step in the process to communicate and educate employees on the value of ROI created an impetus for moving beyond training as a solitary change strategy to a more holistic and systematic approach to performance improvement.

Guthrie's commitment to support ROI strategies as a system is evidenced in the following ways:
- the formation of a partnership between HOD and finance to assist in demonstrating and monitoring financial value
- the growing awareness that each employee must partner with GHS in assisting the organization to survive and grow

- the systemwide support to assist managers in identifying critical knowledge and skills required for individuals and teams to succeed in accomplishing the tactical goals of the department in which they work
- the systemwide support to assist management in finding, identifying, or developing cost-effective methods for employees to learn needed knowledge and skills
- the firm commitment of the system to develop and promote valid and useful ways to measure the return on its investments.

Phillips conducted ROI training sessions in December 1997. The certification focused on developing the skills necessary to perform ROI studies on Guthrie Healthcare System initiatives. The desired outcome of this training was to become competent not only in performing the ROI methodology but also in leading the integration of ROI within GHS.

Although members of the training group shared a common goal, there was much diversity among the participants. Members of the group represented a myriad of the roles found within many health-care organizations. Individuals within the group consisted of a cross-functional team with members representing senior administration, finance, adult learning, human resources, information services, audiovisual services, nursing administration, and nursing education. The diversity enabled participants to establish links between human resources, education, training, administration, and the core business of providing patient care. Table 3 lists the individuals who participated in ROI training.

The training program taught much-needed lessons. The first lesson was that no amount of ROI reading material could compare with Phillips's ROI knowledge, experience, and skill. He made difficult ROI case studies seem easy. Adopting and implementing the ROI process throughout the system was not going to be an easy task. The second lesson was that GHS's work-related projects, learning labs, and action research projects were critical to the learning process. The third lesson was that calculating ROI was imperative if GHS was committed to improving the bottom line, transitioning from event-based training to results-based training, bridging performance gaps, and aligning training and development to core business strategies. Improvements could take the form of eliminating programs that do not add value, educating managers on the benefits of calculating ROI, developing Guthrie Healthcare System ROI skills, and concentrating resources on those projects, initiatives, and programs that add value.

Table 3. ROI training participants.

Participant	Department
Christine Burt	Manager, human resources
Connie Coles	Director, education and health, Tioga Nursing Facility
David Cleveland	Manager, audiovisual services—HOD
Susan Hall	Director, staff development—HOD
William Muth	Nursing systems manager
Bonnie Onofre	Nursing education coordinator
Sally Parr	Staff development trainer
Rick Rava	Information services manager
Roberta Sabitus	Vice president, human resources—HOD
Michele Sisto, co-chair	Vice president, finance
Pauline Stamp, co-chair	Senior vice president

Year 1 Projects

With a goal of systemizing the ROI process, the certification class decided to look at three pilot projects—the Ancillary Aide Program at the Tioga Nursing Facility, the Management Development Technology Initiative at Guthrie Healthcare System, and the ROI on the ROI certification process. The class subsequently broke into three groups.

Project 1

The participants examined the program to increase retention of aides in the Ancillary Aide Program at GHS's Tioga Nursing Facility. One group studied a 10-month (September 1996 to July 1997) period of ancillary aide training and nursing aide training programs. They evaluated four training classes—two with ancillary aides and two without. Twenty-eight individuals were trained for Tioga Nursing Facility; nine had been ancillary aides for a two- to three-week period prior to the Nursing Aide Training program.

The objective of the ROI study was to determine if ancillary aide experience improved retention of employment and if it was a cost-effective means of addressing temporary staffing relief issues.

LEVEL 1: REACTION AND SATISFACTION. The method of evaluation was a questionnaire. The evaluation demonstrated no issues with instruction in the nursing aide training program and no differences in satisfaction with the program depending on experience as ancillary aides.

LEVEL 2: LEARNING. The method of evaluation was a self-assessment questionnaire. Our objective was to demonstrate understanding of the certified nursing aide job description. Out of 18 questionnaires distributed, only five were completed and returned, a 28 percent response rate. Of the five responses, three were ancillary aides and two were not.

LEVEL 3: JOB APPLICATION. The evaluation method was a supervisor evaluation. Interim and 90-day evaluations were analyzed and averaged for a single number result. Of the 28 employees studied, the 19 who did not have ancillary aide experience had an average evaluation score of 3.4 of a possible 5. The nine employees who had worked as ancillary aides had an average score of 3.0.

This may indicate that the ancillary aide experience did not help in performance. The ancillary aides actually performed, as a group, lower than their classmates.

LEVEL 4: BUSINESS RESULTS. Business results encompass the cost to recruit and train, turnover, and loss of investment.

- *Cost to recruit and train.* The total investment in ancillary aides, from recruitment through unit orientation, is $1,582 per employee. The total investment in nonancillary aides, from recruitment through unit orientation, is $1,123 per employee. The Ancillary Aide Program results in an increased cost to the facility of $459.
- *Turnover.* Of the 28 employees at Tioga Nursing Facility who participated in the nursing aide training course, seven have either been terminated or have resigned. The ancillary aide group accounted for 57 percent of the turnover.
- *Loss of investment.* Loss of investment due to terminations and resignations for ancillary aides is $6,328; for nonancillary aides, $3,369, for a total cost of $9,697. Ancillary aides accounted for 65 percent of the loss.

During the average two-week preclass time that ancillary aides worked on the nursing units, the facility saved $12.30 per day ($120 for the two-week period) for each ancillary aide. To staff the units with Level 2 certified nurse's aides would cost $51.83 per day; by using ancillary aides it cost $39.53 per day.

PRELIMINARY CONCLUSIONS. Preliminary conclusions indicated that the Ancillary Aide Program did not accomplish its objective and may not be a benefit to the facility. Although the members of the project felt the study was too short and the data inadequate, the project was dissolved. The project was an excellent learning experience for the task force.

Project 2

The Management Development Technology Initiative (MDTI) at Guthrie Healthcare System was designed to provide all members of the Guthrie management and leadership team with access to technology and better information to facilitate decision-making, enhance communication, and improve management performance. The initiative involved delivering desktop microcomputers to 160 managers as well as providing a standard management suite of software. The initiative included the development and implementation of an MDTI training plan that applies to the needs of management. This training plan involves defining and developing competencies measured by using personal computers and the standard management suite of software. The initiative also includes the development and provision of a support infrastructure that emphasizes good customer service.

The MDTI was implemented in two phases, each with 80 managers. Phase one rollout of technology was complete with training and evaluation ongoing at the time of the ROI training. Phase two rollout of technology was scheduled for year 2 of the project. ROI was measured throughout the initiative and will be finalized at the completion of the second phase.

Project 3

The ROI on ROI was a project to calculate the return-on-investment for the five-day certification program. This project included the costs of the certification course and included the Ancillary Aide Program and MDTI Program data. Because of the length of the MDTI project, the ROI on ROI project was scheduled for the early part of 1999.

Year 2 Objectives
The Pilot Project

As outlined in the goal to maximize ROI, we decided to use the MDTI as our systemwide ROI project for 1997-1998. MDTI was part of a plan designed to propel the organization to higher levels of performance through information technology. This initiative would become the cornerstone in our efforts to assess bottom-line impact. The following issues drove the MDTI training strategy:

- How do we link individual technology learning needs to work processes?
- How do we determine whether participants have transferred training to their jobs?
- How do we determine whether training has resulted in organizational improvement?
- How do we measure ROI?

Managers participating in the MDTI were partnered with an instructor from the staff development area of HOD. The instructor acts as an advisor to the manager, and together they perform an assessment of the training needs for that manager. This Individual Technology Development Plan (ITDP) is designed to focus on building competencies in the areas identified through the assessment process. The plan is designed to help create a learning track to close the gaps identified and to begin the journey toward improved performance. The ITDP outlines learning objective and learning resource and strategies. In the plan, they include targets for completing the competency-building process and methods used to measure success.

Six months following the initial assessment, the managers are asked to complete an evaluation, shown in figure 4, to determine knowledge and skills transfer to the job. In addition, the impact of technology, training, and support are measured to determine business results of the MDTI. This information will then be utilized to calculate the ROI on the initiative.

Learning Partners

Individuals who participated in the ROI workshop have since paired together to begin the education process with the senior executive team. Each pair is responsible for presenting ROI concepts to their senior staff partner as well as providing ongoing support on potential ROI projects identified within their realm of responsibility.

The concept of forming partnerships and establishing a coaching relationship with senior staff members further supports our efforts to drive the organization to high performance through learning.

System Education and Awareness

ROI has not only become the buzzword of the 1997-1998 budget year but also is outlined in the goals of the Guthrie Healthcare System and further supported in the goals of HOD. In addition, in December 1997, a leadership forum was to set the stage for ROI implementation throughout GHS. Managers and supervisors were to re-

Figure 4. MDTI evaluation.

What happens when participants leave training and return to their jobs? How much transfer of knowledge, skills, and attitude occurs? That is what we are attempting to find out in the following eleven items.

This questionnaire will help the MDTI Task Force determine the extent to which those who have participated in the MDTI have applied the knowledge and skills learned throughout this initiative to their jobs. The results of this survey will help us assess the effectiveness of this initiative and identify ways in which it can be made more practical for those who participate in the future. Please be frank and honest in your answers.

Instructions: Please circle the number that applies. Use the following scale in responding to the items below.

1. To a large extent
2. To some extent
3. Do not use
4. Not applicable

1. To what extent have you used the following skills? Please circle the number that applies.

A.	Opening multiple software applications using the Start Button and using the Taskbar to move between applications.	1	2	3	4
B.	Finding, opening, and printing files.	1	2	3	4
C.	Reading, deleting, and printing mail.				
	• Internet	1	2	3	4
	• Lotus Notes	1	2	3	4
	• IDX E-mail	1	2	3	4
D.	Composing, sending, forwarding, and replying to mail messages.				
	• Internet	1	2	3	4
	• Lotus Notes	1	2	3	4
	• IDX E-mail	1	2	3	4
E.	Creating, organizing, navigating, and deleting folders.				
	• Windows 95	1	2	3	4
	• Internet	1	2	3	4
	• Lotus Notes	1	2	3	4
	• IDX E-mail	1	2	3	4
F.	Maintaining Address Books.				
	• Internet	1	2	3	4
	• Lotus Notes	1	2	3	4
G.	Finding, exploring, and bookmarking Web sites.	1	2	3	4
H.	Creating, editing, saving, and printing Lotus notes database documents.	1	2	3	4

continued on page 70

Figure 4. MDTI evaluation (continued).

I. Applying various formatting techniques   1   2   3   4
    to Windows software programs
    (i.e., margins, tabs, font size, italics, color, etc.).

J. Using cut, copy, and paste techniques among   1   2   3   4
    Windows software programs.

K. Attaching files and working with file attachments.   1   2   3   4

L. Using Word to develop and maintain documents   1   2   3   4
    (i.e., edit, save, spell check, etc.).

M. Using Excel to develop and maintain spreadsheets.   1   2   3   4

N. Using PowerPoint to develop and maintain   1   2   3   4
    presentation materials.

O. Using Access to develop and maintain databases.   1   2   3   4

2. To what extent have you used the reference and resource materials provided during this initiative?

> To a large extent _____   To some extent _____   Do not use _____

3. Please identify factors in your work environment and realm of responsibility that have influenced or motivated you to apply the knowledge and skills learned during this initiative.

4. What technology applications have been most useful to you? Rank in order all that apply with "1" being the most useful.

Windows 95	_____	Internet	_____	Access	_____
Lotus Notes	_____	Word	_____	Excel	_____
PowerPoint	_____	IDX E-Mail	_____		

5. Which 90-Minute Workout series was most helpful to you?
    Rank in order all that apply.

Windows 95	_____	Internet	_____	Access	_____
Lotus Notes	_____	Word	_____	Excel	_____
PowerPoint	_____	IDX E-Mail	_____		

6. Has the level of support provided by each of the following been appropriate for your needs?

	Yes	No	N/A
A. Advisement/Assessment Session support	_____	_____	_____
B. Training support	_____	_____	_____
C. Help Desk support	_____	_____	_____
D. Technical/PC support	_____	_____	_____
E. Software support (spreadsheet/database)	_____	_____	_____

Please comment if necessary. _____

continued on page 71

Figure 4. MDTI evaluation (continued).

7. What percentage of your learning for this initiative was attributed to the following: (Total should equal 100%)

Prior knowledge	____%
Actual technology	____%
Help Desk support	____%
H.O.D.D. Staff Development support	____%
Self-learning packets	____%
Trial and error	____%
One-on-one	____%
Classroom training (90 Minute Workouts)	____%
CD ROM Tutorial	____%
Coaching (peers)	____%
Internet	____%
Audiovisual materials	____%
Other	____%
Total	**100%**

8. Which of your work processes have benefited as a result of this initiative? (Check all that apply)

Analyzing/Budgeting	_____
Planning	_____
Communicating (Electronically)	_____
Presenting	_____
Creating Policies and Procedures	_____
Problem Solving/Decision Making	_____
Customer Service	_____
Purchasing	_____
Managing Projects	_____
Researching	_____
Meetings	_____
Staffing/Scheduling	_____
Organizing	_____
Training	_____

9. Please describe specific situations in which you have effectively applied the knowledge and skills learned to your work processes since your participation in this initiative.

10. Please describe previous work practices, procedures, etc. that you have stopped performing since your participation in this initiative.

11. Please describe any changes in you, your work, or your upward-downward relationships that are a result of this initiative.

continued on page 72

Figure 4. MDTI evaluation (continued).

In items 12-17, we are evaluating the results of the MDTI to organizational improvement. Some of the results that can be examined include cost savings, work output improvement, and quality changes.

Instructions: In regard to the following results, what changes have been noticed since your participation in this initiative? Rate the individual benchmarks listed below.

12. Performance Benchmarks

Performance Benchmarks	Much Better	Somewhat Better	No Change	Somewhat Worse	Much Worse	Don't Know
Computer literacy						
Efficiency in accessing applications						
Efficiency in managing files and folders						
Accessing information						
Level of support						
Other:						
Communication						
Communication						
Collaboration on projects						
Speed at which information is exchanged						
Other:						
Job satisfaction						
Stress level						
Outlook						
Other:						

continued on page 73

Figure 4. MDTI evaluation (continued).

13. As a result of this initiative, what do you estimate to be the increase/decrease in your personal effectiveness, expressed as a percent?

Performance Benchmarks	% Increase	% Decrease
Time savings		
Meeting time		
Travel time		
Job tasks		
Telephone usage		
Other:		
Cost savings		
Paper waste		
More efficient work processes		
Other:		
Quality improvement		
Rework		
Work errors		
Other:		

14. How did you arrive at each of the estimates above?

Time savings (i.e., meeting time, travel time, job tasks, telephone usage)
Cost savings (i.e., paper waste, more efficient work processes)
Quality improvement (i.e., work errors, rework)

continued on page 74

Figure 4. MDTI evaluation (continued).

15. As a result of applying technology skills on the job, please estimate (in dollars) the amount of money you have saved the system (increased efficiency, reduced meeting time, reduced travel, etc.) as a result of this initiative? **Please provide an annual estimate.**

Performance Benchmarks	% Increase	% Decrease
Time savings		
Meeting time		
Travel time		
Job tasks		
Telephone usage		
Other:		
Cost savings		
Paper waste		
More efficient work processes		
Other:		
Quality improvement		
Rework		
Work errors		
Other:		

16. In relation to the time savings benchmark above, how have you utilized the additional time?

17. After reviewing all the data provided, what confidence, expressed as a percentage, can you put in your estimate? _____% (0 = No Confidence, 100 = Complete Confidence)

Please feel free to add any additional comments.

NAME _____
(Optional)

ceive education on the five levels of evaluation and learn a variety of approaches for calculating ROI. Members of the original ROI training group will assist managers in finding, identifying, and developing cost-effective methods for employees to learn needed knowledge and skills, and to help support management's role in determining training's impact.

Challenge of Sustainability

One thing remains certain—the 11 Guthrie employees involved in the original ROI training and the senior executive team are, as a result of that training and continued work, convinced of its potential value and are committed to its adoption as a policy practice of GHS. Guthrie has identified itself as a learning organization, and the group trained in ROI has readily accepted the concept of ROI measurement. The task of demonstrating and selling the concept of ROI, or any new program, requires sustained enthusiasm and sustained progress. The biggest challenges we have faced involve our own inexperience with ROI and the incorporation of ROI projects into busy schedules.

Members of the group have felt frustration with their own inexperience, which may have manifested itself in the projects selected. One group's project may have been too small, making it difficult to obtain credible statistics. Another's may be too large, involving an entire initiative rather then a particular training program.

Members of the group have found support in each other and have found their own belief in the value of ROI to keep them moving forward. As we develop our expertise and see the successful completion of our projects continue to work and partner with managers and the senior executive team, we feel confident that our enthusiasm and success will help sustain us through implementation throughout the system.

Moving Forward

In moving forward, our goal is to affect the Guthrie Healthcare System culture in such a way that understanding, accepting, and adopting ROI are routine. To ensure our success, we have begun working with the senior executive team on selected ROI projects. Our goal is to have all Guthrie Healthcare System managers comfortable with the ROI process. This will be accomplished by assisting department managers in conducting front-end needs assessments, providing learning opportunities on the ROI process, and partnering with them on subsequent ROI projects.

Conclusion

One of the toughest challenges facing organizations today is the pressure to demonstrate value in return for investments made. The call for cost-effectiveness is becoming louder and more persistent throughout the Guthrie Healthcare System. This renewed emphasis on financial accountability can be clearly traced to the strategic goals of GHS and the Human and Organizational Development Department. In addition, there has been a systemwide shift from activity-oriented training as the means or intervention of choice to fix problems, to a new focus on results-oriented activities that enhance performance and support Guthrie's core business strategy to demonstrate results and add value. In our commitment to become a high-performance learning organization, key contributors throughout the system have been asked to identify goals and standards required for all employees to reach top performance levels. To accomplish this required a shift in how we view teaching, learning, assessment, and measurement. For the first time, we are being challenged to answer this question: What knowledge, skills, job orientations, and attitudes will our employees need in order to prepare for the competitive challenges of health care in the future? As a result, a new awareness and appreciation for assessment and evaluation as a means to enhance learning and performance has emerged. More frequently, the message being communicated and integrated in our day-to-day work is that corporate and individual learning is best facilitated when assessment and evaluation are intimately linked to and integrated with other organizational initiatives such as corporate strategy, policy development, compensation and reward systems, information technology, and management development.

The ultimate responsibility for demonstrating value and achieving outcomes that translate to bottom-line results does not fall on the shoulders of a single individual or department. Accountability for adding value is now considered the responsibility of everyone in the organization. ROI is a systemwide philosophy.

Questions for Discussion

1. How is ROI being utilized to aid in the transformation to create a high-performance learning organization? What are your reactions to this approach?

2. Was the Tioga Nursing Facility project a valid ROI study? Why or why not?

3. How was ROI introduced and implemented in GHS? Do you agree with this approach?

4. What were the desired outcomes of the five-day certification training program? What lessons did the attendees learn?
5. What is your assessment of the Year 1 objectives? What is your assessment of the Year 2 objectives? What changes would you make?

The Authors

Pauline L. Stamp entered the Guthrie Healthcare System in July 1992 as senior administrator of the Donald Guthrie Foundation for Education and Research. In 1993, Stamp was named president of the Mansfield University/Robert Packer School of Health Sciences, School of Nursing. In addition, in 1995 she was promoted to senior vice president of the Education and Research Division and Human and Organizational Development Department. In this capacity, Stamp is responsible for all departments and companies within the division, including the Guthrie Research Institute; the William C. Beck, M.D., Library and Resource Center; EAP Staff Development and Training; Mansfield University/Robert Packer School of Nursing and Allied Health Sciences; Audio-Visual Services; Human Resources and Human and Organizational Development.

Stamp received her undergraduate degree in education from Northeastern University in 1985. She received her master's degree in health education from Boston University in 1987 and a master's degree in organizational development in 1996 from the Fielding Institute. In 1991 she received a Certificate of Advanced Studies in education administration from SUNY-Cortland. In July 1997 she received her doctoral degree in organizational systems from The Fielding Institute, with a focus on organizational change. She can be contacted at the following address: Guthrie Healthcare System, One Guthrie Square, Sayre, PA 18840; phone: 717.882.4621.

Michele Sisto is the vice president of finance in the Guthrie Healthcare System. She is responsible for the For-Profit and Education & Research divisions of the system, and is acting as finance lead on all tax matters. She holds a B.S. degree in business administration with a concentration in accounting from Duquesne University in Pittsburgh.

Roberta Sabitus joined Robert Packer Hospital in 1984 as employment manager. In 1988 she was appointed employee relations manager, in 1989 she was promoted to director of human resources, and in 1994 appointed to vice president of human resources for GHS. She holds a B.A. degree from Wilkes College and received a Graduate Credit Certificate in industrial relations from Cornell University School of Industrial and Labor Relations.

Christine Burt presently holds the position of human resources manager of Guthrie Healthcare System. She earned a B.A. degree in business administration from Elmira College and has been employed in the field of human resources for 24 years, both in health care and industry. She is currently developing the human resource information system for GHS.

Richard Rava is the information services manager research, development, and education at Guthrie Healthcare System. He is responsible for the research of new computer technology and the development and education of computer technology skills within information services. He holds an M.S. degree in education from SUNY College of Technology at Utica, New York, and a B.A. degree in computer science from Potsdam College at Potsdam, New York.

William Muth's position with GHS is that of nursing systems manager. He has been a registered nurse in Trauma/Cardiac ICUs for more than 14 years, an assistant nursing division manager for eight years, and an ICU manager for three years. He is presently working on his master's degree in informatics at Syracuse University.

Susan Hall is a member of the Human and Organizational Development Department for GHS where she is responsible for planning, coordinating, implementing, and evaluating a wide range of training and development activities within the organization. Prior to joining GHS, she taught for many years at Broome Community College in her hometown of Binghamton, New York. In addition to her teaching experience, she has had extensive experience coordinating adult education programs. Hall received her undergraduate degree in business and education in 1974 from the State University of New York at Albany. In 1979 she earned her master's degree in education from the SUNY, Albany.

Bonnie Onofre is a nursing education coordinator within the Department of Nursing Education and Research at the Guthrie/Robert Packer Hospital. She is responsible for assessing, developing, conducting, and evaluating educational programs and activities for nursing department personnel. Onofre has over 20 years of experience in a variety of settings, including nursing education, management, and clinical practice. She has a B.S.N. from Alfred University, is an M.S.N. graduate of Syracuse University, and has completed a post-master's certificate as a family nurse practitioner from Binghamton University. In addition to her current role, Onofre coordinates a variety of clinical performance improvement projects and research initiatives within the organization.

Bibliography

Argyris, C. (1993). *Knowledge for Action: A Guide to Overcoming Barriers to Organizational Change.* San Francisco: Jossey-Bass.

Bennis, W. (1996, January-February). "The Leader as Storyteller." *Harvard Business Review,* 154–160.

Bennis, W., & B. Nanus. (1985). *Leaders: The Strategies for Taking Charge.* New York: Harper & Row.

Burgoyne, J.G. (1992). "Creating a Learning Organization." *Royal Society for the Arts Journal, 140* (5248).

Garvin, D. (1993, July, August). "Building a Learning Organization." *The Harvard Business Review, 71*(4), 78–91.

Gayeski, D. (1993). *Corporate Communications Management: The Renaissance Communicator in Information-Age Organizations.* Woburn, MA: Focal Press.

Pedler, M., J. Burgoyne, & T. Boydell. (1991). *The Learning Company: A Strategy for Sustainable Development.* London, England: McGraw-Hill.

Schein, E.H. (1993, Winter). "How Can Organizations Learn Faster? The Challenge of Entering the Green Room." *Sloan Management Review.*

Senge, M.P. (1990, Fall). "The Leader's New Work: Building Learning Organizations." *Sloan Management Review.*

Stamp, P. (1997). *Journey from Concept to Practice: One Company's Experience with the Learning Organization.* Doctoral dissertation, University of Michigan, Ann Arbor, MI.

Watkins, K., & V. Marsick. (1993). *Sculpting the Learning Organization: Lessons in the Art and Science of Systemic Change.* San Francisco: Jossey-Bass.

The Results-Based Approach of Evaluating Learning

First Union's Commercial College

Debra Wallace

To understand the current learning evaluation process in the Commercial College at First Union, you must first understand how the group originated. First Union is the sixth largest bank in the United States with over $163 billion in assets, over 50,000 employees, and a franchise that stretches from Key West, Florida, to Hartford, Connecticut. First Union's Commercial Bank consists of approximately 2,500 employees and has a presence in all of First Union's major markets. First Union is characterized by aggressive growth through acquisition and expansion into nontraditional banking arenas.

Background

In 1994, First Union reengineered its Commercial Bank and created a Commercial Bank training function. The two key objectives for this new training group were to align itself with customer requirements for new business imperatives, and to do it faster, better, and cheaper than ever before.

Additionally, in 1995, the human resources group also reengineered, creating a new division called First University, which was responsible for creating a learning organization within First Union. The Commercial College was created at that time by merging the Commercial Bank training team into it to meet the learning needs of First Union's Commercial Bank.

After the Commercial Bank reengineering training in late 1995, it became obvious that old techniques for designing, developing, and

This case was prepared to serve as a basis for discussion rather than to illustrate either effective or ineffective administrative and management practices.

implementing training would not equip the team to meet the client's key objectives. Therefore, the team established two key goals:

- to adopt a consistent and effective approach for designing and delivering appropriate learning opportunities to the client that truly addresses specific business issues
- to develop a process for evaluating the effectiveness of its learning opportunities to provide both a tool for performance consulting with clients and to continuously improve products and services.

To address the first goal, the entire team was certified in mid-1996 in Robert Mager's criterion-referenced instruction process of instructional design. After completing this certification process, the Commercial College learning specialists were better prepared to consult with internal Commercial Bank clients on performance issues and to prescribe solutions that were focused on improving individual and team performance. This approach differed from the old one of often meeting client needs by simply delivering what they asked for, whether or not the learning solution was the appropriate intervention.

The second goal was addressed by selecting Performance Resources Organization (PRO) as a consultant. PRO would both work with the Commercial College in conducting a study to determine the impact of a major learning initiative and to provide Commercial College team members with the skill and knowledge they need to conduct internal impact studies.

The result of adopting Mager's approach of instructional design and PRO's approach of evaluating learning is an effective and integrated results-based process that more clearly links individual programs to specific business needs. All learning opportunities must be directly linked to business needs, and must be designed, developed, and implemented with the goal of improving business measures.

At the heart of this approach is a multiple-level evaluation framework where learning opportunities are evaluated on the basis of several inputs and measures. Evaluation begins with an assessment of the reaction of participants to the program. Next, measures of specific learning are developed while the program is being implemented. After implementation, changes in behavior on the job and changes in business performance are monitored. The ultimate evaluation level is the return-on-investment where the cost of the program is compared to the economic benefits. The Commercial College routinely calculates the return-on-investment for a select group of learning opportunities.

The implications of this results-based approach are updated roles and responsibilities for all individuals and groups involved in initiating, designing, developing, delivering, and supporting learning opportunities. The concern for results begins in the needs assessment and performance analysis phase as client partners who are assigned responsibility for performance consulting with specific client groups in each First Union franchise state uncover business problems or opportunities. During design and development, designers and vendors must develop materials that are directly linked to the measurable and criterion-referenced business objectives. Facilitators must focus their presentations, exercises, and activities on important business issues and needs. Managers must reinforce and support the learning process with a variety of involvement activities and initiatives. The ultimate responsibility for the success of a learning opportunity must rest with the management group. The Commercial College shares in this responsibility in a supportive and collaborative role.

The Commercial College routinely creates impact studies to document the results of learning opportunities at various levels. Program owners or client partners present these impact studies to many different parties in the Commercial Bank, as appropriate, including participants, participants' managers, Commercial Bank senior managers, and the Commercial College Advisory Board. The client is slowly introduced to this philosophy by seeing results as opposed to being presented with theory that may seem unrealistic.

The Results-Based Approach of the Commercial College
Philosophy

The purpose of learning opportunities offered by the Commercial College is to achieve corporate, business unit, and individual goals. Programs should offer tangible and intangible returns to the client and to the short- and long-term performance improvement of the Commercial Bank. The evaluation of programs and services will provide measurement of the desired improvement.

What It Means

The results-based approach of the Commercial College has several important features:
- Learning opportunities are initiated, developed, and delivered with the end in mind. A clearly established business need must be linked to a new learning opportunity before it is developed and implemented.

- A measurement and evaluation plan is developed for each learning opportunity. Some programs will require a very comprehensive plan, whereas others will require a more simplistic approach.
- A performance support tool is developed for each learning opportunity. The purpose of this tool is to describe to the participant's manager
  —what the employee will be able to do after the learning opportunity
  —what the employee must do prior to the learning opportunity
  —what the manager should do prior to the learning opportunity
  —what the manager can do after the learning opportunity to assist in transferring learning to on-the-job performance improvement.
- Business impact or return-on-investment (ROI) evaluations are regularly developed each year in the Commercial College. The Commercial College Advisory Board will provide guidance as to which programs will be evaluated at this level.
- Participants understand their responsibility to achieve results with learning opportunities. It is important for each participant engaged in a program to accept responsibility to successfully apply learning to achieve results.

Collectively, these five elements make up a results-based framework that has become an important foundation of the Commercial College's approach to developing and implementing successful learning opportunities.

Evaluation at All Levels

The success of each learning opportunity will be evaluated to ensure ultimate success and to provide effective performance-consulting information to all groups involved in the process. Although evaluations may not be conducted at all levels, the capability and the process will be in place to evaluate at all of the levels outlined in figure 1.

Collectively, these five levels of evaluation provide a comprehensive measurement and evaluation process for the Commercial College. This process follows the work of Kirkpatrick (1994) and Phillips (1996). Because evaluation at all five levels is time-consuming and expensive to develop, a small number of learning opportunities will be targeted for the more comprehensive evaluation levels. Specific targets are established and will be revised regularly.

Evaluation Targets

To ensure that there is a comprehensive system of evaluation and the resources available for evaluation, specific targets are set for each level of evaluation. This process requires that a certain number of

Figure 1. Levels of evaluation.

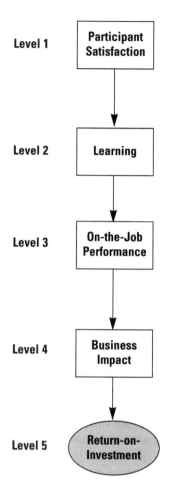

Level 1 — Participant Satisfaction

As the learning opportunity is implemented, participants provide information about their reaction to the program in terms of key variables such as the effectiveness of the facilitator, usefulness of the materials, and the relevance of the content. Level 1 evaluation information serves as important client satisfaction data from the participants, and also provides critical data needed to make adjustments in the learning process.

Level 2 — Learning

The Commercial College's programs are designed to build skills, increase knowledge, and/or enhance attitudes of employees. For Level 2 evaluation, learning is measured in terms of the acquisition of skills and knowledge and changes in attitudes.

Level 3 — On-the-Job Performance

It is critical to apply the skills and knowledge acquired in the learning opportunity to the job, and measures are taken during follow-up periods to judge the success of on-the-job applications. With Level 3 evaluation, specific measurements gauge the success of on-the-job applications as well as barriers to successful applications.

Level 4 — Business Impact

With learning opportunities linked to business needs, it is important to measure the changes in specific business measures that have been influenced or driven by the learning opportunity. At Level 4 evaluation, a variety of business measures are monitored and linked to the programs.

Level 5 — Return-on-Investment

Because the cost of training programs can possibly exceed the specific benefits, the ultimate level of evaluation is a measure of return-on-investment, where the monetary values of the benefits are compared to the cost of providing the program. For this Level 5 evaluation, the cost versus benefit comparison is developed using a standard ROI formula.

programs be evaluated at each level. Targets for the three curriculum teams in the Commercial College (Business Development, Products and Business & Industry; Financial and Credit Skills; and Interpersonal, Leadership, Management and Coaching) are shown in figure 2.

Commercial College uses several criteria to determine which specific courses are selected for advanced levels of evaluation. These include the following:

• The program is part of a Commercial Bank strategic initiative.
• An executive requests that the program be evaluated.

Figure 2. 1997 evaluation targets.

Business Development, Products, and Business & Industry
1997 Evaluation Targets

Level of Evaluation	Percent of Programs Evaluated at This Level
Level 1: Reaction and planned action	100%
Level 2: Learning	50%
Level 3: Job applications	4 courses
Level 4: Business impact	2 courses
Level 5: Return-on-investment	1 course

Financial and Credit Skills
1997 Evaluation Targets

Level of Evaluation	Percent of Programs Evaluated at This Level
Level 1: Reaction and planned action	100%
Level 2: Learning	50%
Level 3: Job applications	4 courses
Level 4: Business impact	2 courses
Level 5: Return-on-investment	1 course

Interpersonal, Leadership, Management, and Coaching
1997 Evaluation Targets

Level of Evaluation	Percent of Programs Evaluated at This Level
Level 1: Reaction and planned action	100%
Level 2: Learning	50%
Level 3: Job applications	4 courses

- The length of time the learning opportunity is expected to be viable.
- The learning opportunity has a high level of visibility.
- A comprehensive needs assessment has been conducted.
- The target group is large.
- The cost of the program is high.
- The program cuts across business units or geographic regions.
- The program's vendor is interested in assisting in the evaluation.
- Level 4 baseline data are available.
- The cost and time of evaluating at this level is reasonable.

These targets and criteria provide guidance for a complete evaluation system. For evaluations planned at Level 5, a Level 4, 3, 2, and 1 evaluation must also be planned to ensure that a chain of impact has occurred that indicates that participants learned the material, applied it on the job, and obtained the desired results.

Developing Costs

Capturing costs is an important issue because the costs must be accurate, reliable, and realistic. Although the total Commercial College direct budget is usually a number that is easily developed, it is more difficult to determine the specific costs of a single program, including the indirect costs related to it. To develop a realistic ROI, costs must be accurate and credible. Otherwise, the painstaking difficulty of developing the monetary benefits will be wasted because of inadequate or inaccurate costs.

The Commercial College has adopted a conservative approach at calculating ROI by fully loading all costs associated with the learning opportunity. With this approach, all costs that can be identified and linked to a particular program are included. When an ROI is calculated and reported to target audiences, the process should withstand even the closest scrutiny in terms of its accuracy and credibility. The only way to meet this test is to ensure that all costs are included.

Major cost categories include:
- needs assessment and performance analysis
- design and development
- acquisition costs (costs to acquire programs from vendors)
- delivery costs including:
  — salaries of facilitators and coordinators
  — program materials and fees
  — travel, lodging, and meals
  — facilities
  — participant salaries and benefits
  — evaluation costs
  — overhead.

Results-Based Model for Implementing Learning Opportunities

Figure 3 illustrates the process that the Commercial College follows when either designing new programs or revising existing programs. It is a further expansion of the model adopted after attending the Mager training on criterion-referenced instruction.

The Commercial College's results-based approach has a dramatic effect on new or proposed learning opportunities. Because learning

Figure 3. New program design/revision of existing program process.

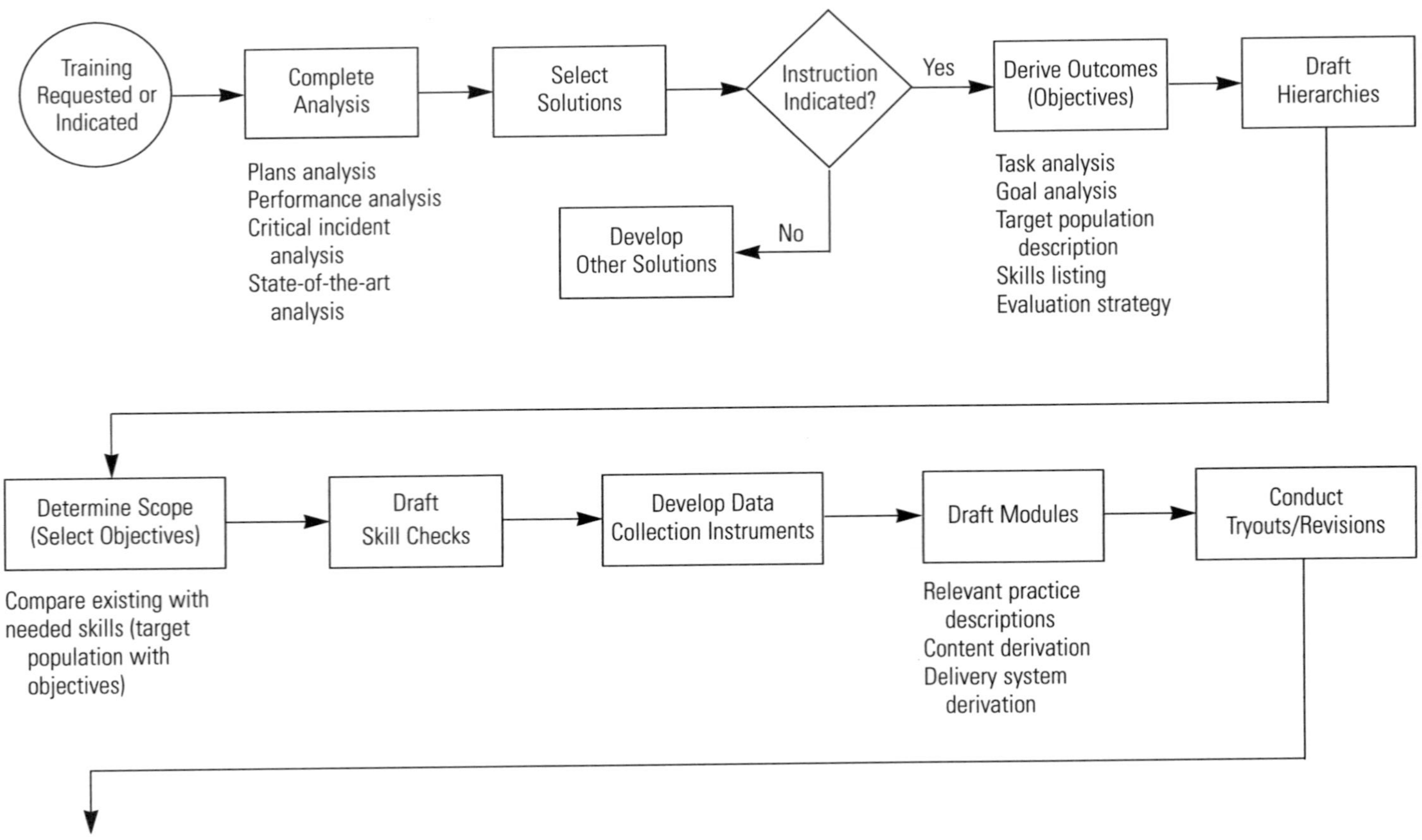

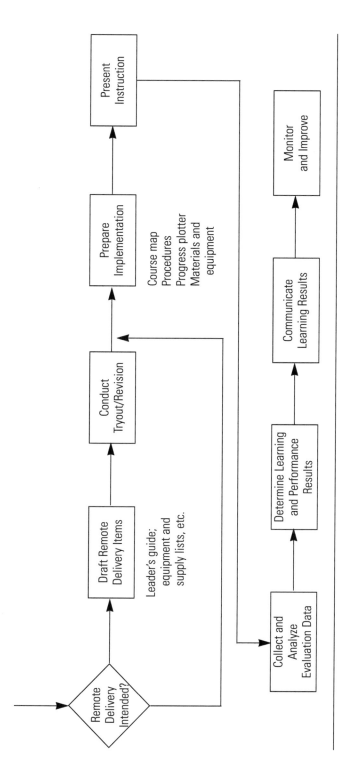

opportunities must be linked to business needs, a thorough needs assessment is required. A precise business need must be identified that will be enhanced, influenced, or corrected by the intervention. In addition, specific behavior changes needed in the future must be identified. This requirement moves needs assessment beyond the traditional assessment of skills, knowledge, or attitudes to true performance analysis that assesses on-the-job performance, business problems, and opportunities. With this approach, the college will not pursue a new or proposed learning opportunity unless it directly addresses a legitimate business need and is changing behavior linked to the performance issue.

Communication With Clients: A Focus on Performance

The results-based approach requires a change in the nature and character of communication with clients. Previous communication focused on issues such as what participants need to learn, how many participants will be involved, and the reaction of participants to the learning opportunity. Although these are important issues, they do not reflect the ultimate accountability of the learning opportunity. Typical communication with clients will involve the following issues:

- *Linkage with business needs.* Because new programs must be linked to the Commercial Bank's business needs or the specific measures in a business unit, or both, client communications must focus on problems, concerns, and opportunities as they relate to specific business measures. When programs are implemented or completed, the impact on specific improvements in business variables will be discussed, reviewed, and reported.

- *Specific behavior changes.* Because the culture and the climate of the Commercial Bank is constantly changing, new and enhanced behaviors are required at all levels in the organization. The college's dialogue with clients focuses on the expected change in behavior, rather than actual behavior. Planned behavior change should support specific business needs.

- *Developing and approving terminal objectives.* All learning must have one or more specific terminal objectives that are directly linked to the business issue. The client must be involved in establishing and approving these objectives. Terminal objectives describe the skill or competence representing the final outcome of a related group of performance objectives.

- *Developing and approving performance objectives.* In concert with the development of terminal objectives, clients must help set specific objectives for desired behavior change or performance of participants as they are engaged in various learning opportunities. Desired, expected, and actual data will be regularly explored and discussed with the client, and senior management will have the responsibility for approving the objectives.

- *Collecting data.* At times, the client will be required to collect evaluation data or assist in the collection of data. Above all, the client must support data collection. Active client involvement in evaluation will enhance the understanding and success of the process.

Responsibilities

Measuring the effectiveness of learning opportunities is a shared responsibility of several important groups. The Commercial College, through the direction of the advisory board, has the overall responsibility to:

- manage the evaluation process from the needs assessment and performance analysis to communicating the results of evaluation
- ensure that an appropriate needs assessment and performance analysis is conducted before proceeding with a new learning opportunity
- identify application objectives (Level 3) and business impact objectives (Level 4) for each new learning opportunity
- set targets for evaluation for all programs at each level
- develop an evaluation strategy for each learning opportunity
- develop learning opportunities with evaluation procedures in place to measure results
- provide participants and managers with information about the evaluation process and expected results from each learning opportunity
- coordinate the data-collection process
- coordinate or conduct data analysis
- interpret results and review evaluation reports
- communicate evaluation results to selected target audiences
- modify or eliminate existing learning opportunities based on evaluation results.

Learning specialists have the responsibility to:

- ensure that terminal objectives and performance objectives are developed for each new program early in the design process
- develop content that is relevant to jobs and linked to business unit issues
- design exercises and activities that link to the business environment, needs, and issues

- when possible, develop evaluation tools within the learning opportunity for self-assessment and for reporting results
- communicate the results-based focus to vendors who design and develop learning opportunities and tie vendor compensation to evaluation results when appropriate
- revise and redesign programs on the basis of the results of previous evaluations.

Support staff is responsible for:
- ensuring that participants and managers have appropriate materials related to measurement and evaluation
- assisting in the evaluation process as required to ensure that it flows smoothly and timely
- assisting in collecting data when required
- distributing evaluation results to various target groups.

The evaluation staff is responsible for:
- monitoring the measurement and evaluation process for the Commercial College
- coordinating significant activities and efforts involving the measurement and evaluation process
- reporting progress on measurement and evaluation to appropriate target audiences
- securing appropriate resources to keep the measurement and evaluation process on track and meeting goals and targets
- reviewing results of significant evaluations
- participating in communications of evaluation information to appropriate target groups.

Instructors and facilitators have the responsibility to:
- ensure the participants understand performance of the program
- reflect business issues in illustrations, cases, exercises, and discussions
- insist that application and business impact are regularly discussed and integrated throughout the learning opportunity
- assist with Level 1 and Level 2 data collection, when required
- explain Level 3 and Level 4 data-collection requirements, when required
- constantly stress the change in behavior and attainment of results as part of the learning opportunity.

Clients have the responsibility to:
- ensure that the learning specialist is aware of the desired performance improvement from learning opportunities
- identify employees whose participation in the learning opportunity is critical for the desired business improvement

- provide appropriate direction to the Commercial College to ensure that learning opportunities are linked to business unit needs
- keep the Commercial College apprised of future developments and trends so that programs can be available to assist the implementation and meet new business challenges and requirements
- review evaluation results and provide feedback to the Commercial College.

Participants' managers have the responsibility to:

- partner with their employees in enrolling in learning opportunities intended to improve business performance
- discuss the program with the participant using the performance support tool for the program prior to attendance or involvement to determine expected outcomes
- conduct a personal follow-up for the program results
- reinforce behavior after the program has been implemented and provide positive feedback and rewards for successful application of the learning opportunity
- assist in the planned formal follow-up activities of the learning opportunity
- be proactive in identifying and removing barriers to the application of learning opportunity.

Participants in learning opportunities have important responsibilities. They must:

- participate fully in learning opportunities to learn as much as possible
- explore ways in which learning can be applied on the job
- partner with the manager to choose training programs that can best improve business performance
- enter into the learning opportunity with an open mind and be willing to learn new concepts and develop new skills
- take responsibility for success of the application of the program
- when requested, provide information and feedback on success of the program and the barriers to implementation
- partner with the manager to identify and remove barriers to the application of the program
- have the determination to achieve success with the learning opportunity in the face of many obstacles to application and improvement.

Implementation Issues and Targets

The implementation of the results-based approach has not occurred quickly; it has been evolving for some time and will take several years to be fully operational. The timing of the implementation is very critical because changes in approaches are needed, along with a redirection of resources. To keep the implementation on target and the Commercial College staff in focus on this important transition, the following targets were set:

- A results-based cross-functional needs assessment and performance analysis will be conducted for 100 percent of new learning opportunities initiated after December 31, 1996. This requires that needs assessment and performance analysis will be focused on Level 3 and 4 data and from this data, Level 3 and 4 objectives for the learning opportunities will be developed.
- By January 1, 1997, all new learning opportunities will have a data-collection plan. The plan will include the following items:
  — objectives
  — data-collection methods
  — timing
  — responsibilities.
- By December 31, 1997, all learning opportunities will have a Performance Support Tool in place. This tool will document in a concise format the following information to the participant's manager:
  — What participants should do *prior* to the learning opportunity
  — What participant's managers should do *prior* to the learning opportunity
  — What participants will be able to do *after* the learning opportunity
  — What participant's managers should do *after* the learning opportunity to assist with transfer of training
- Evaluation at Levels 3 and 4 will include a strategy for isolating the effects of training.
- Evaluation at Level 5 will include strategies for converting the data to monetary values and tabulating the cost of the program.

The above targets are ambitious, but are essential to make the transition to a results-based approach within a reasonable time frame.

Benefits of a Results-Based Approach

The results-based approach has five important and very significant benefits:

- *The efficient use of resources.* This approach ensures that learning opportunities are only undertaken if they are adding value to the Commercial Bank and that all parts of the learning process are focused more specifically on the important goals, strategies, and objectives of the business unit.

- *Improved business impact of all learning opportunities.* Because the process focuses on important business unit needs, the success of learning opportunities are enhanced to show improved business impact.
- *Increased client satisfaction.* All clients involved in the learning process should be satisfied with this approach. Participants will clearly see the results of their efforts and the connection to business performance. Managers who support learning in a variety of ways will be more satisfied with the results they obtain from these programs.
- *Increased support and commitment from senior management.* The results of the learning opportunities, as they are applied to help business units reach their goals, will be welcomed by senior management. Increased support and commitment will follow.
- *Stable funding.* The results-based approach provides senior management and the Commercial College with an enhanced view of the contributions of learning opportunities. Linking learning with business outcomes should contribute to a stable funding level that consistently meets the needs of the business.

Progress With Process

Reaction to this approach has varied. Although learning specialists see the value in the discipline this process requires, it has been a challenge to precisely follow the process in all cases. The up-front time investment required to follow the process has been the biggest barrier to implementing this approach. This process requires the same inspection of expectations we suggest to our clients on significant performance improvement initiatives. This inspection process does not confine itself to the Commercial College dean, but also to all team members who must constantly remind, support, and give peer feedback to ensure its success.

The Commercial College Advisory Board has advocated the approach, and currently focuses interest primarily on Level 3 results. It will take several examples of Level 4 and 5 results to fully educate both our board and our client on the benefits and validity of the higher levels of evaluation.

Vendors have been both very interested in and quite intimidated by the expectations this process creates for the products they supply to the Commercial College. For many, they have never had to develop true criterion-referenced objectives and struggle through the initial process only to realize that it was worth the effort. For others, their compensation is tied to evaluation results that create both a strong desire to provide the appropriate learning intervention and intense anxiety about the results.

As stated earlier, our goals for implementing this approach have been aggressive. We have made significant progress toward our goal, and must stay focused on the foundation of the approach, which is conducting thorough and accurate needs assessments and performance analyses, and then developing in-depth Level 3 and 4 objectives as the basis for our learning opportunities. With this focus and client support, we are confident we will have a positive impact on our client's bottom line.

Questions for Discussion

1. Many factors influence a successful transition to a results-based approach of designing and evaluating learning. Do the members of your training team have the critical performance-oriented instructional design skills required to make a transition to a results-based approach? If not, how will you go about acquiring the new skills or knowledge needed to make the transition?
2. Has your organization established a fundamental framework for designing and evaluating learning opportunities? If not, what steps will you take to begin the process?
3. Has your organization established evaluation targets to ensure that all members of the team are striving to make evaluating learning a key component of any learning opportunity? If not, what industry benchmarks will you use to establish first-year goals?
4. Critical to the success of a results-based approach is client and management support, participation, and advocacy. What obstacles will your organization face as you "market" and obtain buy-in for this approach? How will you handle these objections?
5. How can you effectively educate and communicate with consultants or vendors who work with your team to develop learning opportunities to ensure adherence to the results-based approach? How will you handle their resistance to this approach?

The Author

Debra Wallace is a learning specialist and vice president in the Commercial College, part of First University (the training division for First Union Corporation). She has been in the banking business since 1986, first with NationsBank for eight years in a variety of line support positions. Her last position there was as manager of the Training and Systems Division supporting the special Assets Bank. Since joining First Union in 1994, Wallace has focused on managing training-related projects including major process reengineering and strategic learning system initiatives. She is currently focused on developing a strong learning evaluation framework and process for the Commercial College, along with conducting studies to determine the impact of learning opportunities delivered to First Union's Commercial Bank. Wallace has a B.S. in accounting with an emphasis in tax from Clemson University in Clemson, South Carolina. She can be contacted at the following address: First Union—Commercial College, 301 S. College Street, NC-0957, Charlotte, NC 28288.

References

Kirkpatrick, D.L. (1994). *Evaluating Training Programs*. San Francisco: Berrett-Koehler.

Phillips, J.J. (1996, February). "ROI: The Search for Best Practices." *Training & Development, 50,*(2), 42–47.

Building Accountability Into a Start-up University

Illinova/Illinois Power Company

Connie J. Schmidt and Jack J. Phillips

This case provides the reader with key issues and decisions that the company made to build and implement a successful, systematic, and comprehensive evaluation process within a start-up corporate university. It details how the organization successfully approached the evaluation challenge using creative means while tackling the barriers for successful implementation by building key relationships and partnerships both internally and externally. This case provides real-work situations and lessons learned from key stakeholders in the process.

Background

"Not so long ago, electric and gas utilities were rewarded by the marketplace for being conservative, slow, imitative, and unimaginative. Not anymore. Increasingly, utilities are rewarded by the marketplace for being bold, quick, aggressive, and creative" (Illinova/Illinois Power Corporation, p. 12). The utility industry is faced with the need to become more competitive as deregulation is occurring in some market segments and is imminent in others. Traditionally, in regulated environments, customer market share was protected. There was an obligation to serve customers in the franchise area, and costs were passed on to customers in a manner that guaranteed regulated profit levels. This led to the development of a corporate culture within regulated utilities where there was a lack of emphasis on efficiency and a false sense of reality on costs, profit maximization, customer

This case was prepared to serve as a basis for discussion rather than to illustrate either effective or ineffective administrative and management practices.

needs, and market dynamics. However, business strategies in a deregulated environment require placing more emphasis on customer satisfaction, quicker decision making, flexibility in services and pricing, and becoming a low-cost provider.

Illinova/Illinois Power Company (hereinafter known as Illinova) has been operating for more than 50 years as a publicly owned utility located in the Midwest. Illinova has grown primarily through selling off original interests from the early days and retaining only core gas and electric functions. With deregulation imminent, however, recent growth strategies have spawned the development of two nonregulated subsidiaries and expansion of existing gas fields. Illinova Generating, the independent power subsidiary, more than doubled its generating ownership during 1996. Illinova Power Marketing grew from a standing start in 1995 to a $45 million business in 1996 and "expects to grow eightfold in 1997" (Illinova/Illinois Power Corporation, p. 8). Restructuring of the corporation has led to annual revenues of nearly $1.7 billion, and future growth is planned at an increasing rate.

To survive in competitive markets, Illinova realizes that it must continue to grow while maintaining profits. In addition, Illinova must continue to increase efficiency of gas and electricity delivery, implement increasingly innovative approaches in marketing and customer retention, and develop and expand employees' skill base. Illinova employees must continually change their perception of jobs, customers, and business principles.

Building the Corporate University

Illinova University was conceptualized in the early 1990s shortly after the current CEO, Larry Haab, became president. In an increasingly changing environment, Haab knew that, as Darwin said, "It is not the strongest of the species that survive, nor the most intelligent, but the one most responsive to change." Preparation for competition required a shift in the current conservative culture to one that would encourage employees to take risks, be proactive, and be the best at what they do, ultimately improving market share and customer service. To ensure continued success, every employee would need to share the same vision.

To begin the culture change process, senior management conceived Illinova University (IU) to offer a curriculum that would help employees understand the business and industry. They had begun to view training as an investment in the company, its people, and the future of the business. Training was perceived as a way to provide the knowledge and skills necessary to remain competitive; enhance and maximize the company's most valuable resource—people; align the workforce with corporate beliefs, vision, and long-range goals; and promote innovation and initiative throughout the company. In short, IU was to be a change agent for the organization. Illinova's success would, in part, be determined by how committed the IU staff are to driving change.

Staffing of Illinova University began in 1996. As a part of the strategic action plan, the infrastructure for IU was formed by establishing a board of directors consisting of officers from each key business group. Senior management approved the mission, strategic plan, and proposed board structure, and provided funding, commitment, and support. Staff at IU together with cross business unit teams assisted in developing university guidelines, communications, and resource sharing. A plan was developed for the university to add value and support the objectives of the business groups.

IU began as two business institutes, the Leadership Institute and the Business Institute. A primary part of the infrastructure is assessment and evaluation, which support both units. The mission of Illinova University is to meet corporate needs by simulating and sustaining change, developing leadership, and promoting a results-based approach toward continuous improvement and learning within Illinova.

Drivers for Measurement and Evaluation

Illinova/Illinois Power Company views IU as a large investment for Illinova corporation, and, as such, IU must be accountable to the board by demonstrating that programs are not only changing attitudes and behaviors, but also contributing to the bottom line—hence, the need to evaluate early. IU's 1997 Strategic Action Plan calls for the establishment of a comprehensive system of evaluation and measurement for all university activities.

Increasingly, evaluation is viewed as a catalyst for organizational learning instead of a supplement to learning. Evaluation provides the framework for accountability. The collection of evaluation data provides a basis for more informed decisions regarding the acquisition and application of the skills and knowledge. Program results can be shared with others to promote continuous improvement.

Staffing for evaluation posed an interesting situation for IU. Evaluation responsibilities are varied, and staffing is limited to one full-time specialist. The role of the evaluation specialist is broad and includes technical expert, consultant, problem solver, initiator, designer, developer, coordinator, cheerleader, communicator, process monitor, planner, analyst, interpreter, and yes, even teacher (Phillips, 1997b). Within IU the most critical skill needed in the evaluation position became understanding the current culture, and the most important part of that was the ability to expand relationships throughout the organization. Building these relationships is critical to the future success of IU. Technical expertise could be developed provided these other key skills were evident.

A search for a consulting firm to assist IU in the development and implementation of evaluation became a primary driver in early 1996 and was the first challenge for the assessment and evaluation specialist. Three critical factors were developed as criteria in the selection of a consulting firm. The consultant must:

- be skilled in a results-based approach using a recognized, quantitative method of evaluating programs at the return-on-investment (ROI) level
- be willing to partner with IU to develop staff skills and other key individuals to use a results-based approach
- be a recognized, leading expert in the field.

The search led to the consulting firm of Performance Resources Organization (PRO).

Goals and Strategies

The primary drivers behind establishing evaluation targets early in Illinova University's start-up are IU's need to ensure that each program will be evaluated at the appropriate level and its desire to continually measure for improvement. History has shown us that we cannot continue doing the same things and expect different results.

Using a results-based approach to evaluation has enabled IU to prepare for the future by providing critical leadership, business knowledge, and skills linked to business goals and objectives, and individual development plans. As a critical step in this process, evaluation plans for each offering are designed to measure business impact (Level 4) and when appropriate, cost-effectiveness (Level 5). Implementation of the results-based approach is directly linked to performance compensation of all university staff members.

The purpose of evaluation is to link offerings of each institute to business objectives by developing specific purposes for each offering (that is, is the solution accomplishing the objectives of the program; what are the strengths and weaknesses of the program;

what is the cost-benefit ratio of the program; what is the correct audience). As part of the 1997 Strategic Action Plan, a goal of developing and conducting multiple-level (Levels 1 to 5) evaluations for offerings in each institute was established. By December 1997, the following targets were set:

- Level 1 (reaction and planned action): 100 percent of all programs
- Level 2 (learning): 50 percent of all programs
- Level 3 (job application): 30 percent of all programs
- Level 4 (business results): 20 percent of all programs
- Level 5 (return-on-investment): 10 percent of all programs.

Responsibilities, Staff and Development, Coordination

The assessment and evaluation (AE) specialist for IU has specific responsibility for all aspects of evaluation. Other key staff members include the dean, a director for each of the institutes, a curriculum design specialist for each of the institutes, a management assistant, and one other support employee.

Everyone needed evaluation skills, or at least an understanding of the process. In February 1997, the AE specialist attended an ROI certification program, offered by its consulting firm, to begin the process of becoming certified to provide internal consulting and training on measurement and evaluation, including the ROI process.

In March 1997, the principal consultant conducted a four-hour workshop for IU staff members, providing an overview and understanding of IU's results-based approach.

Policies and Procedures

Policies and guidelines, considered an important part in implementing the measurement and evaluation process, provide prototypes for conducting all five levels of evaluation. They provide direction for the IU staff and ensure consistency in the application of the results-based approach. The IU staff assigned the AE specialist the responsibility of developing the policies and guidelines for evaluation for IU. The development of the policies and guidelines was a joint effort of the AE specialist and PRO. Work began on the policies and guidelines in February 1997. The initial draft of the policies and guidelines contained six sections covering the following:

- policy and explanation of the results-based approach of IU (philosophy, defining the need for accountability, linking training programs with Illinova business needs)
- evaluation at all levels

- implications for new and existing training programs, and the attainment of new skills and knowledge
- communication with IU clients and monitoring the process
- implementation issues and targets
- payoff for IU.

After the first draft was formulated in June 1997, the entire IU staff reviewed the draft to offer input. Their review resulted in several changes, including placing increased emphasis on the important facts that IU was setting its policy itself and that IU would adhere to these policies. An additional section defining evaluation terms was added.

Distribution of the policies and guidelines began by circulating copies to other internal trainers of Illinova and asking for feedback. Copies were distributed to key organization members including managers who are not directly involved in training. This accomplished two purposes: first, to solicit their input for changes, and, second, to obtain buy-in from key organizational members for the results-based approach to evaluation.

ROI Projects

In March 1997, the AE specialist, working with PRO, began the work of identifying the programs that might be taken to the ROI level of evaluation. It was essential that an impact study be conducted because the board of directors of Illinova University charged the staff with the challenge of proving return-on-investment for the programs IU offered.

The selection process began by first examining programs IU would offer during 1997 that would meet the criteria for Level 4 and 5 evaluations. These criteria include the following:

- The length of time a program is expected to be viable.
- The program has a high level of visibility.
- A comprehensive needs assessment has been conducted.
- The target group is large.
- The cost of the training program is high.
- The program cuts across business units.
- Level 4 baseline data are available.
- The cost and time for evaluating at this level are reasonable.

Two programs were initially identified; one in the Business Institute and another in the Leadership Institute. Together the AE specialist and PRO determined that a team approach would be used to ensure that the process, techniques, methodologies, and technologies would be transferred to IU staff. Using a team approach, PRO consultants conducted the studies during 1997; PRO and the AE specialist will jointly conduct them during 1998; and during 1999, the AE specialist will conduct them with PRO reviewing the studies.

The objectives of the impact studies were determined and the first phase of each project included a thorough review of the documentation, including expected outcomes, enhancements for transfer of training, and program context. It also included an analysis of the expectations from the various groups involved (Phillips, 1997b).

The key steps for successful data collection include developing Level 3 and 4 measures and objectives, selecting the appropriate data-collection methods, and determining the timing of and responsibility for data collection. For the ROI analysis, several critical steps are necessary, including selecting the feasible strategies for isolating the effects of the program, identifying the appropriate strategies for converting data to monetary values, tabulating fully loaded program costs, identifying intangible benefits, designing the instruments for data collection, collecting and tabulating the data, developing application results, calculating the ROI, developing the impact study report, and presenting the results to management and other appropriate audiences (Phillips, 1997b).

Two impact studies provide clear evidence of the connection between programs and shareholder value, thus satisfying IU board members of the value of IU programs. In addition, this provides an opportunity for IU staff to gain the skills, techniques, and processes to conduct similar impact studies as needed.

Implementation Plan

Implementation of the results-based process began in February 1997, during the certification workshop that the AE specialist attended. The philosophy of implementation is to meet corporate needs by stimulating and sustaining change, developing leadership, and promoting a results-based approach toward continuous improvement and learning within Illinova. The AE specialist drafted an implementation plan to include an evaluation plan for each program designed to measure business impact. The plan also ensured that new offerings would be linked to business objectives. Also, the success of the results-based approach is directly linked to performance compensation of university staff members.

The AE specialist together with other IU staff members and PRO established specific goals for implementation during 1997, which included developing policies and guidelines for all levels of evaluation, conducting an impact study on 10 percent of the programs at the ROI level, and developing skills of staff and other key individuals.

Partnership Identification and Development

Corporate universities must ensure that all training, education, and development programs are connected to business needs and are achieving the desired measurable results. IU determined very early that it would be necessary to partner with key organizational members for a results-based approach to be successful. IU believes the best way to achieve its mission of providing the highest quality human resource development possible for employees is to balance the teaching staff with full-time experts and some part-time trainers. The part-time trainers are Illinova employees from a variety of disciplines and organizational levels who have achieved a strong track record of superior job performance, are dedicated to their current work, and have a strong interest in training. In August 1997, extensive training would be provided for those individuals who support Illinova University in either a direct or supportive role. Objectives of this results-based training were

- to develop the skills, knowledge, and behavior necessary to initiate, design, develop, and deliver programs that focus directly on business needs and measures
- to implement a system for accountability of all programs so that management will know if programs are successfully achieving objectives
- to provide a process for participants to achieve certain standards of excellence necessary to initiate, design, develop, and deliver results-based training.

The AE specialist and PRO jointly developed the results-based training program. The process was initially titled Train-the-Trainer and contained several key elements. One of these elements includes a follow-up session, scheduled approximately three months after the initial workshop. This follow-up session allows the participants to report specific alignment and progress as identified from the action plans created during the initial workshop.

IU and the participants were each making a significant investment in this program. So that each participant would fully understand the necessary commitment, IU developed a partnership agreement. The partnership agreement, shown in figure 1, specifically outlined the results-based process including objectives and the specific commitments needed from the participants. Each participant and his or her supervisor signed the partnership agreement prior to the certification workshop.

Initially, IU staff was uncertain how this workshop would be received and if there would be anyone interested enough to commit to it. The response to the initial invitation was overwhelming, with over 62 employees submitting applications.

Participants' initial reactions to the process were favorable. One participant said, "If Illinova University succeeds in implementing these strategies, we will have a partner that will support our efforts to be competitive." Another reaction was, "The training was excellent! It provided both the framework in which to assess and evaluate training and the important linkage to business results. With the Company's increased focus on training and development, these are critical tools that can be used to measure the effectiveness of training and the associated return on our investment."

The impact of this initial training will not be known until after action plans are complete. Judging from the action plans that participants submitted, however, IU expects very favorable results. At a minimum, partnerships have been developed with key organizational members that will assist in ensuring that a results-based approach to training will be successfully implemented at Illinova.

Executive Briefing

An executive briefing is planned for the board of directors of IU. This session, lasting approximately a half or a full day, will present the results-based framework and show how programs are linked to bottom-line measures, ensuring that IU board members develop an understanding of, and an appreciation for, the process to capture the return-on-investment.

This executive briefing will be conducted during the last quarter of 1998, when the results of the impact studies are available. During this session with the board, the results of the impact studies, in addition to the executive briefing, will be presented.

Manager Development

Line management support is critical to any corporate initiative, and evaluation is no exception. Line managers provide resources, data, organizational contacts, budget dollars, time, and subject matter expertise to make evaluation possible. Additionally, the need for management support was also identified in the Train-the-Trainer program.

A one-day manager workshop will be conducted several times beginning in 1998. These workshops are designed for managers who sup-

Figure 1. Partnership agreement.

Illinova University
Partnership Agreement

Name:_____

Location: _____

Thank you for your support of Illinova University! The mission of Illinova University is to provide the highest quality human resource development possible for our employees.

In partnership with Illinova University, you will be involved in a Train-the-Trainer Program to develop a leadership role for Results-Based Training. This certification process will meet three important objectives:

1. Enhance the skills, knowledge, and behavior necessary to initiate, design, develop, and deliver results-based programs which focus directly on business needs and business measures.
2. Implement a system for accountability of all programs so that management will know if programs are successfully achieving objectives.
3. Provide a certification process for participants to achieve certain standards of excellence necessary to initiate, design, develop, and deliver Results-Based Training.

The certification process will require your commitment (and the commitment of your supervisor) to the following:

1. Complete pre-work materials prior to the workshop to develop a common understanding of key issues and important challenges.
2. Participate in two workshops. First, a comprehensive four-day workshop for participants is scheduled from August 18-21 at The Radisson Hotel in Bloomington (information included).
3. After the workshop, apply the concepts, practices, and tools, on-the-job and report the reactions, successes, and concerns at a later time. This ensures that each participant, whether in a direct or supporting role, transfers the skills and knowledge from the certification process to on-the-job application. Action planning will be used to facilitate the participants' application of the above concepts and practices on-the-job.
4. Participate in a follow-up session, scheduled approximately three months after the first workshop. This session provides an opportunity for participants to report specific alignment and progress as they have utilized the results-based approach to assist Illinova University in fulfilling its mission. This session will be scheduled at a mutually convenient time for participants and Illinova University.
5. Dedicate at least 8 hours of time to Illinova University during each quarter of 1998 and 1999 for delivery or assistance with one or more programs. This time commitment may be met in a variety of ways.
6. Serve as a proactive partner with Illinova University to:
    A. Share concerns about operational policy issues.
    B. Provide suggestions for improvement in all areas.
    C. Offer guidance to Illinova University staff members.
    D. Provide assistance on special projects when requested.

continued on page 109

Figure 1. Partnership agreement (continued).

E. Reinforce objectives of specific programs, when appropriate.

F. Support goals, mission, and initiatives of Illinova University.

You and Illinova University are making a significant investment to this certification process. Therefore, please sign and return this agreement to Connie Schmidt at E-07 prior to August 11, 1997. Please have your supervisor sign as well.

Illinova University has significant goals and plans for the remainder of 1997 and all of 1998. Your assistance will greatly enhance the quality of Illinova University and contribute to the success of Illinova/Illinois Power as we move toward the next millennium. We hope you are as excited as we are about future opportunities.

Participant Signature	Date
Supervisor's Signature	Date
Supervisor's Telephone No.	Location

A return envelope is provided for your convenience. We look forward to your commitment and involvement as a key partner of Illinova University.

port Illinova University more from a functional perspective than an active involvement role. These managers send participants to programs, request new programs, and provide input into a variety of issues with the university. Although not necessarily mandatory for the entire managerial group, ultimately, all managers will probably cycle through the workshop. This should occur naturally, as some of the more active supporters are the first groups to attend the workshops.

This workshop is perhaps the most critical element of the process as it attempts to build management support. The workshop is designed to change four misconceptions of management groups. Managers usually believe: (1) that training adds little or no value from a monetary perspective; (2) that training is not their responsibility, but the responsibility of the training and development function; (3) they should not be involved directly in training and development; and (4) that training is primarily a delivery process and that other parts of the process are secondary to the actual delivery. Obviously, if managers have these perceptions, support will not materialize. Using a variety of exercises, cases, and actual data, this workshop will dispel each of these misconceptions. More important, it will show how Illinova University will demonstrate that training does add value, that managers have the primary responsibility for training and development, that managers must be actively involved in a process, and that delivery is only a minor part of what must be accomplished to make the process effective.

These workshops offer an important way to effectively use the resources of the company and keep the disruption to the organization at a very minimum. At the same time, these workshops should build an important resource base and increase management commitment and support for Illinova University's goals, programs, and strategies.

Annual Reviews

To keep the process on target and to access progress, an annual review is planned for the results-based process. This review, conducted by the external consulting firm, is designed to determine the extent to which the implementation process is progressing, to identify the actual progress made and the barriers to implementation, and to provide recommendations for adjustments, if necessary. This annual review will be prepared for the board of directors of Illinova University and will attempt to collect detailed information on each of these four areas. Included in this review are the actual statistics around the targets and a survey of managers and participants, which will determine the level of customer satisfaction.

Barriers and Obstacles

As with any complex process, there are always barriers. Some are real, and others often have their basis in misconceptions. Support from IU staff members for this process is strong and will be invaluable as this process is implemented. The IU dean sees the results-based approach to training as vital to the success of the university. The curriculum designers view this process as a means of ensuring that programs are developed to meet the objectives of contributing to business measures, through transfer of learning to the job. In addition, the IU staff members perceive this process to be a continuous learning tool that will enable them to constantly monitor their progress in achieving corporate and university goals. The IU staff recognizes that even negative results can be a valuable learning tool. If a program is not working or is not producing the desired results, it can be modified or canceled. Making needed adjustments quickly will increase the credibility and respect of the university.

The best way to address barriers and obstacles is to recognize that they will occur and to formulate a plan, in advance, on how to analyze and respond. In addition, it is prudent to anticipate barriers and remove them in the development stage before objections can arise. It is also important to recognize that barriers and obstacles can be used as guideposts to identify gaps and errors in the plan. They should be viewed as opportunities to improve instead of roadblocks to implementation.

Illinova University has experienced some initial barriers and obstacles, including objections to curriculum, objections to who will be trained, a resistant attitude (Is this the latest flavor of the month?), what to do first, and cost. One of the greatest barriers is the outdated paradigm that training is a reward for good performance instead of an investment in the individual and company. The expectation of a return-on-investment and the fact that training results can and will be quantified and measured have caused some resistance to the process. Faced with the possibility that sacred cows with special perks could be eliminated, barriers and roadblocks were quickly erected. Patience, consideration of the issues, detailed explanations, and logical presentation of the process have removed most of these concerns. Examining the consequences of not using this process has caused some resistance to diminish.

An example will illustrate how a barrier was minimized. Additional barriers to the implementation of the results-based approach were identified on the first day of the Train-the-Trainer program. Participants of the program were concerned that they had signed up for more than they had bargained. At the mention of calculating ROI, several participants raised the issues of "Am I in the right place?" or "Are you sure you want me involved in this training?" The AE specialist immediately addressed these questions and provided the participants with an accurate picture of their role in the process. These participants will assist the university by:
- serving as champions of the results-based process
- providing a maximum level of service to the university
- assisting in identifying skills and competencies needed in their own areas of expertise
- ensuring that programs will be designed to develop the necessary skills and competencies with Level 3 and 4 objectives
- serving as ambassadors for the University by speaking to others both internally and externally about the value of using a results-based approach
- acting as advisors to the university on important issues and concerns.

Participants received assurance that they were indeed in the right place. A key element of successful implementation is showing participants how to identify and remove barriers that might prevent the successful transfer of training into the workplace. It will be crucial to the company's success to maximize the intellectual capital in each area or function of the organization and to assist the company in meeting challenges in the future. "When managers begin to concentrate on what employees are doing and are becoming, they contribute to the professional and personal development of every individual" (Phillips, 1997b).

A concern from most Illinova managers is the amount of time spent in training. IU staff is responding to this challenge in a variety of ways. Participants deliver training throughout the service territory thereby reducing "windshield" time for travel. IU staff is currently investigating delivering training through alternative or less traditional means (that is, distance learning, utilizing computer-based programs, partnering with local colleges and universities to deliver programs, and utilizing internal electronic mail systems).

Because of the support and commitment of top management to Illinova University and an initial curriculum design presented to all levels of employees, IU has experienced fewer barriers than possible and enjoyed the positive response from partners.

Early Progress and Reaction

Initial reactions to implementation of results-based training are quite favorable. Because of this process, Illinova's current culture is focused more on accountability than at any time in the history of the company. The external environment is forcing the company to examine where dollars are being spent and the return on the investment. Managers involved in the Train-the-Trainer program view the results-based approach as a method of measuring improvement, enhancing the transfer of training to the workplace, and enforcing accountability for transfer of learning to both participants of programs and the managers of participants. More important, managers involved in this process view it as credible.

Reaction from vendors also has been positive. Vendors also realize that more companies want "proof" that what they are selling will be effective. Results-based training offers proof that programs are valuable and achieve intended objectives. The AE specialist is creating partnerships with vendors and working with them to create Level 3 and 4 objectives for each program during the design stage. In the case of existing programs, adjustments are made to program objectives where necessary to support Level 3 and 4 objectives.

Conclusion: Lessons Learned

The initial year of implementation has shown university staff members that implementing a results-based approach to training will be a gradual process. The goal is to ensure that this process is integrated seamlessly into the organization. To do this will take time.

However, several actions were successful from the beginning. Evaluation was viewed as a necessity, and funding was immediately established to enable evaluation at multiple levels. The need for a leader to drive the process was recognized early in the university's start-up. IU established evaluation targets in the initial planning. Vendors were brought into the process from the beginning and provided guidelines on expectations. Two impact studies are being conducted during the first year of operation, allowing the university to address accountability issues quickly and create support needed to move forward.

Without the support of the CEO, a corporate university cannot be successful. From the start-up, the CEO at Illinova has supported it. More important, he is supportive of a process that will show measurable bottom-line results. His support and the support of other key individuals are critical to the success of the results based approach.

It quickly became apparent that more needs assessments will be necessary prior to development of programs. Additional funding for needs assessment will ensure that programs are developed only when they are needed and that they are focused on results. This additional funding should be offset by a reduction in development and delivery expenses.

Overall, the point of view of all constituents and all stakeholders is that the process is on track and is successful. The effort has been significant, and the time allocated has been worthwhile. Although successful and necessary, it still represents a major change effort that requires constant attention, discipline, and follow through, just like every other successful change effort. As one key IU staff member said, "This is not as easy as it appears but absolutely necessary. It is a process that will reap returns for many years in the future."

Questions for Discussion

1. Most start-up corporate universities do not address the accountability issue early, waiting until programs are in place. What problems could develop with this approach?

2. Why is the ROI process, as described in this case, critical for a corporate university?

3. Why is university staff development critical to the success of ROI implementation?

4. Multiple responsibilities for evaluation are essential. How does this work in practice?

5. What role do policies and procedures play in a successful ROI implementation?

6. The IU partnerships were considered to be critical to the success of the university and the ROI implementation. Explain the critical role of this initiative.

7. Building management support for training and development and the ROI process is often overlooked (at least on a formal basis), yet it can have a tremendous impact. Explain.

8. What barriers to implementation are expected with this type of process? How can they be overcome or minimized?

The Authors

Connie J. Schmidt has 20 years of corporate experience in the fossil and nuclear side of the utility industry, finance and accounting, human resources division, and training areas of Illinova/Illinois Power Corporation. She is currently with Illinova University as an assessment evaluation specialist.

Schmidt is an active member of the International Society for Performance Improvement and of the ROI Network™, of which she is a founding member and president of the ROI Network.™ The ROI Network™ is an elite organization of practitioners and experts in the field of evaluation research, and its goal is to help members continue to grow and learn from each other and together succeed in the expanding and rapidly evolving field of evaluation. She can be contacted at Illinova/Illinois Power, 370 South Main Street, E-07, Decatur, IL 62523.

Jack J. Phillips has 27 years of corporate experience in five industries (aerospace, textiles, metals, construction materials, and banking) and has served as training and development manager at two *Fortune* 500 firms, senior human resources officer at two firms, and president of a regional federal savings bank.

References

Illinova/Illinois Power Corporation. *Illinova 1996 Annual Report.* Decatur, IL: Author.

Phillips, J.J. (1997a). *25 Global Training Trends.* Houston: Gulf.

Phillips, J.J. (1997b). *Return on Investment in Training and Performance Improvement Programs.* Houston: Gulf.

Phillips, J.J. (February, 1997c). Personal communication.

Schmidt, C.J., and R.D. Stone. (1997). Illinova University Policies & Guidelines, unpublished.

Building Evaluation Into External Education Services

Medical Assurance

Patricia D. Davis

This case outlines the development of a comprehensive approach to evaluation of the Education Services operation of a professional liability insurance company. The commitment to this project evolved from the company's achievement of accreditation to provide continuing education for physicians as well as other health-care professionals, along with a strong commitment to establish criteria by which to measure the impact of the educational programming provided to customers.

Background

The development of the evaluation approach detailed in this case study emerged because of two main events. First, our organization, Medical Assurance, achieved accreditation as a provider of continuing education from several key organizations that have required measurement of outcomes. In addressing the issue of measuring outcomes of educational programming, several other business applications of this methodology emerged as well. Next, the company identified that customers who participate in education activities or purchase education services, or both, could benefit from the processes involved in measuring educational outcomes and, ultimately, measuring the return on their investment of education dollars.

As an accredited provider of continuing education for several groups of health-care professionals, it is vital that evidence be available about the effectiveness of programming activities. The evalua-

This case was prepared to serve as a basis for discussion rather than to illustrate either effective or ineffective administrative and management practices.

tion of educational activities is an important component of each accrediting organization's requirements. Specifically, all accrediting agencies require evaluation at the reaction and learning levels. One group of health-care professionals also recommends evaluation at the job application level. However, it became clear over time that the capacity to evaluate programming activities at higher levels could contribute to the organization in several ways:

- The organization would exceed the expectations of all accrediting agencies, thereby achieving a level of excellence beyond expectations.
- Customers could utilize these methods to monitor and evaluate the effectiveness of their educational activities with Medical Assurance.
- The evaluation data, when combined with claims and risk management information, establish benchmarking information for all customers as well as specific information regarding the performance of individuals and organizations resulting from education and risk management interventions.
- Company growth is leading to expansion of education activities and a clear need to assure that the ever-expanding educational activities are monitored for both quality and effectiveness, as a quality assurance mechanism for accrediting agencies and as a method of ensuring that customers are receiving the most service and quality for their investment.

The process to implement this initiative has met with several significant barriers. First, there is a general lack of knowledge about the components of the evaluation process among both colleagues and customers. Next, the investment required to position the company to implement this project has been significant. Further, the needs assessment component of the evaluation process also had to be designed and implemented as a component of the process—a very laborious and difficult task. In addition, the implementation of the necessary links with customers to achieve the higher levels of evaluation for education programming is an ongoing challenge. Finally, the process of organizing and operationalizing the methods for comparisons and analyses with claims and risk management information continues.

Organizational Profile

The nature of Medical Assurance creates an ideal environment for such a project. The corporate commitment to improvement of patient outcomes in health-care organizations as well as the availability of real-time information regarding performance, errors, and patient-care outcomes establishes a rich source of evaluation information for study and analysis.

Medical Assurance is a professional liability insurance company established in the mid-1970s by Alabama physicians in response to a malpractice insurance availability crisis. Many such insurance companies were established throughout the United States. Medical Assurance has grown over the 20 years of its existence to its current status, which involves a client base of over 70 percent of the private practicing physicians in Alabama, almost 40 percent of hospital beds in Alabama, and ownership of companies in the Midwest and Southeast. In 1991, the company made a transition from its roots as a mutual company to begin a new era as a public company, traded on the NASDAQ. In early 1997, the company made two further transitions, changing the name of the holding company to Medical Assurance, Inc., and moving to the New York Stock Exchange, where it is now traded under the symbol *MedAsr.* The company's success can be attributed to the vision of its leadership to provide:

- a strong commitment to defend all nonmeritorious cases against its insureds
- an environment that seeks to insure both the health-care organization and physicians to provide for a joint defense
- the most highly trained and qualified defense attorneys with strategies for defending insureds in a plaintiff action
- risk management services to help prevent adverse outcomes that can lead to medical malpractice lawsuits
- educational seminars and other services that can assist insureds to identify personal or organizational practices and behaviors with the potential to lead to lawsuits, and strategies for changing these practices and behaviors.

The Education Services department, with the goal of meeting the challenge of providing educational seminars and other services, has undertaken a number of initiatives. Over the past six years, this department has grown from a productivity of nine seminars for Alabama physicians annually to its current productivity of over 400 seminars annually for physicians as well as nurses, health-care executives, physician practice administrators, and other health-care professionals in at least 15 states. In addition, the accreditation as a provider of continuing education for a variety of health-care professionals has elevated the operation of the department to a level of accountability that contributes to the credibility of both the educational endeavors of the department and the company as a whole.

Industry Profile

The professional liability insurance companies that physicians establish and own are unique in many ways. Medical Assurance has been dedicated to the defense of its insureds in every case where physician colleagues can determine that no negligence has occurred. This dedication is played out today in the organization of the Physician Claims and Underwriting Committees that exist to protect patients through responsible and careful underwriting and to protect physicians by thorough investigation and evaluation of claims. A similar organization exists for the evaluation and management of claims against insured health-care organizations.

Decisions regarding resolution of claims are made exclusively on the merits of the claim rather than on the financial considerations of defending versus settling of the claim. This defense philosophy is crucial to the success of the company because of the vitally personal nature of the claims for insured physicians and other health-care professionals. Pressures that bear on these individuals include the very real concern about injuries to patients as well as the potential damage to their personal and professional reputations, their practices, and the consequences of reporting a significant judgment—either through a trial or a settlement—to the National Practitioner Data Bank.

The evaluation of claims and risk management data is a concern of the industry and the company. For the company, this concern has led to the development of a computer system that allows for even more consistent and specific data collection, management, and analysis. With the implementation of this database, performing sophisticated evaluations of educational endeavors has become an imperative. In the industry, there is a growing emphasis on outcomes measurement. In fact, this aspect of health-care management has become one of the most dominant concerns and areas of inquiry in the health-care industry today. Medical Assurance's efforts to contribute to the collection and analysis of evaluation data on educational activities should assist insureds to demonstrate their commitment to and effectiveness in evaluating themselves and their activities.

Key Players, Issues, and Events

The impetus for this project can be attributed to accrediting agencies with established criteria for evaluating educational programming. The initial identification of the need to implement this project evolved as a strategy for compliance with these criteria and standards. The overall responsibility for compliance with these accreditation standards lies with the vice president of Education Services who reports to the senior vice president for Insurance Operations, who is responsible for the claims and risk management operations of the company. The vice president of Education Services has significant experience in both formal and continuing education for health-care professionals.

The decision to seek accreditation as a provider of continuing education for physicians, nurses, health-care executives, and others arose from the overall decision to expand the company into states beyond Alabama's borders. The seminars for physicians, which have been a consistent part of the company's services for over 15 years, have traditionally been approved for continuing medical education (CME) credit in collaboration with the state medical association. With the company's expansion, this collaboration would no longer be possible. Therefore, Medical Assurance embarked upon the path of national accreditation. It became evident very quickly that significant efforts could be beneficial in both the needs assessment and evaluation areas. Although the level of activities in place early on were sufficient to achieve accreditation, the potential for significant contributions to the education process and the company as a whole were identified, and the decision was made to pursue a higher level of both needs assessment and evaluation activities than was absolutely required for achieving and maintaining accreditation.

Identifying this need to create a formal approach to evaluation and needs assessment, the senior vice president authorized the investment required to seek consulting services from Performance Resources Organization for the purposes of designing overall needs assessment and evaluation plans and providing assistance and expertise in the optimal implementation of these plans.

Because of the large and growing scope of the education operation and the general difficulty in measuring the impact of risk management education on patient outcomes and malpractice litigation trends, it was important to implement systems that could demonstrate measurable, bottom-line results. Also, it was important to establish a multidimensional system, allowing for needs assessment and evaluation input from a wide variety of sources including the audiences served, company management, physician and other advisory committees, customers who purchase education services, risk management and claims professionals in the company (both in Alabama and other states), industry issues and trends, and speakers used in educational programming for Medical Assurance. In addition to accreditation and other imperatives, the intriguing challenge of isolating the effects of education on claims and the challenges associated with measuring the impact of participation in seminars and other education activities for customers also contributed to the decision to embark on this project.

Overall issues and goals of this project included:

- identification of significant input sources for evaluation information
- determination of customers who have the greatest potential to benefit from the focus on evaluation
- identification of variables to be measured
- design of an approach for evaluation of each group of activities at the selected levels of evaluation
- revision of existing forms, policies, and procedures
- creation of new evaluation forms to seek input at higher levels, in different ways, and from different audiences
- creation of a plan for implementing Levels 4 and 5 evaluation strategies for selected programs and customers as a part of contract education programming
- organization of evaluation components and methods into a cohesive, consistent evaluation program that includes policies and procedures, exhibits, and an implementation plan and schedule
- creation of a strategy for "marketing" contract education programming with the addition of evaluation and needs assessment services
- development of a plan and strategies for conducting the research necessary to determine the influence of physician and other loss prevention education activities on adverse events and resulting medical malpractice lawsuits.

Identification of Significant Input Sources

In determining the need for evaluation of the Education Services operation, department management along with company leadership and the Physician Advisory Committee identified that the evaluation processes to be developed should address not only seminar programming, which is done among a variety of audiences, but also the department processes, reactions from speakers, input from advisory committees, input from company management, accreditation concerns, methods for measuring and comparing influences on claims, and the like. The management of the department also established targets for evaluating programming at each level. For example, 100 percent of programming will be evaluated at Level 1 and 5 percent at Level 5, and so forth. In addition to these sources of input, other elements to be included are numbers of repeat customers for contract education, attendance, income, and expense trends. As previously discussed, an additional element of the evaluation process will be the effect of educational programming on claims in selected audiences.

Determination of Customers With the Greatest Potential to Benefit

Consistent and ongoing evaluation of education services has the potential to allow customers to monitor and manage selected aspects of their products and services. These customers include physicians, physician office staff, clinics, hospitals, and other health-care organizations that could benefit from risk management education toward reducing adverse events. Because both physicians and health-care organizations are being called upon to measure their effectiveness and to report this information to increasing numbers and varieties of agencies and consumer groups, the ability to both measure the impact of risk management education on patient outcomes and the return-on-investment (ROI) in actual dollars should appeal to a wide variety of Medical Assurance customers.

Identification of Variables to Be Measured

Determining the variables to be measured will be a part of the process of needs assessment for each customer. In addition, there will be standard variables to be measured with each program type, audience, and level of evaluation. These sets of variables have been spelled out in department policy.

Design of an Approach for Evaluation of Each Activity Set

The methodology for evaluating each type of activity, including the levels of evaluation, the components to be evaluated, the forms to be used, and preliminary information to be gathered, has been established in department policy. In addition, samples for each method are included in the overall evaluation plan. Further, the targets for each evaluation approach become an element of strategic planning so that it will be assured that each task is accomplished during the year.

Revision of Existing Evaluation Forms

Performance Resources analyzed all existing forms and revised them to more accurately and effectively evaluate the elements each is intended to evaluate. Each form is being converted to a scannable format so that the entire evaluation process can be automated for ease in tabulation, analysis, and reporting.

Creation of New Evaluation Forms

New forms have been created for the purpose of eliciting information at higher levels from the various input sources and by new methods. These forms have been designated for their appropriate and intended use and are included in the departmental evaluation plan.

Creation of a Plan for Level 4 and Level 5 Evaluations

Contract education is a growing component of the Education Services operation. This service involves the provision of education services on a fee-for-service basis for health-care organizations and others interested in risk management and malpractice liability prevention education. This service is provided in a variety of ways, and is customized to meet the individual needs of the customer. Because evaluation at Levels 4 and 5 are crucial to the strategies for increasing the contract education market share, it has been a strong focus of the efforts to develop this approach to ROI evaluation.

Customers who participate in this aspect of programming will be guided through the process of needs assessment, program planning, evaluation planning, implementation, and the actual evaluation process. A significant component of this process is the series of follow-up evaluations over the months following the implementation of the education program. For customers who are insured by the company, this evaluation process extends to include comparative analysis of claims, event reporting, and other indicators of performance. In addition, Medical Assurance offers benchmarking services for insureds as a component of the evaluation process.

Organization of Evaluation Components and Methods

The entire scope of the evaluation program and plan has been formalized into a reference document that is readily available for review. This document is contained within the department policy and procedure manual. The plan is scheduled for review on an annual basis with necessary additions, deletions, and revisions undertaken as identified or warranted. Not only is this method of documenting and organizing information designed to provide consistency and continuity of the process, regardless of leadership changes, but the plan is also a critical component of the compliance documentation process for various accrediting agencies, which demonstrates the commitment of the Medical Assurance Education Services department to a well-designed, ongoing process of evaluation.

Creation of a Marketing Strategy for Contract Education Programming

The availability of needs assessment and evaluation components to our contract education customers (fee for service) sets this company apart from many others. The challenge is to identify a suitable strategy for marketing these services. In order for the company to achieve success in this endeavor, customers must recognize the value of conducting meaningful needs assessment and evaluation and be willing to commit the resources to pursue an evaluation process over time. Medical Assurance now includes the needs assessment and evaluation services as part of the contract for education services. The benefits of choosing to participate in this aspect of contract education programming are significant. Therefore, the methods we identify and select to communicate these benefits to potential contract education customers are critical.

Development of a Plan for Research

As this program grows and expands, it will be necessary to monitor and measure the effects of this intervention on the frequency and severity of adverse events, and, subsequently, claims for malpractice. The determination of this correlation will be accomplished over time, with careful attention to isolating the effects of the educational programming from the effects of other interventions or events. The methods for achieving this goal are still under consideration and will be adjusted as necessary from one program or customer to another.

Models and Techniques

The methodologies for implementing this evaluation plan include needs assessment tools and seminar evaluation forms that collect data at Levels 1, 2, and 3. Further, for contract education customers who desire further emphasis on evaluation, needs assessment as well as follow-up evaluation surveys elicit information unique to the organization and program topic. The evaluation plan also includes guidelines for developing follow-up evaluations.

The evaluation plan includes tools for collecting input and information to evaluate the services that the Education Services department provides to speakers, advisory committees, internal customers, and company management. The Education Services department prepares an annual report that summarizes all information gathered and offers action plans to correct any systems problems that are identified as well as the issues to improve services for the coming year. This process is another accreditation requirement.

Costs

The costs for implementing this program, other than the cost of consulting and equipment purchase, will be relatively minimal. The claims information is gathered for other purposes, and will be analyzed in the course of regular duties. The contract education evaluation program will require minimal additional effort on the part of the Education Services staff, and will be integrated into existing customer services. The same is true for the evaluation of the Education Services operation. The elements of this evaluation are integrated into existing responsibilities as a component of ongoing accreditation readiness.

Summary

The process for development and implementation of an evaluation plan for Medical Assurance will allow the Education Services department to more fully analyze its contribution to the company. Further, the availability of needs assessment and evaluation services to contract education customers will allow these customers to actually measure the costs versus the benefits of their investment of education dollars with Medical Assurance. The ultimate analysis, determining the effects of education on adverse patient outcomes and claims for medical malpractice, will be of critical importance in deciding the future direction of the Education Services function throughout our market service area.

Questions for Discussion

1. What are the most beneficial measures of evaluation for health-care organizations?
2. What elements of patient care would most readily lend themselves to measurement as appropriate indicators of the effectiveness of educational programming?
3. What are the key components of a comprehensive evaluation program for a department of education that has more external than internal customers, in broadly divergent locations, and with a wide variety of product and service lines?
4. How can the validity of this evaluation plan be measured?

5. How should the critical reports for each element of this plan be formatted?

6. What are the potential barriers to and facilitators for success in such a plan?

The Author

Patricia D. Davis is vice president, Education Services, with Medical Assurance, Inc. She has an extensive background in health care, including almost 15 years in a faculty role in three major universities and responsibilities for continuing education in a university school of nursing and hospitalwide education in a large rehabilitation hospital. She received both bachelor's and master's degrees in nursing from the University of Alabama at Birmingham. Her responsibilities with Medical Assurance involve management of almost 800 seminars per year targeted to physician, dentist, nurse, and other health-care professional audiences. Medical Assurance is accredited by the Accreditation Council for Continuing Mutual Education to sponsor continuing medical education for physicians. Medical Assurance is also approved as a provider of continuing education for nurses, dentists, and health-care executives. Davis can be contacted at the following address: Medical Assurance, 100 Brookwood Place, Suite 500, Birmingham, AL 35209; e-mail: patdavis@main.com. More information about Medical Assurance Education Services can be found on the web at www.medicalassurance.com.

An Evolution of Evaluation of Training and Education

Duke Energy Corporation

Derrick Allman

Duke Energy Corporation is a growing energy services company based in Charlotte, North Carolina. In 1996, the company received final approval for completing a merger with Pan Energy Corporation of Houston. These organizational changes resulted in the consolidation of all training and education services into a shared services format. Although we at Duke Energy are still adjusting to this form of organization, we still pursue the evaluation of training and education services.

The objective of this case study is to present the history of Duke Energy training evaluation and share some of our experience in hope that you may avoid some of the pitfalls we have experienced.

Background

Duke Energy Corporation is a large energy solutions provider headquartered in Charlotte, North Carolina. The company's business units include a wide range of services ranging from raw material acquisition and power generation to complex engineering services and telecommunications. The company employees approximately 22,000 people in 37 of the contiguous United States and in 44 countries around the globe.

The primary objective of this case is to assist in helping others by sharing the adventures the company experienced in the course of evaluating our training and education programs. Because most readers are familiar with both Donald Kirkpatrick's and Jack Phillips's mod-

This case was prepared to serve as a basis for discussion rather than to illustrate either effective or ineffective administrative and management practices.

els of evaluation, I will dispense with reviewing the different levels and steps in each model. This case will, however, recant much of the background, progress, and future direction of evaluative processes at Duke Energy. These activities can be arranged into three groups I call the formalizing evaluative processes, the two-year test period, and future plans and strategies.

Formalizing Evaluative Processes

Duke Energy's training and education functions were made up of four primary divisions prior to the fall of 1997. This arrangement was the result of a corporate-wide study performed in 1991–1992, which indicated a need for training functions to be closely aligned with business unit services. The arrangement was for training divisions to become more accountable to those organizations where services would be delivered. As a result, training divisions came into being with solid line reporting relationships to the named organization and a dotted line relationship with each other. Business unit organizations included corporation and corporate group specific education needs, customer delivery needs, power generation needs, and electric system support needs. With this arrangement, a loose confederation resulted in which training and education (T&E) professionals frequently communicated with counterparts in other areas of the organization. However, the desire to maximize impact and minimize costs through the capitalization on economies of scale and consolidation did not develop. So, although the T&E functions were improving products and services, we continued to be wasteful and duplicative in services. Eventually, the four divisions failed to develop relationships necessary for survival in the organizational changes that would eventually take place when Duke Power merged with Pan Energy in the summer of 1997.

On a more positive note, training divisions did employ various strategies for evaluating training. All training divisions used various representations of each of the five levels of evaluations that Phillips and Kirkpatrick presented. For the most part, staff continuously used end-of-class evaluations (smile sheets) to assess class reaction. However, there were no consistent questions or methods for analysis applied to the review of the data collected. In many cases the information was the sole possession of the course instructor. Unfortunately, we lost vast amounts of data that we could have used to demonstrate continuous improvements.

Other areas were more advanced in their evaluative processes. Power Generation and Electric Systems Support used the most methodical Level 2 evaluation process. In these areas, excellent evaluative processes evolved as a result of the exhausting analysis, development, and implementation requirements established in the nuclear utility industry, and through peer evaluation and accreditation processes. Customer group training used Level 2 evaluations in a sophisticated electronic performance support system (EPSS). In this division, learning transfer was tracked through automated data collection and analysis. Finally, at the corporate training division, we were busy delivering end-user computer training, safety, environmental, management development, professional development, and other education to the point where we were not using any evaluation method or process with any degree of consistency.

However, after all of the effort, we still were not acting responsibly with the corporate trust we had been granted. At the end of 1995, we could still not answer the questions of how much we were spending on training and education, what improvements were recognized as a result of the investments, and where could we demonstrate positive business results. This led to a "two-year" test period in which the training and education functions began to assess the impact and contributions we were adding to the bottom line of the business. It was a two-year test without anyone ever being told!

The Two-Year Test

In the years following the organizational changes of 1992 and 1993, evaluation processes at Duke Energy Corporation took many turns. The corporate focus turned to preparing for the era of aggressive competition in the energy services market. Much of the efforts put forth during this time involved the objective of determining the value that learning and development contributes to the business. An essential element in the valuation of learning and development is the gathering and analysis of evaluation data associated with learning events. Yet, we didn't know what to measure, let alone where to acquire the information. A few areas had initiatives directing that the training function would operate more like a business. However, it became nearly impossible to perform like a business from within a regulated utility shell. If for no other reason, the criteria with which we had to work were far too confining and stifled the idea of entrepreneurial approaches to running the business.

It was not until 1994 that Duke Energy sought to quantify the value of learning in the organization. Corporate training and education was asked to analyze and trend the experiences in order to monitor continuous improvement of programs. At that time, the initiating queue did not come from within the training and education function. The queue came from quality initiatives surrounding the self-evaluation of the company using the Malcolm Baldrige National Quality Award (MBA) criteria. In the early 1990s, Duke Energy had a strong focus toward continuous improvement and quality performance measures. As a result, criteria for pursuing the MBA was adopted as a standard from which all corporate programs would be measured. It was thought that the Baldrige criteria should be used for several reasons:

- *Standardized.* The award criteria are a standard by which we could directly compare our performance with that of other corporations across the country.
- *Available.* A systematic process for evaluating programs was well-established, including a network of examiners that would allow us to perform self-evaluations.
- *Successful.* The prevailing view was that compliance with Baldrige criteria would naturally result in excellence, although it was later realized that excellence in all aspects of the business allows the corporation to succeed, not the use of artificial criteria with which we were attempting to align practices.

As a result of this effort, the training and education function was asked to produce reports in response to four areas of training. Later we learned that the four areas outlined in the MBA were actually the four levels of evaluation posed in Kirkpatrick's model for evaluating training and education. We also learned that Phillips' return-on-investment (ROI) model was also included through reference. It was at this point that several huge steps were accomplished in understanding the value of training, the volume of training, and the cost of training. After conducting several benchmarking exchanges, the corporate T&E function established a small evaluation team that began to apply some proven analytical models to determine cost, volume, and value.

In the fall of 1995, the first reports were generated for training and education. These included the following results: First, a total of 983,000 hours of training were delivered to 116,000 participants from within the company. This results in approximately 80 hours of training annually for each employee. Approximately 88 percent of all training that year was delivered through traditional classroom-style situations. We also learned that we could account for nearly $55 million in direct training-related costs. The $55 million was made up of $32 million from costs associated with all training functions and $23 million in salaries and associated expenses. Yet with all this information, we still could not be sure of three things:

- Was the cost only $55 million as reported?
- How did we compare with other similar organizations?
- Do we do enough to maintain the investment of our employees?

In addition to monetary and volume measures, we set about implementing a common Level 1 evaluation process. In a matter of weeks we went from using an ordinary smile sheet to collecting data on a continual basis. In turn, we analyzed these data for trends to determine the various influencing factors on training delivery. The result of this awareness led to the development of a more sophisticated database system for scanning, converting, and analyzing data. At the center of this project were four criteria: develop standard questions to apply across the enterprise, develop a process for electronic gathering of data to reduce the human interface required, secure the data in a manner so as to prevent any bias or tampering with results, and be able to report the results of any event based on criteria important to the management of the training and education function. Within six weeks of the initial request, we had an operational database program capable of gathering data using an electronic scanner, analyzing data by course, instructor, location, and generating general and confidential reports for management.

When Duke Energy training set about the development of a standard Level 1 reaction sheet, we knew that by their nature the questions would be very subjective. This indication of the mood of participants as they leave training is essential toward understanding part of the data gathered in subsequent evaluations. It was proposed, therefore, that a rigorous analysis of well-defined questions at the first level of evaluation could be an indicator of how well knowledge or skills would be applied, and the results that would be achieved. If true, then the Level 1 could also be indicative of the positive or negative ROI that might be realized.

Therefore, the goal of Level 1 evaluations became, "Measure participants' perception (reaction) to learning experiences relative to a course, content, instructor, and relevancy to job immediately following the experience in order to initiate continuous improvement of training experiences." As a result, our project established three primary objectives:

1. Questions developed for the reaction level evaluation MUST measure the course, content, instructor, and relevancy to the job. These are four areas considered essential to successful training programs.

2. The form and delivery of the Level 1 evaluation must communicate a link between quality, process improvement, and action. Participants MUST be made to feel as though their individual response is a factor in the continuous improvement process.

3. Action plans should be initiated to address identified weaknesses without regard to owner, political correctness, or other bias. If the results indicate poor quality, then appropriate action should be taken to correct. If excellence is indicated in an unlikely place, then reward and celebration should be offered commensurate with the accomplishment.

In addition to the primary objectives, several secondary objectives evolved. First was the charge for the identification of prerequisite processes that must be accomplished with each learning event. It became evident that the success of the evaluative process is directly linked to the proper completion of prerequisites for a course. Second, postmeasurement activities should be addressed by subsequent teams. During the initial database design, the team knew that certain reports would be required, and others desired. Most all reports were prepared during the first phase of development.

The initial computer project deliverables included the following:

- Proposed questions to be included on the Level 1 evaluation.
- Proposed measures from which management will determine actions to be taken when analyzing evaluation results.
- Recommendations for deployment of the process within corporate T&E including roles and responsibilities.
- Guidelines for data collection, cycle times, reports, and analysis of data.
- Schedule for developing, delivering, and measuring the responsiveness of participants (generic Level 1 assessment of course).
- Database and input program for manually gathering data.
- Plans and scope document detailing a second (phase 2) project for automating the data acquisition process. This document should include plans for using data collected in multiple ways. That is, it should include requirements that header data be used to confirm enrollment and attendance, automated course completion on the company's payment and records management system, Level 1 automated analysis and reporting, and so forth.

Along with the development of the computer program, a team worked on drafting an initial set of questions for the standard Level 1 reaction sheets. These questions included the following:

1. Overall, my impression of this course was excellent.
2. The course objectives were clearly stated using understandable terms.
3. This course met the defined objectives.
4. Both the facility and equipment used met ALL needs of the class/course.
Note: Please describe any facility or equipment needs that did not meet your expectations!
5. The course materials were both useful and easy to follow.
Note: Please describe any material that was not useful or easy to follow!
6. The instructor(s) demonstrated thorough knowledge and understanding of the topic.
Note: The instructor(s) would be the facilitator(s) of any video, CBT, or audio tape.
7. The instructor(s) presented information in a clear, understandable, and professional manner.
Note: The instructor(s) would include the facilitator(s) of any video, CBT, or audio tape.
8. The amount of time scheduled for this course was exactly what was needed to meet the objectives.
9. This course relates directly to my current job responsibilities.
10. I would recommend this course to other teammates.

These were measured using a five-point Likert scale with a value of 5 being assigned to strongly agree and a value of 1 being assigned to strongly disagree.

A test period from November through December 1995 was used to shake-down the system and remove any bugs. On January 1, 1996, the first electronic Level 1 evaluation instruments were formally used. During the first month, fewer than 200 Level 1 reaction sheets were returned for processing. In the ensuing months, acceptance and use of the questions as a basis for illustrating the effects of training grew. All of corporate training began using the Level 1 reaction sheet to gather end-of-class data by March 1996; volume grew to nearly 1,000 evaluation sheets per month. By the end of 1996, corporate training of Duke Energy had recorded over 12,000 evaluations on the reaction to training. By the end of 1997, the number using the standardized Level 1 reaction sheet grew to over 25,000 participants. Analysis of the data began to reveal some very interesting trends. The growth also revealed the need to adjust the corporate training unit.

As we analyzed the data and produced reports, training management came to the realization that, "...the reaction to training and education is directly linked to the operation and business management aspects of the training unit." This led to the formation of a team to monitor business management and education quality. In theory, we concluded that the two are inseparable in determining areas of continuous improvement, measuring the success of programs and program participants, and ensuring that corporate investments in training are providing an appropriate return-on-investment.

Plans and Strategies

Duke Energy training stands at the threshold of a whole new era in evaluating the effectiveness of training. As we continue to analyze the "reactions" people have toward training, we are beginning to see indications in the trends that suggest a direct correlation between reaction (Level 1) and transfer to the job (Level 3). If the investigation of these trends is correct, then the use of sophisticated techniques for analyzing participant reaction will be warranted. If all we are able to glean from the data are suggestions for areas to improve, then we are still able to implement corrective actions in programs before they are long forgotten. When used effectively, analysis of Level 1 evaluation data can help in the early detection of areas that need improvement, or support the conclusion that an excellent job is achieved.

Questions for Discussion

1. Identify and discuss at least three issues that may result when a formal process for evaluating services is not implemented.
2. Discuss the impact that failing to think and act like a business partner has on the training and education unit.
3. Identify five positive results that can be expected from changing the mindset of the training function from one of a corporate financial burden to one of corporate business partner.
4. Although Level 1 evaluations are generally considered to be smile sheets with little relative importance, step outside of your normal train of thought and compare at least five effective uses of Level 1 data in monitoring the T&E business for indicators.
5. Discuss how the rigorous analysis of large quantities of Level 1 training data can lead to greater understanding of the business climate, result in the ability to perform predictive analysis for Levels 3 and 4, and provide insight into the expected ROI that may result when measurements are taken.

The Author

Derrick Allman is a member of Duke's Corporate Training Computer and Technical Education Services unit. He is responsible for educational quality and business management. In fulfilling this assignment, he had seven areas of responsibility: qualification and certification activities, budget management, training measurement and evaluation, training process definition, training quality issues including delivery and benchmarking activities, work management, and reporting of aggregate training performance for the Duke Corporation.

Allman joined the Duke team in 1979 as maintenance technician serving the company's fossil, nuclear, and hydroelectric stations. In 1982, he accepted a position in Nuclear Mechanical Maintenance Training at Duke's McGuire Nuclear Station. While there, he achieved several notable goals including becoming a fully certified training staff instructor. In 1990, he joined the corporate training team and became involved in new computer application training deployment. In addition, he established a curriculum for materials management training and corporate safety training.

Allman possesses a B.F.A. in business management from Belmont Abbey College. He can be contacted at Duke Energy Corporation, 422 South Church Street, Charlotte, NC 28242-0001.

Part II

Specific Evaluation Techniques

Implementing ROI: Creating a Strategic Framework to Link Training to Business Results

Toronto-Dominion Bank

Brian Howard, Connie Karlsson, Brenda Chong,
and Kim Japp-Delaney

This case study details the role that program evaluation plays in support-ing the defined strategic business needs of a major bank in Canada. It shows the steps used in positioning program evaluation as a front-end strategy in the training process, the value of leveraging the lessons learned in implementing program evaluation across multiple projects, and the steps necessary to gain organizational buy-in to program evaluation activities from a performance consulting perspective.

Background
The Organization

The Toronto-Dominion Bank is one of the five large Canadian Banks. It has a 900-branch network distributed across 3,000 miles with two different key language groupings in the organization. Until the late 1980s, the head office function was mainly composed of prod-uct groups that distributed their products through the branch net-work. The businesses of the bank up to 10 years ago were largely deposit, credit, and corporate and institutional investment related. To sup-port these activities, the bank was predominantly transactional in na-ture with a very limited sales focus. The branch network has been run by eight largely autonomous line divisions.

In the past 10 years, the bank has been restructuring to include a key suite of new businesses such as mutual funds, personal and cor-porate trust, wealth management, and discount and full-service bro-

This case was prepared to serve as a basis for discussion rather than to illustrate either effective or in-effective administrative and management practices.

kerage services. This diversification has been accompanied by a shift from a predominantly transactional focus to more of a relationship and sales banking focus. This change is consistent across all businesses.

Education and Training at the Bank

Historically, the bank's education and training function was decentralized with training design, development, and delivery largely determined at a divisional level. Although this structure supported a more localized implementation of training in the regions, there was a limited focus on the broader training solutions in support of strategic business directions of the organization. To provide more tactical support for broader business changes in the bank and to exercise cost efficiencies where necessary across the organization, the education and training function was centralized to the Corporate Education Centre.

This consolidation facilitated a number of key paradigm shifts for training at the bank:

- There was a shift from a reactive mode to a proactive role in meeting the training needs of the existing and emerging businesses of the bank.
- A curriculum-based methodology was adopted, moving away from an event-drive model.
- A reliance on classroom-based delivery as the primary mode of training was diminished, and a distance-based technology-facilitated paradigm was introduced.

In tandem, with the shift from a reactive role to a proactive supporter of the business needs of the organization, there was also an increasing need to provide tangible evidence that training provided a sustained improvement in the skills, knowledge, and behavioral changes required to meet emerging business demands. The program evaluation function was reinvented along more tactical lines to test the residual value of training applications introduced for internal customers.

A closer integration of the curriculum development and program evaluation functions allowed the Corporate Education Centre to provide training solutions that were more customized to each individual business area. A direct benefit of this approach was the increased salience and relevance of defined training for the businesses. The model for aligning education and training solutions to the unique needs of the businesses is summarized below.

The Strategy

The Corporate Education Centre recognized that to support the bank's continued success, it had to do four things: (1) Align itself with strategic initiatives; (2) link training to improved on-the-job performance; (3) develop training solutions that gave employees all the knowledge and skills required to do their jobs; and (4) demonstrate that training had a positive impact on business results.

Linking Training to Business Results

It was recognized that all these objectives could not be achieved at once, but on a step-by-step basis. The following steps were undertaken:
1. A defined owner of the training was identified. This person was responsible for providing a clear definition of the business objectives. This person was also key to identifying and resolving implementation issues.
2. The training was based on specific business results. The performance required to generate the business results was defined. Organizational Development created job models for all positions required to implement the business strategy, and these models were developed for all levels of the organization that were critical to the success of the business initiative.
3. A comprehensive curriculum was developed on the basis of the performance requirements of all aspects of each job function.
4. Training was delivered starting with the most senior people in the organization and down throughout the organization. This approach ensured that managers had the knowledge and skills to support their employees when the employees started to apply their training on the job.

Demonstrating Results

To support the strategic shift in a results-oriented paradigm for training at the bank, changes had to be undertaken at the Corporate Education Centre. The steps, noted above, resulted in training that had an impact on business results. Now the program evaluation process needed to be expanded to measure the results. The following steps were undertaken to ensure effective measurement of results.
• A separate program evaluation department was established with its own resources. It was responsible for the effective implementation and evaluation of training initiatives. Its key functions were to:
— work with business owners to define the specific measures and the tracking systems to be used to measure the results of the initiative

— work with the various stakeholders to ensure that the performance and business goals were the correct ones to achieve the business strategy

— help the stakeholders to identify and manage the other factors that would have an impact on the successful implementation of the initiative

— work with the various stakeholders to collect, report, and analyze the results.

• Program evaluation design was changed from a back-end process to a front-end process. It then ran parallel to the development and delivery process. The program evaluation group worked with the business customer to ensure that all objectives were measurable and that systems existed to collect the data.

• The levels of evaluation were expanded so that the measurement of the success of training was the same standard as that used to measure the success of the business—that is, return-on-investment (ROI). To do this, Jack Phillips's model of evaluation was adopted. Figure 1 shows the different levels of evaluation in this model and their relative value. This model builds on Kirkpatrick's four levels of evaluation by adding a fifth level that ties the business results to the ROI to be generated from the initiative. This additional level provided a method to show business owners how training was linked to ROI. It also demonstrated why they should monitor for a clear definition and achievement of business and performance results.

• Measurement tools were introduced to evaluate the different levels as follows:

Figure 1. What to measure.

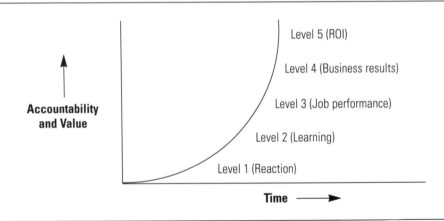

— *Level 1, reaction.* Assessed the learners planned actions back on the job as well as their reaction to the training.
— *Level 2, learning.* After each component of the training, learners were tested for knowledge and skills comprehension, using a question-and-answer format. Formalized performance assessments were conducted in a simulated work environment for behavioral objectives.
— *Level 3, on-the-job performance.* During the training, participants and their managers were informed of their on-the-job performance goals. They were also given tools to measure their progress. They then monitored and reported on their progress once they were back on the job.
— *Level 4, business results.* Business goals were established for all employees and monitored and reported up through the management structure.
— Level 5, return-on-investment. ROI is the only consistent measure of success used across all businesses in the organization. Calculating the ROI of training allowed training's impact to be reported in the same manner as the success of an operating business was reported. In this way, the value of training could be demonstrated to all senior stakeholders.

A forecast of ROI was undertaken before training development started. Based on expected business results, the revenue value of the business results generated from training was calculated with the assistance of the business group. Training expenses were deducted from the revenue to obtain the net ROI. This forecast was used to confirm that the training intervention was likely to generate the intended ROI. If the forecast did not indicate a positive ROI, alternate strategies could be considered before funds were spent on training. After the training was delivered, ROI was recalculated on the basis of the results achieved.

Postimplementation reviews were conducted, initially at about six months after the launch of a program. Data for all levels were collected. Initially, the Program Evaluation department collected on-the-job performance data and analyzed it in conjunction with the business results. As the postimplementation reviews started to demonstrate the links connecting training, on-the-job performance, and business results, the business units increasingly took ownership of the collection of on-the-job performance measures. The Corporate Education Centre accessed these data in order to conduct a comprehensive review. Outstanding issues were highlighted so the appropriate stakeholders could address them.

Copies of the postimplementation reviews were also sent to Corporate Finance personnel so they could see the methodology used and the results generated by training. This resulted in better access to funding for training when it was tied to strategic business initiatives.

Building Support

Linking training to business results and ROI were new concepts for all stakeholders. It was therefore necessary to educate all stakeholders on the value of this approach and how to implement it. The issues that needed to be addressed for each of the stakeholders are noted below.

Human Resource Executive

The first person whose support was essential was the human resource executive responsible for training. This executive's support was critical as he had to champion and communicate the concept to the business owners at the start of the initiatives. In order to obtain his support, a presentation was made to him which described:
- the different levels of evaluation and their links
- the need for specific measures and data collection systems at each level
- the importance of the clear definition of the business strategy and its measures before training development started
- the benefits to human resources of using this training strategy including:
  — adding value to the implementation of the business strategy
  — ensuring the direct link of training to ROI
  — obtaining the best use of training dollars by assessing, up front, if the training is likely to generate a positive ROI.

After the presentation, the human resources executive agreed to champion the process to business owners requesting training.

The Business Owner

To achieve the successful implementation of this process, the senior business executives, who were actually held accountable for ROI, needed to support it strongly. They were the only ones who had the influence to ensure that all aspects of the process were put in place. Presentations to these executives focused on the following:
- The need to estimate the potential ROI of the training initiative, at the start, in order to ensure highly focused, cost-effective training.
- The need for specific performance and business objectives and related measurement systems.

- The goal of training was not successful training but a sustained change in on-the-job performance in order to generate improved business results.
- The need for all levels of the organization to have their own training, performance, and business goals and measures. This permitted them to fully understand what they were expected to achieve personally and to monitor their progress.
- The value of the business incorporating both business and performance measures in the management reporting process so that progress could be continuously tracked.

As business owners understood the benefits of the process, their support was generally forthcoming.

Education and Training Staff

The education and training staff had to execute and champion the process if implementation of the ROI program evaluation process was to be successful. Training was provided to all employees of the group. The issues covered included:
- how mapping specific business objectives and performance objectives down to the skills and knowledge required permitted the tighter definition of the training required
- why each training and performance objective needed to have a specific method of evaluation
- the value of incorporating these measures into the training for easier data collection
- the need for the training to include discussions with the participants of their training, on-the-job performance, and business goals. This ensured that participants knew what results they were expected to achieve
- the types of collection instruments that could be used
- the role of the training group in the process and the roles of other stakeholders
- how the measurement process assisted in the achievement of the overall business strategy.

Line Employees

The idea that participants were responsible for generating specific performance and business results as a result of training had not been formalized before. The active involvement of managers to support the generation of results after training was also a new concept for some people. To assist in their understanding and acceptance of the concepts, their training was expanded to include the following:

- why measurement of results was necessary
- what the different levels of objectives were and how the achievement of the different objectives was linked to achieving business results
- what each participant's objectives were for each level
- how results were to be collected and reported.

Using Program Evaluation for Performance Consulting

As program evaluation is integrated into the learning process, two factors repeatedly emerge as having a strong impact on the effectiveness of the transfer of learning to on-the-job generation of results. One factor is that although the business owners have solid strategies for improving the business, the business and performance results and the related measurements are often not clearly articulated. The second factor is the nontraining issues that must be changed in order to achieve the new performance levels on the job are often not addressed at the outset. As a result, when the employees try to apply the knowledge and skills on the job, their work environment does not support their actions.

The training group has developed two tools to help clarify these factors. When working with a business owner on a new initiative, the evaluation department uses the business strategy and performance worksheet, shown in figure 2, to map all the components of the business strategy and the performance required to support the strategy. If gaps are identified, they are used as a basis of discussion with the business owner to help ensure that these issues are clarified prior to the start of the development of training.

As part of the training needs analysis, the Corporate Education Centre completes the needs analysis summary flow, shown in figure 3, to ensure that all components required for a successful implementation of the business strategy have been identified. The center uses this form to monitor the following:
- That concrete measures have been defined for all levels of evaluation.
- That systems exist to collect the measurement data at all levels of the organization. (Without these systems, it would be very difficult for the management structure to monitor for the achievement of target results.)
- That all training needs have been identified.
- That all nontraining needs that will have an impact on employees' ability to generate results have been identified.

Figure 2. Business strategy and performance worksheet.

ROI = (Business Goals x Value) - (Cost of Acquisition)

Business strategy

Target customer	Customer's needs	Products and services	Target improvement for products and services	Measures of improvement	Delivery systems

Performance required

Define and identify audience	Define products	Sell product	Process products	Transmission	Adjudication

Delivery system (complete per each delivery system)

Implementation steps to achieve performance

Evaluation of results

Figure 3. Needs analysis summary flow.

Business Needs

Business objectives	Business measures				Revenue benefit ($)	Data collection systems	
	Description	Current level (baseline)	Desired level	Gap (value of intervention)		Business measures (Level 4)	Revenue measures (Level 5)

Performance Needs

Business objectives	On-the-job performance	Performance measures				Correction objectives		Data collection systems
		Description	Current level	Desired level	Gap	Training	Nontraining	Performance measures (Level 3)

Training Needs (Education and Training Process)

On-the-job performance	Training objective	Training solution	Mastery level				Data collection systems
			Description	Pretraining	Posttraining	Improvement	Training measures (Level 2)

Nontraining Needs (Corporate and Line Customers" Process)

On-the-job performance	Nontraining objective	Nontraining solution	Mastery level				Data collection systems
			Description	Pretraining	Posttraining	Improvement	Nontraining measures (Level 2)

The Corporate Education Centre discusses the form with the business owner. Although the center is not responsible for nontraining needs, by providing the business owner with a summary of all issues, the business owner has a tool to monitor the implementation of all aspects of the strategy.

These tools have helped to ensure that all factors required for the successful implementation of a business strategy and training are in place. By formalizing these steps and reporting the results to the business owner, the Corporate Education Centre is perceived to be adding value for the business customer.

Results

Taking the steps noted above has resulted in training being viewed as successful and key to the implementation of new business strategies. The training budget is now based on what is required to support strategic business initiatives and has been increasing annually for the past three years. The Corporate Education Centre is now brought in at the front end of new initiatives to help identify key issues required for the successful launch of a strategy. It also helps define comprehensive measurement systems that will monitor for the continued generation of the desired performance and business results. And, most important, training is now linked to the generation of business results.

Questions for Discussion

1. What are the benefits of defining the expected business and performance outcomes prior to the development and delivery of training?
2. From an ROI perspective, what are the benefits of evaluating programs that have comprehensive curriculums tied to strategic business initiatives?
3. To help ensure a positive ROI from training, who, organizationally, are the two most important stakeholders to take ownership of the ROI evaluation process?
4. Should the primary role of the program evaluation group be to evaluate the effectiveness of training after its delivery or to work with business owners to ensure that objectives and their measures, at all levels of evaluation, are defined at the start of development?
5. Should it be the responsibility of program evaluators to go out and sell the ROI process?

The Authors

Brian Howard has over 20 years of experience with the Toronto Dominion Bank in both branch and corporate functions. For the past six years, he has been part of the education and training team. As manager of program evaluation, he is responsible for working with internal clients to ensure that training and development programs achieve their business and performance goals. Howard has a B.S. from the University of Toronto and a certificate of training and development from Ryerson University, and he has completed the Certification Program for Measuring Return on Investment for Training and Development. He has completed a master's degree in education at the University of Toronto, specializing in program evaluation and computer-mediated learning. He is an associate of the Institute of Canadian Bankers and has his C.S.C. (Securities) designation. He can be contacted at the following address: The Toronto-Dominion Bank, Education Centre, 68 Yonge Street, 10th Floor, Toronto, Ontario M5E 1L1.

Connie Karlsson, project leader, training research and development, is responsible for developing evaluation tools and managing various research projects. She has completed the Certification Program for Measuring Return on Investment for Training and Development as well as certificates in training and development and courseware design and development. She also holds a diploma in applied social research.

Brenda Chong, training evaluation analyst, program evaluation, is responsible for data collection, compilation, analysis, and reporting of results. She has completed the Certification Program for Measuring Return on Investment for Training and Development as well as certificates in training and development and human resources. Chong also holds an honor's degree in sociology.

Kim Japp-Delaney, assistant manager, Evaluation and Administration, is responsible for the financial costs for the ROI process. She has completed the Certification Program for Measuring Return on Investment for Training and Development and has her C.S.C. (Securities) designation. She is currently completing the certificate program in training and development.

References

Kirkpatrick, D.L. (1994). *Evaluating Training Program—The Four Levels*. San Francisco: Berrett-Koehler.

Phillips, J.J. (1991). *Training Evaluation and Measurement Methods* (2d edition). Houston: Gulf.

Phillips, J.J. (1997). *Return on Investment in Training and Performance Improvement Programs*. Houston: Gulf.

Robinson, D.G., and J.C. Robinson. (1995). *Performance Consulting: Moving Beyond Training*. San Francisco: Berrett-Koehler.

Measuring and Evaluating Training at the Technical Education Centers

Nortel (Northern Telecom)

Salvatore V. Falletta and Jill Murphy Lamb

This descriptive case study examines the implementation of a large-scale training evaluation initiative in a global telecommunications company. The company is Nortel (Northern Telecom). This study presents the use of the Kirkpatrick training evaluation framework and the instructional design process within a milestone framework. The evaluation initiative in this case study represents a training evaluation system and process that was implemented in five technical training centers across North America.

Background

The Telecommunications Act of 1996 is profoundly affecting the way in which the telecommunications industry does business. Prior to its enactment, telecommunications service providers were limited to the provision of local or long-distance telephone service. With this restriction on service potential lifted, telephone companies were able to compete in both local and long-distance services as well as in product and service arenas outside the traditional marketplace (for example, Internet access, video on demand, multimedia applications). The purpose of the Telecommunications Act was to increase competition and lower costs to customers by deregulating the industry.

Undoubtedly, this act has marked the beginning of a period of industrywide change in telecommunications. The legislation is shaping the way in which telecommunication companies are operating and conducting business with their customers and suppliers. As a result,

This case was prepared to serve as a basis for discussion rather than to illustrate either effective or ineffective administrative and management practices.

telecommunications companies can no longer rely on operational excellence alone to satisfy customers as they have in the past. The new market demands innovative and higher quality customer service. Customers today are also much more savvy and demanding with regard to the products and services they purchase. In effect, customers now expect world-class service in the telecommunications industry.

Corporate Profile

Nortel (Northern Telecom) is a leading global provider within the telecommunications industry; Nortel's consolidated revenue exceeded $15 billion in 1997. Nortel operates principally along four global lines of business: broadband networks, enterprise networks, public carrier networks, and wireless networks. With a workforce of more than 70,000, Nortel works closely with customers worldwide to offer a wealth of new and innovative networking possibilities. Within the different product lines, Nortel offers a broad range of solutions for designing, building, and integrating networks for communications, information, entertainment, education, and commerce.

Nortel's customers include local and long-distance telecommunications companies, cellular mobile radio and personal communications service providers, businesses, governments, cable television companies, competitive local access providers, and other network operators around the world. Customers purchasing Nortel products often opt to include service agreements as part of a total product package. Such service agreements cover product installation, maintenance, technical support, documentation updates, software releases, and technical training to support the product.

Technical Training as a Performance Intervention

Technical training on Nortel products is one way for customers to acquire knowledge of the new technology they are utilizing within their companies and institutions. Technical training has been the primary strategy to address performance needs related to new technology. With the emergence of alternative performance improvement strategies (such as job aids, online technical documentation, and performance feedback systems), the technical training enterprise is under increased pressure to provide innovative, timely, and cost-effective training products and services.

To remain competitive in the industry, technical training solutions must be effective in transferring product knowledge and skills to customers who purchase Nortel products. To maximize customer learning and performance, the technical training enterprise must continually improve the quality of training and provide evidence of its value and worth to customers. This need for training evaluation and continuous improvement is apparent in the new global marketplace (Brown & Seidner, 1998). By designing and implementing effective evaluation systems and processes, Nortel is able to maintain its competitive advantage.

The senior leadership at Nortel's Technical Education Centers (TEC) has recognized the importance of offering performance-based technical training and implementing a systematic process for measuring and evaluating training quality and impact. In 1996, during the time of the enactment of the Telecommunications Act, TEC developed a business case to acquire the human and fiscal resources necessary to design a strategy for implementing a measurement and evaluation system.

Organizational Profile

TEC offers technical product training for Nortel's public carrier networks and broadband networks product lines. TEC is Nortel's largest training enterprise, with nearly 250 professional staff located in five training centers across North America. TEC has a 140,000-square-foot training facility in Raleigh, North Carolina, with 43 classrooms and 31 labs. Additional training centers are located in Sacramento, California, and in Toronto, Montreal, and Ottawa, Canada. In addition to these five training centers, TEC offers on-site training to customers. In total, TEC serves more than 20,000 students annually across a training portfolio of more than 200 courses. TEC designs, develops, and delivers technical training to external customers (for example, telecommunications service providers) as well as internal Nortel employees. TEC uses a wide variety of media, including leader-led courses, computer-based training (CBT), interactive distance learning (IDL), virtual classroom technology, and self-paced video and workbook training.

TEC is striving to become a process-centered organization, although the organizational structure at TEC remains relatively functional. Of the nearly 250 professional staff, TEC has one assistant vice president (AVP), seven senior managers, 35 managers and internal consultants, more than 30 course designers and developers, and approximately 100 instructors. The remaining staff work in support groups. The different functional groups within TEC and relevant to this case study include the following: customer service, design and development, delivery, media production and logistics, customer accounts, instructional materials (that is, editing and publishing), marketing and communications, and organizational performance. The measurement and evaluation function resides within the organizational performance group. In addition to measurement and evaluation, the Organizational Performance Department is responsible for employee and organization development initiatives, employee satisfaction solutions, ISO and quality programs, and internal communication for TEC. The department manager and two senior evaluation specialists are primarily responsible for leading the evaluation initiative.

Evaluation Strategy and Philosophy

As mentioned, the senior leadership at TEC recognized the importance of implementing a systematic process for measuring and evaluating technical training. After acquiring the necessary resources, TEC hired two senior evaluation specialists to assist the organizational performance manager with formulating a strategy and philosophy of evaluation. To begin, the evaluation team performed a benchmarking study of major companies in the telecommunication and computer industries to obtain information on best practices in training evaluation. The team conducted telephone interviews with 10 leading companies to collect the benchmarking data on training evaluation practices. This study indicated that all but one company was applying Kirkpatrick's training evaluation framework (that is, Levels 1 through 4) in the measurement of training quality and outcomes. Only one company reported a process that did not directly involve the Kirkpatrick framework.

Selecting an Evaluation Framework

The training industry uses various frameworks in the conceptualization of training evaluation. Frameworks such as Kirkpatrick's four-level model and Phillips's five-level approach, which includes return-on-investment, provide a common language for communicating, reporting, and marketing training evaluation activities within the corporate setting (Kirkpatrick, 1994; Phillips, 1997a). Although other useful frameworks, taxonomies, and approaches exist (for example, Brinkerhoff, 1987; Falletta & Combs, 1997; Holton, 1996), TEC chose to conceptualize the evaluation initiative using Kirkpatrick's four-level framework due to its simplicity and ease of use. This framework is recognized and widely disseminated by the American Society for Training & Development (ASTD). Most important, TEC's key stakeholders and customers were familiar with the Kirkpatrick framework, and the evaluation team felt stakeholder familiarity would minimize the resistance associated with the implementation of the evaluation initiative. Kirkpatrick's four levels are

- *Level 1, reaction:* expert reaction toward the training; participant satisfaction or dissatisfaction, or both, with the training
- *Level 2, learning application:* knowledge and skills acquired from the training
- *Level 3, on-the-job performance:* participant application of what was learned in training to the job (that is, transfer of training to the work environment)
- *Level 4, organizational results:* training impact on organizational results.

The Kirkpatrick framework makes it possible to evaluate training at any one or more of the four levels.

In selecting the Kirkpatrick framework as a guide for future evaluation activities, the evaluation team recognized the shortcomings of this particular model. One of these shortcomings is the implied causal linkages between the levels of the model (Alliger & Janak, 1989; Holton, 1996). Another shortcoming is the fact that the framework is not actually a model at all, but rather a taxonomy of training outcomes (Holton, 1996). Given the widespread familiarity of the framework within corporate settings, the evaluation team agreed to use Kirkpatrick's approach nonetheless.

Strategic Stakeholders

Stakeholders are those individuals who are interested in or affected by training, including trainers, training participants, designers and developers, supervisors, managers, senior managers, executives, and customers (Falletta & Combs, 1997). In the early stages of the evaluation initiative, the evaluation team identified strategic stakeholders to support the initiative; these individuals were design and development managers, delivery managers, senior managers, and the AVP. The manager of organizational performance held active working sessions to achieve the involvement of these stakeholders, and they were fully involved in the creation and endorsement of an evaluation strategy and philosophy (that is, the evaluation process and documentation).

In terms of formulating an evaluation strategy, the evaluation team recognized that there was no other way to implement a successful evaluation initiative than to engage stakeholders in discussion over the specific purposes of the initiative. Team members thought that stakeholder dissatisfaction and disillusionment with the evaluation process would result if stakeholders' needs were not met by the initiative. The evaluation team also recognized that stakeholders' perceptions of the usefulness of the evaluation data would be a strong indicator of the success of the initiative. Again, if evaluation information did not meet stakeholders' informational needs, the stakeholders would not view the initiative as successful. Hence, the evaluation team focused considerable time and energy into clarifying the evaluation philosophy with stakeholders.

Philosophical and Ethical Issues

Three major issues emerged in working sessions on the development of the evaluation philosophy. The first issue involved the relative importance of formative (process) versus summative (outcome) evaluation activities. The second issue concerned whether to report data in individual as well as aggregate form. The third issue involved the use of evaluation information in the management of training staff and performance appraisal. The discussion over these three issues ensued for several months.

The first issue of debate was whether evaluation activities would be primarily process oriented or outcome oriented. Most stakeholders agreed that the evaluation initiative should focus on the measurement of training outcomes rather than processes in order to demonstrate training effectiveness. A few stakeholders, including the evaluation team, suggested measuring both training processes and outcomes simultaneously to improve training quality as well as to assess the impact. This issue was resolved relatively quickly through an educational and consultative approach. The evaluation team presented the benefits associated with both process and outcome evaluation and explained the varied purposes evaluation might serve.

The second major issue, the use of individual evaluation data, was not so easily agreed upon. The data collected to evaluate training often includes individuals' assessment scores, attitudes, ratings, social security numbers, and professional positions, all of which is private information. Given the sensitive nature of these personal data, the evaluation team felt that trainees would participate in the evaluation process only if they were assured that this information would be kept private and confidential (Newman & Brown, 1996).

The evaluation team was also concerned that harm to individuals and to the entire evaluation initiative might result if individual data were not kept secure. This harm might involve direct or indirect damage to individuals' credibility or self-esteem. Further, the lack of security of the data might lead to suspicion and feelings of vulnerability surrounding the evaluation initiative. The potential misuse of such data might even lead to legal implications (for example, if the data were used for human resource decisions such as demotion or promotion). Hence, the evaluation team remained vigilant to business and political pressures to release individual evaluation data.

Many of the senior leaders, who are characterized as business oriented due to their ongoing business relationships with external customers, were more comfortable in releasing individual data than were staff professionals (such as, designers and developers, evaluation specialists). These staff professionals, who have little contact with customers, were not comfortable releasing individual evaluation data to customers. The evaluation team continued to advise senior leaders on the ethical implications of reporting individual evaluation data. For guidance on this matter, the team consulted the Nortel Corporate Ethics Department.

The assertion that individual evaluation data must remain confidential and secure is rooted in the practice of program evaluation (that is, evaluators' professional code of ethics; Joint Committee on Standards, 1994; Newman & Brown, 1996). Ethics codes dictate that individuals be informed of the purpose and use of evaluation data, the limits of confidentiality, and their rights to privacy.

In the end, TEC decided not to distribute individual evaluation data to customers due to the legal implications (for example, assessment validity, reliability, adverse impact associated with tests) and ethical implications, as discussed. It was agreed that customers would receive aggregate data (that is, data summarized across all of their employees) and comparative data (that is, overall TEC averages).

The third issue regarding the use of evaluation data involved managing and appraising the performance of TEC training staff. Historically, TEC used Level 1 survey data on instructor effectiveness as a measure of overall instructor performance for performance appraisal purposes. Although such data are useful for immediate feedback, the use of this data for annual performance appraisal is questionable. For example, using this data for reward and recognition encouraged instructional staff to seek to influence high ratings on Level 1 participant surveys at any cost. Although not overt, instructors could bias ratings by virtue of their behavior or comments to the participants completing the surveys. As a result, the data collected on the instructor effectiveness scales were historically inflated, which raised doubts as to the validity of the measure. The AVP was aware of the organizational dependency on Level 1 data for performance appraisal purposes. In fact, she highly encouraged managers to use a more comprehensive approach in managing and documenting the performance of training staff. The AVP called for the use of formal performance appraisal tools and processes, including the observation of classroom performance.

Stakeholders' perspectives, values, business needs, legal concerns, and professional ethics were all taken into account in formulating a clear evaluation philosophy to guide the initiative. The following philosophy was endorsed and enacted:

> TEC's purpose in conducting evaluation is to measure training processes and outcomes in order to improve training product quality and effectiveness. A corollary purpose is to measure the extent to which training outcomes impact on-the-job performance and organizational results. In doing so, the evaluation team will meet stakeholders informational needs and focus evaluation resources on performance-based training interventions, while respecting the confidentiality of training participants.

The evaluation team found that the senior leadership has to discuss, negotiate, and own an evaluation philosophy, if it is to be meaningful (Basarab & Root, 1992). Senior leadership, including the AVP, ultimately endorsed TEC's evaluation strategy and philosophy; it became established policy only after time was devoted to this discussion. The evaluation strategy and philosophy were also incorporated into TEC's standardized ISO 9001 procedures to ensure consistent evaluation practice and quality.

Establishing an Evaluation Culture

Establishing an evaluation culture is no easy task. The evaluation team was aware that implementing a systemwide evaluation initiative would be similar to implementing a large-scale change initiative. The success of such an effort requires the commitment, understanding, and buy-in of stakeholders at all levels. At TEC, much of the groundwork had been laid through the development of the evaluation strategy and philosophy. The next step was education in training evaluation practices for managers and staff. This training provided TEC with a consistent message and approach to implementing an evaluation system and promoting a shared understanding of the benefits of training evaluation. TEC contracted Jim Burrow, associate professor and coordinator of the training and development program at North Carolina State University, to provide evaluation orientations and workshops. Burrow examined the evaluation strategy and philosophy as well as examples of all surveys and measurement instruments that TEC used to customize the sessions. Using Kirkpatrick's four levels of evaluation, Burrow designed and developed orientation sessions, including a special session for senior leadership; customized workshops for designers and developers, which included hands-on activities (for example, constructing knowledge and performance assessments, writing measurable objectives); and instructor workshops on administering and collecting evaluation instruments. The staff actively participated in these sessions. For those who were unable to attend, copies of all training materials, including videotaped sessions, were made available. These evaluation orientations and workshops were extremely successful and valuable in establishing an evaluation culture at TEC.

Evaluation Processes and Procedures

Upon formulating a strategy and philosophy of evaluation and providing an educational foundation, TEC had to develop a process to incorporate evaluation into the existing course development and delivery process. To structure course development, TEC uses a milestone process that reflects the steps of instructional systems design and development (ISD) within a project management framework. ISD is a process-oriented, systematic approach to designing instructional-based interventions (Hannum & Hansen, 1989). The systems approach generally begins with a front-end analysis (in other words, needs assessment, task analysis, and performance analysis) in which training needs are analyzed for groups of trainees within a job function. This is followed by the design phase, in which goals and performance objectives are developed and used to determine appropriate content, methods, and media for delivery. The third phase of ISD is the actual development of instructional materials. The implementation phase follows and involves the actual delivery of the training. Implementation of training (that is, delivery) generally begins with a pilot in which materials and methods are evaluated before they are made generally available. The final ISD phase, evaluation, involves ongoing evaluation of the training product to improve training quality and effectiveness over time.

The Milestone Process

TEC uses the milestone process as a project management tool in the development of courseware. The milestone process includes six distinct project milestones: mile 0 (initiation), mile 1 (planning), mile 1A (design), mile 2 (development), mile 3 (implementation), and mile 4 (evaluation). Project initiation (mile 0) involves assigning the human and fiscal resources to the project and obtaining a project number. A designer/developer and subject matter expert (SME) are assigned to the project during this particular milestone. The project planning milestone (mile 1) involves conducting needs analysis to identify training needs. This milestone is followed by the design milestone (mile 1A), in which a comprehensive job study is conducted. A job study includes the identification of specific job and performance tasks and the development of task inventories. In addition, job tasks that are critical to customers' specific requirements are also identified and documented. The development milestone (mile 2) involves the actual development of instructional materials, including evaluation instrumentation and editing and publishing of materials. Finally, the implementation milestone (mile 3) involves validating the course or courses. Again, during a pilot, the project team—design, delivery, and evaluators—assessed and improved instructional materials before they are made generally available. Evaluation instruments are administered during the pilot implementation to determine whether course goals and objectives are aligned and the appropriateness of the particular methods and media designed into the course. Once the course is generally available, evaluation systems and processes (mile 4) are put in place to support the ongoing assessment and measurement of course quality and effectiveness over time.

The ISD process and milestone process used at TEC are complementary. The milestone process incorporates ISD into a project management framework. It allows TEC to operate in a competitive business environment by providing structure in the management of project resources. Unfortunately, when business pressures arise, the amount of time for course design and development activities may be reduced. The training industry's cliche *quicker, better, faster* accurately characterizes the pressures in today's fast-paced economy.

Evaluation Consultation

The evaluation team within the Organizational Performance Department serves as a support function to TEC. The evaluation team offers consultation on designing evaluation into courseware. The responsibilities of the team include the following: attending project team meetings, conducting evaluation orientations, consulting with various audiences, constructing evaluation instruments, establishing evaluation processes and procedures, capturing data through optical scanning, maintaining an evaluation database, performing data analysis, and communicating and reporting evaluation findings. The evaluation team also provides consultation on other data collection and analysis activities (for example, specialized customer surveys, climate studies, and needs assessments) at TEC.

At project initiation, the manager of organizational performance assigns an evaluation specialist to a project team for the development of a new course or major redesign. Table 1 illustrates the specific evaluation deliverables that evaluation team members are responsible for within the milestone process framework at TEC.

It is evident that the evaluation team has adopted a process consultative approach to evaluating courseware. This approach is necessary given the number of courses in TEC's portfolio (that is, more than 200) and the technical nature of the training intervention. In the area of technical training, a high level of subject-matter expertise is required for course design and development activities. For example, course designers and developers and the SME are the individuals responsible for constructing assessment instruments (Level 2 evaluation instruments). Although evaluation team members may not possess such technical expertise, they do provide substantive input to the construction of assessments instruments. Specifically, evaluation specialists examine Level 2 instruments for ambiguous assessment items, poorly worded assessment items, unfair distracters and unclear response alternatives, and assessment items that do not match the learning objectives. In addition, evaluation specialists thoroughly review the learning objectives in the design document for measurability and to ensure the alignment of the course content and assessment instruments (Mager, 1975).

A significant part of the consultation process involves evaluation planning. During mile 2 (development), a preliminary evaluation plan is drafted in collaboration with the course designer/developer. The evaluation plan includes the level of focus (Level 1 through Level 4), data collection methodology, and data analysis strategy. At mile 4 (evaluation), the designer/developer and delivery manager receive a final evaluation plan detailing all of the above, in addition to final recommendations on revisions to the evaluation instruments.

ISO 9001 and Evaluation

TEC has aligned the evaluation initiative with ISO 9001 requirements. Once a course is generally available, a delivery group owns the course and is responsible for administering all evaluation instruments as indicated in the evaluation plan and TEC's ISO procedures. Descriptive procedures, available to all TEC staff, detail the evaluation system

Table 1. Evaluation deliverables within the milestone process framework.

Initiation (mile 0)
- Evaluation team is notified.
- An evaluation specialist is assigned to the project.

Planning (mile 1)
- Evaluation specialist attends the project meeting and determines whether the course or courses are candidates for evaluation.
- Evaluation specialist provides recommendations.

Design (mile 1A)
- The course design document is reviewed.
- Learning objectives are reviewed for measurability. The learning objectives should include the desired performance, condition, and standard or criteria for performance (Mager, 1975).
- Validation plan is reviewed (internal and external pilot strategy).
- Recommendations are provided.

Development (mile 2)
- Designer or developer is assisted in targeting the major or critical learning objectives to be evaluated.
- A preliminary evaluation plan is developed, including the levels of evaluation, instrumentation, methodology, and data analysis strategy.
- Assistance in constructing and using evaluation instruments is provided. Examples of standardized optical scanning forms are distributed.
- Evaluation instruments are aligned with learning objectives.
- Evaluation instruments are used during internal pilot.
- Statistical analysis of internal pilot is conducted (for example, item analysis).
- Recommendations are provided (for example, revisions, modifications)

Implementation (mile 3)
- Evaluation instruments are used during external pilot.
- Statistical analysis of external pilot is conducted (for example, item analysis).
- Final recommendations are provided (for example, revisions, modifications).
- Corrective action is initiated, if applicable.

Evaluation (mile 4)
- A final evaluation plan is developed for general availability.
- Distribution of final evaluation plan to key audiences (for example, development and delivery).
- Systems and processes are in place for ongoing evaluation, including optical scanner configuration and database file set-up for data analysis and reporting; monitoring course quality and outcomes.

and processes as well as the administration of evaluation instruments. As part of Nortel's quest to compete for the Malcolm Baldrige National Quality Award, TEC has obtained ISO 9001 certification two consecutive years (Russo, 1995).

Evaluation Methodology

The evaluation methods commonly used for measuring the effects of technical training at TEC include questionnaires or surveys, knowledge and performance assessments, observations, performance simulations, focus groups, and structured interviews. Other methods may be used (for example, work logs, action plans, role plays; Basarab & Root, 1992; Phillips, 1997a). The particular method used in any given evaluation will depend on the level of the evaluation according to Kirkpatrick's framework.

Level 1

TEC administers participant reaction surveys on all courseware. For leader-led instruction, a participant reaction form (PRF) is administered to training participants on the last day of instruction. The survey measures the extent to which participants are satisfied or dissatisfied with the training. Using a five-point Likert-type scale, satisfaction is measured on several dimensions, including content, documentation, instructional materials, instructor, training environment, and value. There is also space available for written comments. A shorter, online version of this survey is used for CBT and an interview version is used for virtual classroom courses. The virtual classroom is a technology that allows training participants to access a Nortel product at TEC through an interactive network. With a personal computer, modem, and headset, the trainee can perform hands-on activities from a networked computer desktop (for example, employee workstation).

Level 2

Depending on the type of learning objectives designed into a course (that is, cognitive or knowledge based, or skill or performance based), the evaluation team may plan pre- and postassessments as part of the evaluation process to measure learning acquisition. If the learning objectives are cognitive or knowledge based, preassessments and postassessments are employed, with the same assessment administered on both occasions. Although an equivalent assessment may be developed, it must have the same number of easy, moderate, and difficult items, and must correlate highly with the first assessment (Shrock &

Coscarelli, 1989). However, TEC does not develop or use equivalent assessments. If time is an issue, only postassessments are administered. The use of comparison or control groups, although ideal, are not used at TEC, given business constraints.

Designers or developers and SMEs also construct performance assessments. A list of the most significant skills for the learner to master is prepared from a review of the course learning objectives. The tasks that make up each skill are identified and arranged in a logical sequence. Standards by which the performance (or object) of each skill are judged and designed on the basis of course expectations. A checklist is then used to rate each skill. It allows the observer to record whether the learner "met," "met with assistance," or "did not meet" the criteria for performance. The "met with assistance" category is endorsed when the trainee successfully performs at least 75 percent of the task or objective without assistance from an observer. Team performance assessments are also conducted when there is a lack of equipment or when the situation calls for working in teams. In contrast to performance checklists, rating scales that allow the observer to rate performance or characteristics on a continuous scale can be used on performance assessments. However, TEC is not currently using rating scales for Level 2 evaluation.

Level 3

TEC has recently begun to conduct Level 3 evaluations. A multimethod approach is used in measuring the extent to which trainees apply what was learned in training to their respective jobs. The multimethod approach is ideal and minimizes any monomethod bias associated with using only one type of evaluation tool for data collection. The methods TEC uses for Level 3 evaluation are structured interviews, focus groups, observation, performance simulations, and surveys. The questions on Level 3 surveys address the extent to which learned skills were applied on the job (that is, transferred to the work environment). Although the survey is not the only method TEC uses, TEC considers it an appropriate Level 3 evaluation tool, contrary to what some in the training industry believe. Although direct observation of performance on the job is ideal, it is not easy to accomplish, nor is it cost-effective.

TEC recently conducted a Level 3 evaluation on two high-participation courses. Table 2 presents several items from a recent Level 3 survey. The survey was designed to measure on-the-job performance of tasks across five dimensions. These dimensions on the learner survey were relevancy of the training to the job, opportunity for the learner to perform, the learner's actual performance, the learner's confidence in performing the task or activity, and preparation through the training.

With respect to transfer of training (Broad & Newstrom, 1992), the following three questions pertaining to training transfer were asked on the learners' participant survey.

1. To what extent is your supervisor/manager available to you for coaching or mentoring on the job?

				To a
Not at all				great extent
1	2	3	4	5

2. After taking_____, to what extent did you receive on-the-job training ?

				To a
Not at all				great extent
1	2	3	4	5

3. To what extent are you encouraged to use the new skills you learned in_____ on the job?

				To a
Not at all				great extent
1	2	3	4	5

A similar manager and supervisor version of the Level 3 survey also was administered to measure managers' perceptions of learners' performance after they returned from training. The dimensions on the manager and supervisor survey pertained to the following: relevancy of the training to the job, opportunity for the learner to perform, the learner's success in performing, the manager's opportunity to observe, and preparation through the training. Two additional questions on the manager and supervisor survey pertained to training transfer within the customer organization:

- Is a structured/formal mentoring or coaching program available to employees who have recently completed _____?
  - _____ Yes, Structured/Formal Mentoring/Coaching
  - _____ No Structured/Formal Program
- Is a structured/formal on-the-job training program available to employees who have recently completed _____?
  - _____ Yes, Structured/Formal On-The-Job Training
  - _____ No Structured/Formal Program

Table 2. Example of Level 3 survey items for one performance task.

Task #1	Not at all				To a great extent
A. To what extent is this task relevant to your job?	1	2	3	4	5
B. To what extent have you had the opportunity to perform this task on the job?	1	2	3	4	5
C. Did you perform this task on the job?	_____ Yes		_____ No		
D. To what extent are you confident in your ability to perform this task?	1	2	3	4	5
E. To what extent did the training prepare you to perform this task?	1	2	3	4	5

Certification

In connection with Level 3 evaluation, TEC is implementing a training and certification process for all field installation technicians at Nortel. Installation technicians receive their technical training from TEC, and upon completion, they have an opportunity to perform the tasks learned on the job. On-the-job training is part of the certification process along with formal mentoring. Trainees eventually become eligible for certification after passing on-the-job performance assessments (that is, Level 3). These performance assessments measure trainees' mastery of a minimum set of skills. The performance assessment is a checklist that allows an observer to record whether the trainee met or did not meet the criteria for performance. It includes the skills to be observed and the criteria or standard the performance is judged against; performance ratings actually occur in the field. Although training evaluation and on-the-job certification serve different functions, TEC has effectively aligned its Level 3 evaluation efforts with Nortel's certification needs.

Level 4

To date, TEC has not conducted a Level 4 evaluation largely because a significant amount of TEC's customers are external to Nortel. As a result, the evaluation team does not have access to pertinent business data (for example, performance metrics and financial data) required to conduct this level of evaluation. TEC plans to conduct a

Level 4 evaluation to measure the impact of training on the business results within Nortel. In addition to Level 4, the evaluation team may conduct a return-on-investment (Level 5) study to determine the monetary value of results associated with TEC's technical training interventions in 1998 (Phillips, 1997b).

Data Capture and Analysis

Once the evaluation methods have been determined, the data capture and statistical analysis requirements must be identified. Currently, TEC captures Level 1 and 2 evaluation data through optical scanning technology and CBT diskette. All leader-led courses use the scannable PRF form. Evaluation data from these courses are collected and routed to the evaluation team. Once scanned, the data are converted to ASCII format to be imported into the TEC training evaluation database. Self-paced CBT diskettes are also routed to the evaluation team for data extraction and analysis.

TEC conducts all data analyses in-house. TEC currently uses a FoxPro database for Level 1 analysis and Excel spreadsheets for Level 2 analysis. Level 3 data analysis is performed on a more powerful statistical package (SAS). Simple Level 2 calculations that are easily computed with a spreadsheet application include frequency, percentage, mean, mode, median, range, variance, and standard deviation. For Level 2 cognitive-based assessments, TEC also calculates learning gain index (LGI), which is a more reliable indicator of acquired learning than actual learning gain in that it does not penalize trainees who achieve relatively high preassessment scores. The LGI allows for the calculation of the percentage of knowledge gain following the preassessment (that is, the percentage of the potential gain that was achieved at postassessment; Basarab & Root, 1992). Advanced statistical functions, including t tests and correlations, are conducted as appropriate (Martelli, 1997). Tables 3, 4, and 5 provide examples of Level 2 statistical analysis for cognitive-based learning objectives.

Table 3 includes training participants' preassessment and postassessment scores. The actual gain in learning, potential gain, and LGI are calculated from preassessment and postassessment scores. As mentioned earlier, the LGI provides an overall comparative index of learning that is unaffected by training participants' knowledge prior to the training.

The descriptive statistics in table 4 provide information that is useful in interpreting the training group mean scores. For example,

Table 3. Preassessment and postassessment scores and calculations.

Course #	Company	Pre	Post	Actual Gain	Potential Gain	LGI (%)
101	Telecom	25	97	62	75	82.7
101	Telecom	28	95.5	67.5	72	93.8
101	Telecom	0	68.2	68.2	100	68.2
101	Telecom	0	72.7	72.7	100	72.7
101	Telecom	30	100	70	70	100.0
101	Telecom	42	90	48	58	82.8
101	Telecom	22	85	63	78	80.8
101	Telecom	30	90	60	70	85.7
101	Telecom	8	80	72	92	78.3
101	Telecom	25	86.3	61.3	75	81.7
101	Telecom	25	100	75	75	100.0
101	Telecom	15	91	76	95	89.4
101	Telecom	8	68.2	60.2	92	65.4
101	Telecom	28	91	63	72	87.5

in table 4, the range of scores was broader prior to training than after completion of training. This suggests that although training participants exhibited varying degrees of knowledge at the outset, they had converged in their level of knowledge after participating in the training.

The t test is used to determine whether there is a statistically significant difference between training participants' preassessment and postassessment scores. In this example, table 5 depicts a statistically significant difference between the scores in that the t stat (32.71) are larger than the t critical one-tail (2.65). The t test was calculated at .01 significance level. Hence, one could expect this result 99 percent of the time.

Summarizing Large Amounts of Data

TEC uses bar charts, pie charts, and tables to summarize the evaluation results in reports, presentations, and informal communications. Tables, in particular, allow a large amount of information to be presented in an orderly manner on one page. TEC generally uses tables for reporting Level 3 data. Data from open-ended items are usually typed verbatim into a table, although no information that might identify the individual is included. The responses are then categorized based on themes.

Table 4. Preassessment and postassessment descriptive analysis.

Preassessments		Postassessments	
Mean	20.42	Mean	86.06
Standard error	3.31	Standard error	2.78
Median	25	Median	88.5
Mode	25	Mode	68.2
Standard deviation	12.40	Standard deviation	10.42
Sample variance	153.95	Sample variance	108.68
Range	42	Range	31.8
Minimum	0	Minimum	68.2
Maximum	42	Maximum	100
Sum count	286	Sum count	1204.9
Confidence level	14	Confidence level	14
(99.0%)	9.98	(99.0%)	8.39

Table 5. Test for statistical significance between pre- and postassessment scores.

	T-Test	
	Post	**Pre**
Mean	86.06	20.42
Variance	108.68	153.95
Observations	14	14
Pearson correlation	0.79	
Hypothesized mean difference	0	
Df	13	
t Stat	32.71	
P(<T=t) one-tail	3.57	
t Critical one-tail	2.65	

Communicating and Reporting

TEC uses a powerful relational database for the storage, analysis, and reporting of evaluation data. The practicality of using such a database depends on the extent of data collection, the size of the training enterprise, and stakeholders' needs for information (Falletta & Combs, 1997). Although stakeholders' needs for information are known at this point, it is vital to confirm the format of the information stakeholders will receive, the frequency of reporting, and the preferred media (for example, database-generated reports, PowerPoint slides, bound reports, and statistical summaries; Torres, Preskill, & Piontek, 1996). The evaluation team at TEC formally presents evaluation results each quarter, although informal reporting occurs regularly upon request. In addition, customer reporting is requested on occasion.

TEC's evaluation communication and reporting strategies have evolved over time. In 1998, TEC will implement a state-of-the-art training evaluation database. The application, TEDS, is a comprehensive computer-based program capable of managing various aspects of corporate training (for example, administration, scheduling, assessment, documentation, and evaluation). This application and database will enable TEC to create evaluation surveys and assessments, and to collect evaluation data through a simpler process. For example, evaluation instruments may be administered online to training participants over the intranet or Internet. TEDS can also be used for Level 3 evaluations and can be administered to multiple audiences, including trainees, supervisors, and managers. Because the TEDS database can accept data in ASCII form, data may be captured by multiple methods and imported into the database. Although this new technology will soon become available, optical scanner technology will continue to be used to collect paper-based evaluation data. In terms of data reporting on TEDS, Level 1, 2, and 3 reports may be queried and generated through TEDS on the Nortel intranet. TEDS is designed by CBM Technologies, based in Atkin, Virginia.

Questions for Discussion
1. What similar challenges do you anticipate in implementing training evaluation in your organization or institution?
2. What are the advantages and disadvantages to using the Kirkpatrick framework for evaluating training in your organization or institution?
3. Reflecting on your own values and ethics, how would you respond to requests from customers or senior management to release individual level evaluation data?
4. What are the organizational benefits to using the ISD process within a project management framework? What are the drawbacks?
5. Would your process to implementing training evaluation differ from the Nortel example? Why or why not?

The Authors
Salvatore V. Falletta is a senior performance consultant at the Performance Development Center for ALLTEL Corporate Services. He was previously the Southeast regional manager for training and development at 360° Communications prior to the merger with ALLTEL. Falletta was formerly a senior evaluation specialist for the Nortel Technical Education Centers in the United States and Canada. He is completing a doctoral degree in training and development at North Carolina State University and received his M.P.A. specializing in human resources and organization development from Indiana State University. His publications have appeared in *The American Journal of Evaluation, Contemporary Education,* and *ASTD's Info-line.* Falletta is currently coauthoring a book on measuring and evaluating performance improvement interventions (with Wendy L. Combs) for ASTD. His interests include measuring and evaluating performance improvement, organizational assessment and diagnosis, and talent and knowledge management. His professional memberships include the American Society for Training & Development, International Soci-

ety for Performance Improvement, American Psychological Association, and American Evaluation Association. He may be contacted at 360° Communications, 4000 Regency Parkway, Suite 400, Cary, NC 27511; phone: 919.573.4828.

Jill Murphy Lamb is a senior evaluation specialist for the Nortel Technical Education Centers in the United States and Canada. Prior to joining Nortel, Lamb was a training and development manager at Motorola, where she was responsible for assessing training needs, coordinating and delivering training, and evaluating training effectiveness. Lamb holds a master's degree in training and development from North Carolina State University. She received her B.A. in economics at State University of New York, College at Geneseo. Her interests include training evaluation, self-directed learning, return-on-investment, and human performance technology. Her professional memberships include ASTD and the International Society for Performance Improvement.

References

Alliger, G.M., and E.A. Janak. (1989). "Kirkpatrick's Levels of Training Criteria: Thirty Years Later." *Personnel Psychology, 42*, 331–340.

Basarab, D.J., and D.K. Root. (1992). *The Training Evaluation Process.* Boston: Kluwer.

Brinkerhoff, R.O. (1987). *Achieving Results from Training.* San Francisco: Jossey-Bass.

Broad, M.L., and J.W. Newstrom. (1992). *Transfer of Training.* Reading MA: Addison-Wesley.

Brown, S.M., and C.J. Seidner. (Eds.). (1998). *Evaluating Corporate Training: Models and Issues.* Boston: Kluwer.

Falletta, S.V., and W.L. Combs. (1997, September). "Evaluating Technical Training: A Functional Approach." INFO-LINE No. 9709.

Hannum, W., and C. Hansen. (1989). *Instructional Systems Development in Large Organizations.* Englewood Cliffs, NJ: Educational Technology Publications.

Holton, E.F., III. (1996). "The Flawed Four-Level Evaluation Model." *Human Resource Development Quarterly, 7*(1), 5–29.

Joint Committee on Standards. (1994). *Program Evaluation Standards* (2d edition). Newbury Park, CA: Sage.

Kirkpatrick, D.L. (1994). *Evaluating Training Programs: The Four Levels.* San Francisco: Berrett-Koehler.

Mager, R.F. (1975). *Preparing Instructional Objectives* (2d edition). Belmont, CA: Fearon.

Martelli, J.T. (1997, February). "Using Statistics in HRD." *Training & Development,* 62–63.

Newman, D.L., and R.D. Brown. (1996). *Applied Ethics for Program Evaluation.* Thousand Oaks, CA: Sage.

Phillips, J.J. (1997a). *Handbook of Training Evaluation and Measurement Methods.* Houston: Gulf.

Phillips, J.J. (1997b). *Return on Investment in Training and Performance Improvement Programs.* Houston: Gulf.

Russo, C.W. (1995). *ISO 9000 and Malcolm Baldrige in Training and Education: A Practical Application Guideline.* Lawrence, KS: Charro.

Shrock, S.A., and W.C. Coscarelli. (1989). *Criterion-referenced Test Development: Technical and Legal Guidelines for Corporate Training.* Reading, MA: Addison-Wesley.

Torres, R.T., H.S. Preskill, and M.E. Piontek. (1996). *Evaluation Strategies for Communicating and Reporting: Enhancing Learning in Organizations.* Newbury Park, CA: Sage.

Implementing an
ROI Measurement Process

Dell Computer

Ferdinand Tesoro

This return-on-investment evaluation study determined the business impact of the sales negotiation training course at Dell. The specific metrics used include profit margin and margin attainment percent, units sold and attainment percent, total revenue and attainment percent.

Background

The study used a five-step return-on-investment (ROI) measurement process that Dell Computer uses. The process steps include plan, develop, analyze, communicate, and leverage. This particular case study involved 57 participants who attended the Dell sales negotiation course (DSN) and an equivalent control group. To collect data, the corporate sales information database was used to compare pre- and posttraining metrics for both training and control groups. A cost-benefit analysis was also conducted to determine ROI of the training.

The following are the key findings of the study:

- There was an overall improvement of 17.63 percent in all metrics for the training group. The greatest improvements were in profit-margin volume sales and total revenue sales with 61.56 percent and 41.86 percent, respectively.
- Average quarterly compensation per participant increased by 14.11 percent for the third quarter, over the second quarter of fiscal year 1997.

This case was prepared to serve as a basis for discussion rather than to illustrate either effective or ineffective administrative and management practices.

- The training group performed better than the control group in all metric areas, which means that DSN has had a positive impact on performance and goal attainment.
- The cost-benefit analysis calculated an ROI of 523.25 percent for a three-month period. The total net profit to the company, in margin dollars, was $763,297.
- The projected annual net profits generated by DSN training is about $1.5 million per year.

The recommendations generated from the results of the study include the following:

- The results should be communicated to executive and management staffs for them to recommend the training to those who have not yet attended.
- Coaching and reinforcement efforts for the course have to be stepped up so that these improvements can be sustained.
- Due to the tremendous results of this study, the course should be included in development plans of sales representatives, account executives, sales managers, and regional sales managers.
- A follow-up study should be done to identify specific negotiation skills and tools that are being used on the job.

About Dell Computer Corporation

Dell is the world's number one direct computer systems company in the world. It sells and supports desktops, laptops, workstations, servers, peripherals, software, and other systems solutions in four regions: Americas (including Canada and Latin America), Europe, Asia-Pacific, and Japan. The company pioneered computer Internet commerce and is now generating about $4 million revenues daily through online sales. Dell has approximately 15,000 employees worldwide, two-thirds of whom are based in the Austin, Texas, corporate headquarters.

Sales and Marketing magazine's October 1997 issue recognized Dell for having America's number one sales force. The major criteria used for the award were recruiting, compensation, and training. The award cited Dell's innovative reward systems, aggressive recruiting techniques, and impactful sales training programs. Other companies listed in the top five include Intel, Hewlett Packard, AMD, and IBM.

Dell University is the training (evolving into learning) organization of Dell Computer. Like the company, Dell University has corporate headquarters in Austin and training teams in each region. Dell University's mission is to deliver the right learning solution to the right people at the right time. Its vision is to be the benchmark and be recognized as a key contributor to the success of the business.

About the Sales Negotiation Training Program

The Dell Sales Negotiation course is a two-day interactive, experiential training program. Its intended audience is sales representatives, account executives, sales managers, regional sales managers, and sales directors. In 1996, a total of 315 salespeople attended this training program in Austin, Chicago, and Sydney, Australia.

DSN is designed to help Dell and its people accomplish the following:
- negotiate more profitable agreements with customers
- become more effective at negotiating within the company to gain whatever may be required to negotiate successfully with customers
- shorten sales cycles by eliminating extra negotiation steps during the sales process
- avoid common negotiation mistakes, such as conceding too quickly on price or discount, or entering a customer negotiation without an effective plan
- build increased customer loyalty by crafting agreements that address underlying buyer needs and motives.

Introduction

This case describes the results from an evaluation study that was conducted to determine the effectiveness of the Dell Sales Negotiation training program. The five-step Dell ROI measurement process was developed and used for this purpose. Particularly, the study discusses the impact of DSN to Dell's critical business issues and specific Dell performance metrics such as profit margin and margin attainment percent, units sold and attainment percent, total revenue and attainment percent.

The Dell ROI Measurement Process

The Dell University evaluation team developed this process to define a structure for conducting ROI evaluations at Dell. The process was based on existing literature on ROI measurement written by Phillips, Kirkpatrick, and Basarab, to name a few. The process has the following steps:

Plan

The deliverable for this step is a project plan for the ROI project. The purpose of this step is to identify the direct link between the training program being evaluated, benefits of conducting the evaluation, project goals, business metrics to be tracked, program objectives, project team with roles and responsibilities, timeline with milestones, and resource requirements. The project plan establishes the business case for conducting the ROI and serves as a template for getting management commitment and support to the project. This step also determines which programs are most appropriate for conducting ROI evaluations. Dell used the CLIVE (cost, leverage, impact, visibility, and enrollment) criteria to make decisions on which programs ROI evaluations are most appropriate.

Develop

In this step, the design of the ROI study is identified, including the population, sampling method, sample size, data collection methods, and data templates. These data templates have to be pre-designed so they are easy to collect, analyze, and interpret.

Analyze

Using the data templates from the earlier step, analysis methods are determined in this step. Depending on whether the data received are qualitative or quantitative, the appropriate statistical analysis techniques are identified in this step. It is important to note that evaluation stakeholder needs should drive the decisions on these analysis methods.

Communicate

The communication strategy and tactical plan are the outputs for this stage. The strategy should include the media for delivery of results such as a written report, Web announcements, journal articles, company publications, and face-to-face presentations. Also, the plan should include which stakeholder should receive the different components of the report such as executive summary, full report, brief PowerPoint presentation, or journal article.

Leverage

This is a critical step because it identifies what recommendations and actions have to be done on the basis of the results. This step must be well thought out so that the training program can sustain the improvements that resulted from the program. The type of recommendations that may be developed and implemented during this step includes integrating the training in development plans, providing coaching and reinforcement, conducting a refresher course, and identifying opportunities for improvement.

Business Goals and Metrics

Among the business goals and metrics that link directly with the Dell Sales Negotiation course are

- Exceed product quota attainment.
- Exceed total revenue attainment.
- Increase product volume sales.
- Increase total revenue sales.
- Exceed profit margin quota attainment.
- Increase profit margin volume sales.

DSN Objectives

The performance and learning objectives of the DSN course include:

- Demonstrate ability to "position" products and services advantageously.
- Set high targets and aspirations by setting goals as high as possible within the range of reason.
- Manage information skillfully during negotiations.
- Know the full range and strength of power in negotiation.
- Satisfy customer needs over wants.
- Concede according to plan.
- Make clear, nonpunitive demands of the client.
- Make trades effectively.
- Ask open questions to involve the client, gain information, and uncover needs underlying wants.
- Use test and summarize skills to clarify areas of mutual understanding and areas of disagreement.
- Propose conditionally to generate creative solutions and break deadlocks.
- Handle client negotiation tactics effectively.
- Identify negotiables on the basis of clients' needs underlying wants.
- Extend the range of negotiation by identifying and using low-cost, high-value negotiables.
- Plan effectively for negotiations, completing an evaluation of the situation, and anticipate the major components of negotiation.

Methodology

This project used a design that analyzed the pre- and posttraining metrics of control and training groups. To collect data for the two groups, a request was made to the corporate sales information database department to provide a report on pre- and posttraining metrics such as product volume sales, total revenue sales, quota attainment for each product line and revenues, profit margin, and quota attainment.

Pretraining data were on the basis of second quarter of fiscal year 1992 figures, whereas posttraining figures reflected those for the third quarter of fiscal year 1997. The author then compared and analyzed these figures. If the training group experienced higher improvement levels than the control group, then the cause of such improvement would be DSN.

Training and Control Groups

Dell employees who attended the training in June and July (June 4–5, June 6–7, July 1–2, July 8–9, and July 10–11 training dates) make up the treatment group for this study. The author selected this sample because it will have ample opportunities to apply the skills learned from the training by the end of the third quarter, and the database develops reports quarterly. Likewise, these training dates occurred near the end of the second quarter and in the beginning of the third quarter, which makes the second quarter baseline metric information appropriate.

A total of 90 sales employees attended DSN during the June and July training dates. Approximately 15 percent of them were no shows and dropouts (that is, they did not complete the training). In addition, there were other attendees such as trainers and nonsales employees who were not in the database. As a result, this study is based on 57 participants who have their sales quotas and performance-based compensation systems tracked by the sales information database.

The control group for this evaluation study was composed of an equivalent number of randomly selected sales employees (57) with database records who have not yet attended DSN. An effort was made to ensure that this control group and the sample training group have equivalent positions, job levels, and experience. The probability of having nonequivalent groups for this study will be attributed to statistical sampling error.

Distribution of Training and Control Groups

The following tables describe the breakdown of the training and control groups according to business segment and position. It is worth noting that the control group for the study was determined only after the training group breakdown was finalized to ensure equivalence between the two groups. The detailed results will also be analyzed according to these variables.

Tables 1 and 2 show a balanced representation of four business segments and four sales job families within Dell for both groups. Because of this equivalence, intervening variables such as changes in compensation plans, territories, major discounting actions, transfers, promotions, motivation, and other job-related and personal factors will have an equal impact on the training and control groups.

Results

The results of this Level 4 evaluation study are divided into sections described below. The data are presented in tables, and the interpretation and analysis of results follow each section. The sections are
- overall comparison of pre- and posttraining metrics
- overall comparison of training and control groups
- breakdown of results by segment
- cost-benefit analysis.

Table 1. Training and control group by business segment.

Business Segment	Training Group Number	Control Group Number
Segment 1	12 (21%)	11 (19%)
Segment 2	7 (12%)	8 (14%)
Segment 3	11 (19%)	13 (23%)
Segment 4	27 (47%)	25 (44%)
Total	57 (100%)	57 (100%)

Table 2. Training and control group by position.

Position	Training Group Number	Control Group Number
Regional sales manager	2 (4%)	2 (4%)
Sales manager (I-IV) and account manager	11 (19%)	12 (21%)
Account executive and account representative (I-II)	11 (19%)	12 (21%)
Sales representative (I-IV)	33 (58%)	31 (54%)
Total	57 (100%)	57 (100%)

Overall Comparison of Pre- and Posttraining Metrics

Table 3 describes the comparison of pre- and posttraining metrics for the training group of 57 sales employees and managers.

Analysis of Results Pre- and Posttraining

As shown in table 3, there were improvements in all metrics selected for this study. There were across-the-board increases in quota attainment as well as volume and revenue sales. The average overall improvement for all metrics combined was 17.63 percent, with profit margin and total revenue sales having the greatest improvement with 61.56 percent and 41.86 percent, respectively.

Overall Comparison of Training and Control Groups

Table 4 compares the percentage improvement on each metric for the training and control groups for this evaluation study. The author then calculated the difference between the two, with a positive change reflecting higher improvement for the training group.

Analysis of Results Comparing Training Group and Control Group

A comparison of the control group's improvement with that of the training group, shown in table 4, reveals better results for the train-

Table 3. Overall comparison of pre- and posttraining metrics.

Business Metric	Pretraining (Q2) Results	Posttraining (Q3) Results	Improvement (Post and Pre)
Profit margin quota attainment	121.78%	130.23%	6.94%
Laptop quota attainment	112.32%	119.27%	6.19%
Server quota attainment	95.63%	97.68%	2.14%
Total revenue attainment	114.39%	125.87%	10.04%
Profit margin	$2,436,046	$3,935,692	61.56%
Laptop volume sales	678	731	7.82%
Server volume sales	95	102	7.37%
Total revenue sales	$11,445,377	$16,236,933	41.86%
Overall improvement			17.63%

Table 4. Overall comparison for training and control groups.

Metric	Training Group Improvement	Control Group Improvement	Difference (Training-Control)
Profit margin attainment	6.94%	6.34%	+ 0.60%
Laptop quota attainment	6.19%	5.55%	+ 0.64%
Server quota attainment	2.14%	2.10%	+ 0.04%
Total revenue attainment	10.04%	9.05%	+ 0.99%
Profit margin	61.56%	45.65%	+15.91%
Laptop volume sales	7.82%	7.60%	+ 0.22%
Server volume sales	7.37%	7.24%	+ 0.13%
Total revenue sales	41.86%	28.26%	+ 13.60%
Overall improvement	17.63%	13.59%	+ 4.04%

ing group in all selected metrics. In particular, the greatest discrepancies are in profit margin and total revenue sales with +15.91 percent and +13.60 percent, respectively.

There were almost no differences in the two groups in server quota attainment, server volume sales, and laptop volume sales, which means the training did not have a significant impact on participants' performance in these metrics.

The training group had statistically significant higher improvements than the control group in the areas of profit margin, total revenue sales, and overall percent improvement.

It cannot be concluded that Dell Sales Negotiation training was solely responsible for the significant differences in the metrics. These differences can be due to the fact that, in general, the third quarter (Q3) attainment and volume sales are higher than second quarter (Q2) figures. It would have been a truer comparison if Q3 figures for fiscal year 1996 were compared with those of Q3 for fiscal year 1995. It will be impossible to collect data for this same-quarter comparison, however, because of rapid changes in turnover, head count, position level, and territorial assignments of sales personnel.

Breakdown of Results by Segment

Table 5 describes the breakdown of evaluation results by segment for each metric listed. The overall percent improvement is also provided for comparison purposes.

Analysis of Results—Segment Metrics

There were wide discrepancies in segment percent improvement in metrics such as profit margin and total revenue sales. In these metrics, the segment 2 garnered the highest improvements, followed by segment 1 and segment 4.

The results do not directly conclude that the segment 2 participants to DSN benefited most from the training, whereas the segment 3 group benefited the least. A possible factor that explains these discrepancies can be the fact that for segment 2, Q3 is a better buying period whereas Q2 is better for segment 3.

Laptop and server quota attainment and volume sales for Q3 and Q2 increased slightly across all segments.

Cost-Benefit Analysis and Return-on-Investment

A cost-benefit analysis was conducted to determine the approximate return-on-investment of the Dell Sales Negotiation training to business segments. The following assumptions have been made to calculate estimated costs and benefits in terms of business metrics:

1. The costs to Dell described in table 6 reflect the sum of the training fee of $699 per person, which includes the overhead costs incurred by Dell University. In addition, an estimated evaluation cost of $12,000 was assumed for this study.

2. Opportunity loss is not included in total training costs. This is based on the premise that the system picks up the slack, and participants themselves make up for the time they spent in training.

3. Lost salary and commission are not included in the cost computations because salaries and commission rates remain the same for both training and control groups.

4. It is also assumed that the benefits are based on estimates that are generic to all segments involved. The reality is that there are distinct differences on segment quota systems, compensation and incentive systems, and product-mix. It is further assumed that a trend factor of 30 percent increase in Dell revenues for Q3 over Q2 will be built into computations.

Table 6 shows the detailed calculations for the project's cost-benefit analysis. Profit margin was chosen as the metric that best represents business benefit of the program.

Table 5. Breakdown of metric results by segment.

Metric	Segment Improvement (%)				Overall
	Segment 1	Segment 2	Segment 3	Segment 4	
Profit margin quota attainment	8.26%	1.14%	3.20%	20.03%	6.94%
Laptop quota attainment	NA	8.58%	6.32%	3.67%	6.19%
Server quota attainment	NA	2.02%	0.25%	4.15%	2.14%
Total revenue attainment	NA	26.92%	−1.10%	23.49%	10.04%
Profit margin	51.36%	83.76%	47.31%	27.49%	61.56%
Laptop volume sales	NA	10.23%	7.62%	5.61%	7.82%
Server volume sales	NA	8.55%	4.35%	9.21%	7.37%
Total revenue sales	18.20%	82.49%	29.74%	4.26%	41.86%
Overall improvement	**20.64%***	**29.84%**	**9.38%**	**18.73%**	**17.63%**

*Segment 1 overall improvement % was based on only four metrics.

Table 6. Cost-benefit analysis.

Cost	Benefit	Return-on-Investment (%)
Total cost to Dell = training costs + evaluation costs	Benefit: profit margin	ROI for Dell = benefits/cost
Training cost = $699 per person × 57 participants for training group = $39,849	Benefit = overall % improvement (training group − control group) × change in profit margin = 0.1591 × 2,436,046 × 0.70 (Less 30% Dell increase trend factor Q3 over Q2)	ROI = $271,302/$51,849
Evaluation costs = $12,000		ROI = 523.25%
Total cost = $51,849	Total benefit (increased margin) = $271,302 (for 57 participants)	Net benefit = benefit−cost = $219,453

Analysis—Cost-Benefit

Table 6 shows an ROI of 523.25 percent for the Dell Sales Negotiation course. Total Dell benefits from the training group of 57 participants totaled $271,302, whereas total costs summed up to $ 51,849. The net benefit for Dell for 57 participants is + $219,453.

If extrapolated to include all 313 employees who have attended DSN in 1996, there was a total net benefit of $763,297 for Dell. If this benefit is projected annually, Dell will generate a net benefit of about $1.5 million per year as a result of the DSN course.

In the computations that preceded the calculation of this value, factors such as training costs and Dell University overhead costs have been considered. Thus, when interpreting ROI in this study, other factors that could have had an impact on this improvement can play a part in this ROI computation. Other statistical analyses can be done to isolate the effect of each factor on profit margin.

All things considered, DSN is a training program that is well worth the investment put forth in it. It has immediate impact on participants' performance on the job and a long-term effect on sales productivity for Dell.

Conclusions

The following key conclusions were generated from an analysis of this evaluation study:
- There was an overall improvement of 17.63 percent in all metrics for the training group. The greatest improvements were in profit-

margin volume sales and total revenue sales with 61.56 percent and 41.86 percent, respectively.

- There was overall improvement in all performance metrics for the training group.
- Average quarterly compensation per participant increased by 14.11 percent for Q3 over Q2 fiscal year 1997.
- The training group performed better than the control group in all metric areas, which means DSN has had a positive impact on performance and goal attainment.
- The cost-benefit analysis conducted to calculate the return-on-investment yielded an ROI of 523.25 percent.
- The net benefit of Dell from the training group is $219,453. If extrapolated to include the 313 participants who have attended DSN training so far, the total net benefit to Dell is $763,297.
- Laptop and server quota attainment and volume sales had the lowest increases as shown by Q3 over Q2 figures.
- Dell Sales Negotiation is well worth the investment that segments have to pay for sending their participants to the training.

Recommendations

The following recommendations were developed in light of the conclusions obtained from this evaluation project:

- These significant results have to be communicated to segment executive and management staffs so that they can recommend DSN training to those who have not yet attended.
- Coaching and reinforcement efforts have to be stepped up so that these improvements can be sustained.
- Due to the tremendous results of this study, DSN should be included in development plans of all sales employees in the company.
- It is suggested that a follow-up study be done to identify specific DSN skills that are being applied on the job. This study also will determine the negotiation tools and processes that participants used to improve their job effectiveness. Participants will also be asked to share their success stories so others can learn from them.
- A comparison of same quarter metrics (Q3 fiscal year 1997 versus Q3 fiscal year 1996) will be more valid than comparing Q3 with Q2. However, there are some inherent factors such as turnover and changes in position, territory, and business structures that can present some problems in gathering needed information.
- Further statistical analyses can be conducted to accurately determine the impact of each training variable on overall improvement and ROI results.

Questions for Discussion

1. What is the importance of having an ROI evaluation project plan up front?

2. What other business metrics would have been appropriate for this sales negotiation ROI project?

3. Cite the advantages and disadvantages of including opportunity costs to total training costs.

4. What other statistical comparisons can be made from the results of this study?

5. Why is there a need for reinforcement and follow-up to the training program?

6. What changes can you make to customize the process used in this study for your particular company?

The Author

Ferdinand Tesoro is the measurement and performance improvement consultant at Dell University, the training organization of Dell Computer Corporation. He developed the ROI measurement process at Dell, which was used to evaluate the effectiveness of sales, software, new hire orientation, and other educational solutions at Dell. He is currently managing the design, development, and implementation of the global performance measurement system. His book on Global Performance Measurement Systems, co-written with Jack Tootson, will be co-published by Jossey-Bass Pfeiffer and ASTD Publications in late summer 1999.

Tesoro is incoming president-elect of the ROI International Network and is a member of the American Society for Training & Development, American Society for Quality Control, and the International Society for Performance Improvement. Prior to joining Dell University, he consulted with clients such as Shell Products Training, Amoco, and Texaco, where he evaluated technical, sales, and management training programs. Tesoro has a doctorate in instructional design and quality assurance from Purdue University. He can be contacted at Dell Computer Corporation, One Dell Way, Round Rock, Texas 78682.

Lessons Learned
With Application Evaluation

Exxon

John H. Reed

This case is a practical demonstration of a Level 3 evaluation conducted on training in use of personal computers at a major Exxon site in Louisiana. The evaluation used a survey to gather input from course participants. The case discusses how and why the survey was constructed, the classroom-to-job learning transfer model used, the results of the survey, lessons learned, and the implications for training organizations. It concludes that there are many more factors involved in a successful training intervention than just what occurs in the classroom.

Background

The first personal computer (PC) was placed into use at the Exxon Chemical plant in Baton Rouge, Louisiana, in the early 1980s. From that point on, the number of PCs at the plant grew geometrically. Within a year, it was obvious that PCs were there to stay. They were rapidly being recognized as valuable business tools that would permeate the plant culture and change the way every employee contributed to the business. An astute plant manager spearheaded a drive to develop a computer-literate employee base. His objective was simple. Every employee would be encouraged to take computer training. During those early days of the PC, that meant classes on hardware fundamentals and spreadsheets.

Over a period of several months, a computer-training room was designed and equipped, training materials were purchased and de-

This case was prepared to serve as a basis for discussion rather than to illustrate either effective or ineffective administrative and management practices.

veloped, a volunteer instructor cadre was selected and trained, training schedules were developed, and an administrative and record-keeping system was initiated. Over 1,200 employees were trained in the first year. This was quite an accomplishment when one considers that there were only six PC training stations. All levels of employees received training including plant operators and mechanics, technical and staff support, professionals, supervisors, and managers.

We in the training staff were feeling quite proud of our training efforts until a casual conversation with one of the professional engineers burst our bubble. In a hall conversation several months after he had attended the courses, he was asked how he had applied the training. He responded that he hadn't. When asked why, he replied, "No one ever gave me a computer."

That brought home the most basic lesson in the training business. No matter how good the training, it is of absolutely no consequence if it does not translate into changes in the workplace. There are many ways that a disconnect between the training and the workplace can occur. Lack of equipment is just one. Many other factors can influence training transfer. A few of these include training the wrong participants, organizational culture and support, availability of proper equipment and facilities, technical and staff support, time available for training, physical ability, and motivation. If these links are weak or even detrimental to the transfer, then successes in the classroom may turn into duds in the workplace.

In 1995, our training organization had the opportunity to combine the PC training and administration for our three major Baton Rouge sites: a research facility, a refinery, and a chemical plant. Training, until then, was performed independently at the refinery and chemical plant locations by instructors from a national vendor under separate contractual arrangements. Courses were managed separately by a representative of each location's computer systems department. Course registration and maintenance of the physical facilities were centralized in the training organization. Because of the physical locations of the training rooms and the many people responsible for executing the training, it was difficult to deal efficiently with the sites and the vendor. With the help of the research facility and the two computer systems departments, a uniform contract was executed, a new training room was built to replace the two separate ones, and the training organization assumed responsibility for all aspects of PC training.

One of the steps toward developing a uniform contract was to put the vendor training out for bids. Factors such as service offerings, cost, and reliability were evaluated. Final candidates were asked to teach a one-day computer class that included the course managers and members of the training organization as evaluators. The original vendor was selected, and a new contract was executed that established clear responsibilities and channels of communication. The use of instructor-led training was by conscious choice. Our experience placed weight on the dialogue that occurs among training participants and with the instructor. This choice also afforded us the flexibility to modify the course content to meet our particular organizational needs.

These actions established the physical and administrative structures to perform quality training in the classroom. They could not tell us whether we were successfully connecting the classroom with the workplace. As we learned to ask earlier: "Did the trainees have computers when they went back to work?" Now it was time to develop an assessment to help answer that question. We had to build a model and test it.

Where the Rubber Meets the Road

Kirkpatrick's Level 3, behavior evaluation, is where the rubber meets the road. Did what happened in the training situation translate to reportable behavior in the workplace? If so, how much? It was at this level that we needed to perform the evaluation. We chose three introductory- and one intermediate-level vendor-delivered course offerings for the evaluation. The introductory courses addressed the PC operating environment, a database, and a spreadsheet. The intermediate course was the next level offering for the selected spreadsheet.

To perform a behavior level evaluation, training objectives have to translate to measurable workplace performance. They also must be relevant to the participant's workplace needs and capabilities. There are numerous methods to assess learning transfer, just as there are many personal, job, and organizational factors unrelated to training that can influence it. The assessment methods vary in time, cost, and complexity to administer and interpret. The overall value to the organization of collecting the data will determine the method chosen. It is most important that the evaluation design helps both the business and training organizations examine and understand their influence and roles in producing and supporting meaningful workplace change.

The Classroom Model

We needed to build an evaluation model that linked the classroom with the workplace. It was important to know how relevant the classroom experience was to the participants' jobs and how well it supported their job needs. The classroom side of the model addressed course objectives and selected adult learning principles.

The reasons for using course objectives in the evaluation were twofold. First, the basis of any behavior level evaluation is clear, performance-based learning objectives. Second, because a Level 3 evaluation takes place some time after the training occurs, we felt it was necessary to refresh the participants on the objectives we were measuring. We decided to keep things simple by working with just four objectives, three enabling and one terminal. A terminal objective is the ultimate purpose of the course, such as learning to construct a spreadsheet. Enabling objectives are the intermediate steps used to get to the terminal objective. An example would be learning to perform calculations by adding cells. We used the vendor's stated course objectives for each course and grouped similar objectives together to achieve our limit of four.

Each objective was examined from three perspectives: job relevance, knowledge, and ability. Job relevance was represented by how important the objective was to the participant's job. Knowledge was represented by how well the participant understood the objective. Ability was represented by the participant's confidence to apply the objective. Job relevance, knowledge, and ability were represented by the factors importance, understanding, and confidence, respectively.

The model examined several adult learning principles that could influence the learning process as it related to the job. The first was the opportunity to practice during the class. Practice is used to develop requisite abilities and test understanding. The second was the opportunity for discussion with the instructor and other participants. This is where clarification and personalization take place, and the experiences and needs of the group can be shared. The last was the use of job-related examples in the classroom. Relevant examples link concepts to the participant's workplace, creating the bridge between understanding and application. The factors practice, discussion, and examples represented these adult learning principles.

Figure 1 shows a diagram of the classroom side of the model and how we linked the selected factors together. Several variables represent composites of the ones just discussed. Importance was constructed as the composite of that variable from each of the four separate learning objectives. Interaction was composed of three factors: practice, discussion, and examples. Finally, the factors confidence and understanding were combined into learning. The classroom side of the model then linked the influence of the factors interaction and importance to learning. Learning was then linked to the factor satisfaction, which was defined as how well the course helped the participants to meet their job needs. The relevance of the classroom experience is suspect when the link between learning and satisfaction is weak.

The Workplace Model

The workplace side of the model needed to examine how much job output changed after the participants returned to their jobs from training. The job output factor was created as a composite of reported changes in the factors productivity and quality. This composite was created because it was conceivable that either productivity or quality could change as a result of the training or that combinations of the two might occur. It was also conceivable that job output could decrease due to either inappropriate training or through the influence of other posttraining factors. As such, job output encompassed both positive and negative directions of change. Figure 2 is a diagram of the workplace side of the model.

With job output defined, we were then in a position to test the influence the classroom had on it through the previously defined variable of satisfaction. We also could test selected workplace factors on job output. There were two major groups of workplace factors that we investigated for their impact on posttraining job output: organizational and environmental factors. The factor organizational support was a com-

Figure 1. The classroom.

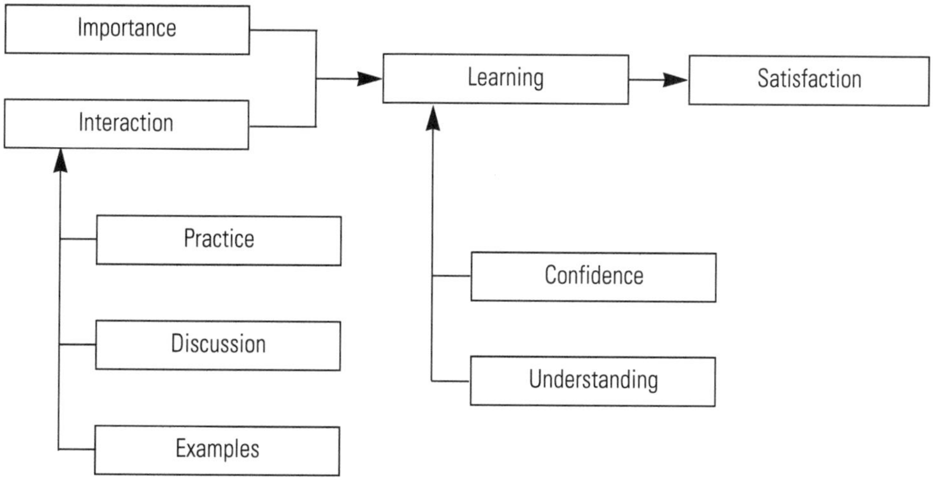

Figure 2. The workplace.

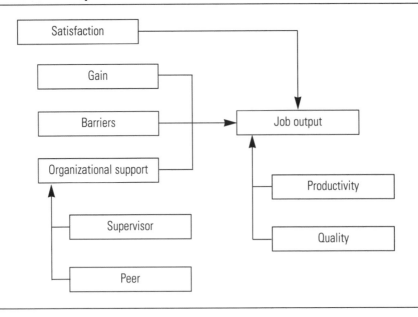

posite of both peer and supervisor support for applying the training. Peers and supervisors can have a significant impact through active moral or technical support or through the establishment of expectations. Subordinate support was not included because it did not appear to play a significant role in this case. Organizational support also can have a negative dimension when a training participant is either actively or passively discouraged from applying the training to the job. Because of this, the model allowed for both the positive and negative dimensions of organizational support. This also maintained consistency with defining positive and negative dimensions for job output.

The environmental factors in the model were defined as potential barriers to applying the training to the job. They included the availability of hardware, software, staff or technical support, and time as well as physical ability to perform the functions and job reassignment after taking the training. In some cases, participants were reassigned to an unrelated job after training and could not report any training transfer. To understand the impact of training on participants' jobs, it was necessary to identify and remove those influences that were not related to training. Barriers were a composite of all of the listed environmental barriers.

One final variable was included in the posttraining section of the model: the percent increase in software usage that occurred after completing the course. For simplicity, we called this variable gain. We wanted to calculate the amount of gain and relate it to job output.

Demographics

We also wanted to investigate the influence of several demographics that may have influenced factors in the model. The first was related to the vendor's instructor cadre. There were several instructors who rotated teaching responsibility for each course. Were they of equal capability, or were one or more significantly different from the others? We chose to investigate for instructor differences in the classroom for all of the factors in the classroom side of the model plus participants' satisfaction with the instructional methods.

The second demographic dealt with the influence of the significantly different cultural climates of the participants' sites. The refinery, chemical plant, and research facility were considerably different in culture from each other. In fact, they were separate companies within the corporation. Would we expect to see differences in software usage—gain—because of these differences? The last demographic that we chose to investigate was whether there were significant differences in gain because of job classification. Course participants belonged to one of five major job classifications. These were wage (process operators and mechanics), technical support (non-degreed), staff support, professionals, and supervisors.

We could work with the vendor if significant differences were found among the instructors for a particular course. If we found differences because of culture or job classification, then we might be able to redesign or modularize the courses to take into account participants' differences. These cultural and job classification demographics addressed the question, "Does the course fit the audience?"

Collecting the Data

Next came the selection of the method for obtaining the data. We chose the survey method for several reasons. It was the least expensive method for collecting and tabulating the data, and it provided us with a quick turnaround. Second, only course participants could provide most of what we were asking. There were no preexisting record systems to tap, and we did not feel that supervisors or peers were in a position to provide comprehensive data. Finally, this method was an easy way to determine if any courses had problems that were significant enough to warrant a more detailed evaluation. One should always establish whether there is a significant problem before spending a lot of time gathering data to solve it.

Most of the data items were scaled from 0 to 5 on a six-point basis, which measured none, low, medium-low, medium, medium-high, and high. For productivity, quality, peer, and supervisor support, participants were asked to indicate whether the scoring was on a positive or a negative basis. For example, if the participant circled *high* and indicated negative for peer support, then it meant that the peer group exerted an extreme influence against having the participant apply the software on the job. The use of scaled items allowed statistical tests and comparisons to be performed on the data.

Participants were given the opportunity to clarify their comments for productivity, quality, peer, and supervisor factors. They also had the opportunity to add to the list of barriers. There were several open-ended questions included at the end of the survey. These dealt with content areas to be added to the course, benefits to themselves or their organizations from taking the course, and what changes they would recommend for the course. The survey also asked participants to indicate the percent of a typical work week that they used the software both before and after taking the course. These data were used to calculate the postcourse increase in software usage that we called gain.

Participants for the survey were randomly selected from attendees of the four courses. An appropriate selection size was calculated to provide a statistical accuracy of ±5 percent for the tests and comparisons that we wanted to conduct. We originally wanted to sample participants who had attended classes within three months after the survey, but extended the period to four months to obtain the required selection size.

University personnel, expert practitioners, and a cross section of course participants reviewed the survey before it was sent to the actual participants. These separate reviews ensured that the survey questions were clear and that there would be no ambiguity in participants' understanding and response.

There was some question about the level of response that we would obtain from the survey. A typical survey response rate can be around 20 percent, but we needed something closer to 50 percent to meet our statistical needs. An individual in our course participant survey group reported an improved survey response rate by sending surveys to supervisors who were then asked to encourage their participants to respond.

We also decided to incorporate a letter explaining what we were doing, why the responses were important, and guaranteeing anonymity. For two of the courses, surveys were sent to participants' supervisors, whereas those for the other two went directly to the participants. With both approaches, supervisors and participants received a letter of explanation. Close to 180 surveys were packaged with return envelopes included, and participants were asked to respond within two weeks. All but a few surveys were returned in this time period, with only an occasional straggler during the third week. The response rates ranged from 39 percent to 64 percent, with an overall response rate of 50 percent. Mailing to the supervisors did not seem to influence the response. We attributed our good response rate to the letter of explanation sent with the surveys.

We compiled the results of the scaled and demographic items into a database for statistical analysis. Responses to open-ended questions were entered into a word-processing document and were summarized into similar categories within each question.

Results

We found no significant differences among instructors teaching the same course. This finding assured us that the instructor cadre was providing a consistent service. We also found no significant differences in postcourse usage of the software due to either site, job classification, or combinations of the two, which indicated that course content addressed the needs of the general population. A statistical technique called an analysis of variance was used to conduct the demographic tests.

No evidence was found that environmental barriers had an impact on job output. The highest average score for any barrier was low, for time available to apply the software on the job. Curiously enough, the usage of the software after taking the course was in the neighborhood of 15 percent to 20 percent, an average increase of 10 percent from precourse levels. This percentage indicated a rather low level of usage in light of the extensive incorporation of computers in the workplace. Further statistical tests to correlate time available as a hindrance to gain showed no relationship. Although we did not pursue an explanation further, this finding raised a question about the actual efficiencies gained by wholesale incorporation of PCs in the general workplace.

There were only rare reports of negative influences on the data, which confirmed that learning the software did not negatively influence postcourse job output. This finding was important because employees were undergoing a conversion to common software at the time of the survey. It also told us that there were no organizational pockets of resistance among peers or supervisors. This was more broadly confirmed by the demographic tests showing no significant site or job classification differences in postcourse gains in usage.

From the open-ended responses for each course, we received recommendations for some changes in content and structure to further improve them. We discussed these comments with the vendor and incorporated the suggestions into the courses. These responses also helped us get a feel for interpreting our scoring system. The scales ranged from none at the low end to high. On the basis of our review and the quality of our vendor, any average score for a classroom variable lower than medium, 3.0, was unacceptable. Scores between 3.0 and 3.5 pointed to the need for substantial rework. Scores between 3.5 and 4.0 indicated some tuning was necessary. Scores at or above 4.0 indicated little or no need to work further with the course. A medium really translates to mediocre or worse and does not represent acceptable performance.

After we collected and summarized the survey data, we needed to decide how to interpret it. Are the results better or worse than one should expect? The same question is asked when comparing the financial reports and ratios of one company with another. A baseline is needed for comparison. One company is usually compared against a benchmark company or a related group of companies. The comparison is made by looking at differences. The same technique was applied to our survey data. We separated the introductory courses from the intermediate one and looked for noticeable differences.

Examining the Differences

Table 1 shows the average scale scores for selected model factors for both groups of courses. From the model in figure 1, interaction and importance influence learning. Learning is linked to job output through satisfaction with how well the course met job needs.

Although importance scores were higher for the intermediate course, there was no difference to speak of in the resulting learning or satisfaction scores. The relatively moderate job output scores tend to substantiate the reported low increase in postcourse usage of the software. Learning and satisfaction scores did not help us to understand job output. We needed another view of the data.

Figure 3 diagrams the relationships of the evaluation model factors for the introductory and intermediate course groupings. As pointed out previously, interaction is the composite survey response for practice, discussion, and examples. Learning is a composite from confidence and understanding responses. Organization support is a com-

Table 1. Average scores by course group for selected factors.

Factor	Score	
	Introductory Courses	Intermediate Course
Interaction	3.6	3.4
Importance	3.5	4.2
Learning	3.6	3.7
Satisfaction	3.6	3.6
Output	2.4	3.0

posite of supervisor and peer responses. Job output is a composite of productivity and quality.

The percents in the two course group diagrams represent the strength of the relationships between various model factors. They represent how closely related two factors are and how much one factor is affected by those that influence it. The higher the percent, the greater the relationship or the influence. The percents are derived from a statistical technique known as a correlation analysis. A correlation of 100 percent means that changes in one or a set of factors fully explain changes in another. They are used to predict how one factor will react to changes in others.

Here's how it worked for the introductory courses in figure 3. The relationships between practice, discussion, and examples ranged from 25 percent to 40 percent. Anything over 30 percent is good. The relationship between understanding and confidence was 65 percent, indicating a very strong link between knowledge and skill. Together, importance and interaction explained 50 percent of the changes in learning. The fact that learning only accounted for about one-third of the change in satisfaction indicated that there were other significant factors influencing satisfaction that were not included in the model.

Look at figure 3 and compare the percents for the same factors in the intermediate course. All of the relationships were much stronger in the intermediate course than in the introductory courses. All but one-quarter of the changes in satisfaction were explained by learning. There was something substantially different in the classroom between the two groups of courses.

Now look at how satisfaction influenced job output between both course groups. Satisfaction with the introductory courses drove on-

Figure 3. Intermediate and introductory courses.

Intermediate Courses

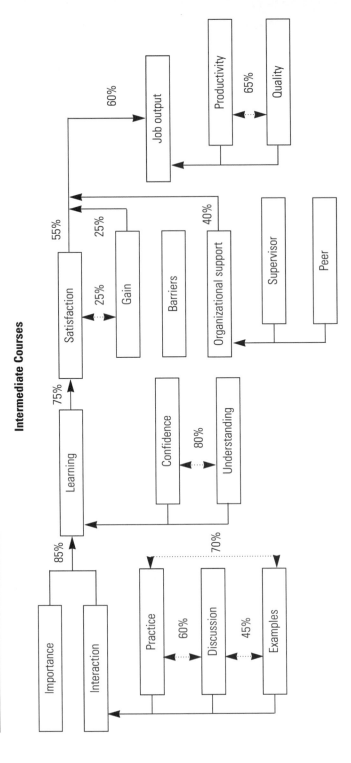

Introductory Courses

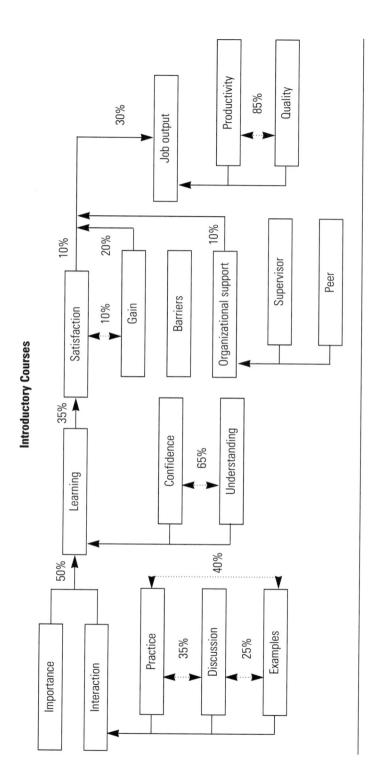

ly 10 percent of the changes in job output, whereas satisfaction drove more then one-half of job output in the intermediate course. Combining gain and organizational support influences with satisfaction in the introductory courses only explained 30 percent of the changes in job output. For the intermediate course, the influence of satisfaction, gain, and organizational support was double that of the introductory courses. The influence of multiple factors on job output is not additive because of some overlap among the factors.

There are two additional points to note in the course diagrams. First, even though the relationship between satisfaction and gain was higher in the intermediate course, the amount of gain and its influence on output was about the same for both course groups. It appears that gain for the introductory courses was driven by something other than satisfaction. Second, there was a high relationship between productivity and quality in both course groups. The survey did not provide a definition for either factor, and the high correlations seem to indicate that the distinction for the participants was not clear.

Lessons Learned

This model was constructed from participant responses after they had an opportunity to return to the workplace and apply the course objectives. It defined learning as an understanding of the course objectives and the confidence to apply them in the workplace. It indicated that learning was influenced by the amount of course interaction and the workplace relevance of course objectives. The model also suggested that the strength of the relationship between learning and satisfaction influenced the link with workplace performance.

Relationships between components of the model were much stronger for intermediate course participants than for those at the introductory level. It may have been that individuals who received training beyond the introductory level had a greater focus on workplace needs. This focus translated directly to higher levels of classroom learning, satisfaction with course content, and organizational support. These factors produced stronger performance results when they were integrated than when they were not.

One could speculate that the introductory course participants were there to familiarize themselves with the software. It may have been that those attending the next course in the sequence had actual applications in mind or under development that improved their focus. If this were true, less time could be spent with introductory courses and more on follow-up courses. This would allow more time to be spent on training those who exhibited a higher level of commitment by returning for further training.

The model also points out that other factors influenced job performance beyond just those examined. Rather than training being the predominant factor influencing job performance, performance results were due to a complex set of interacting training, and personal, organizational, and environmental influences. Relationships were more erratic and performance less predictable when influences were out of alignment.

The Challenge for Training Organizations

These results and observations influence the approach organizations should take when conducting a results-level evaluation for bottom-line impact. This level of evaluation looks to prove that the application of training program content to the job provides a quantifiable value to the organization's bottom-line profitability. Cost avoidance, reduced expenses, increased income, or improvements in the use or need for assets can influence profitability.

Training is not typically an end in itself. More often, it is part of a coordinated set of interventions and feedback loops placed into motion by the business organization to produce a desired outcome in job performance and profitability. Many nontraining factors, planned and unplanned, influence the individual during the training and after returning to the workplace. It would be impractical and sometimes even inadvisable for the training organization to take ownership or stewardship for such components.

Our challenge as training professionals is to distinguish between the influence that training has on performance and influences that come from other sources. The further in time that the training event is from the application, the less direct is the influence it has on performance. Training organizations can provide real value to the business organizations by helping them understand the influence and roles of each partner in implementing a successful workplace intervention.

Questions for Discussion

1. What other factors, training or otherwise, should be included in the model? Why?
2. What are some possible means of measuring these factors?
3. Are there possible explanations for the differences between the introductory and intermediate courses other than the one proposed by the author?

4. What are the implications to the organization of the relatively low percent increase in software usage after participants completed the courses? Is there a PC purchasing and placement strategy suggested by the data?

5. What are some factors that might contribute to a low transfer of training to the job? How would they interfere with the transfer? How could they be reduced or removed?

6. What did the average scale scores of the key model factors hide? How were they useful?

7. Why are demographics important in an evaluation? Name some other than the ones in the model and describe under what circumstances they might be important.

8. How might the terms *productivity* and *quality* have been clarified for the survey respondents?

9. Are there any other methods to improve survey response rates?

10. How much time should elapse between participants taking a course and the behavior level evaluation? Is it always the same amount? What determines any differences?

11. Why is it that the longer the time elapsed between the course and the evaluation, the more difficult it is to relate changes to training?

The Author

John H. Reed is a training advisor for Exxon in Baton Rouge, Louisiana. He holds a doctorate in training and development, a master's degree in business administration, and an M.A. in teaching. He has worked for several major corporations in professional and supervisory capacities during his career. His experience includes positions in systems, financial, and marketing accounting, and training administration, development, and evaluation. He cut his teeth in training and evaluation while serving as a technical trainer, group leader, and departmental analyst in the U.S. Army. Reed can be contacted at the following address: Exxon, ETC-14, PO Box 551, Baton Rouge, LA 70821-0551.

Notes

This case was preceded by another identical set of course surveys. Though not discussed here, one of the outcomes of the survey in the case was to determine whether there were significant changes in classroom factor scores due the course changes made on the basis of recommendations from the first survey. In almost every case, there were statistically significant increases in the scores in the general range of half a point. This result illustrates that a follow-up survey should be made to determine whether changes made were useful.

Another value to the evaluation in this case is that it helped establish benchmarks for other course evaluations. If you don't have any data to begin with, then you have to start somewhere. Each time an additional evaluation is made, lessons are learned and improvements to the process are pointed out.

The evaluation in this case was performed with only two individuals. One was a staff support person who handled all the mailings and compiled the survey data. The other was the author who performed all the statistical tests and analyses. The statistics were kept as minimal as possible and consisted of t tests, ANOVAs, and correlation analyses. These tests were necessary to determine if changes were statistically significant or just due to chance. Simply looking at differences in numbers cannot provide this qualification and can lead to serious errors in developing responses. There was a heavy front end in developing and reviewing the surveys and in writing the statistical programs. The author was able to contribute this expertise to his organization.

It is important to note, though, that the bulk of training organizations do not have this expertise. Nor do they have much depth in personnel. Thus, it is difficult to muster the internal resources for such an evaluation. Training organizations should be encouraged to find this expertise in local external sources such as colleges and universities. Once the initial work and the benchmarking are done, it will require less effort for future evaluations of this sort.

The case makes the point that just looking at scores and compiling open-ended responses to questions can be misleading. Although simple enough for the most unsophisticated staff, key interrelationships can be missed or misinterpreted. Thus, training organizations must always search for the right combination of simplicity and sophistication to match their needs and resources. They should always be looking to stretch themselves just beyond the next corner.

Assessing the Business Results of Management Development Using the Critical Outcome Technique

CIGNA Corporation

Brent W. Mattson, Lawrence J. Quartana,
and Richard A. Swanson

The purpose of this case study is to introduce the critical outcome technique (COT) and describe its utility in evaluating a management development program at CIGNA Corporation. This application of the COT proved it to be a practical and useful evaluative technique, although some aspects require more development to increase its overall effectiveness.

Background

This case introduces the critical outcome technique and describes its utility in evaluating a management development program at CIGNA Corporation. In recent years at CIGNA, we have found that as training expenditures grow, demands from senior management to know the value derived from training efforts increase as well. As practitioners, we have found that this emphasis on business results is a mixed blessing. In one way, it is an opportunity for us to demonstrate our efforts' impact on the bottom line. In another, it is frustrating because we know that assessment of the business value of training initiatives is most effectively accomplished when there is a systematic front-end analysis of the organization's performance requirements (Swanson, 1994). In reality, training programs are developed for a variety of reasons: sponsorship by a senior manager or someone in a position of high influence, unfavorable employee survey results, anecdotal data accumulated by training and development professionals or other human resources (HR) staff, management concern over per-

This case was prepared to serve as a basis for discussion rather than to illustrate either effective or ineffective administrative and management practices.

ceived performance failures (for example, "Those managers aren't coaching their employees! Teach them how!"), and the like. Moreover, a front-end analysis of organizational performance needs and expertise requirements takes time and money, the most coveted resources in any organization. Add to this mix the pressure on managers to respond to the ever-changing, fast-paced, innovate-or-die business environment, and front-end analysis ends up being seen as an expensive and plodding endeavor that will only tell people what they already know intuitively: We need a training program.

Given the need to demonstrate the value of training regardless of the organizational factors, the evaluation team decided to explore alternate methods for determining the business results of training interventions that did not have the benefit of a front-end performance analysis. This case describes CIGNA's use of the critical outcome technique (Swanson & Mattson, 1997; Mattson, 1996) on a pilot basis for its corporate-sponsored introductory management program, Essentials of Management.

Organizational Profile

CIGNA Corporation is a multiline insurance carrier and financial services company with $19 billion in annual revenues and $99 billion in assets. Headquartered in Philadelphia, it is one of the oldest insurance companies in America, having been officially organized in 1792 by merchants meeting in Independence Hall. Training functions within the company reside at the corporate level as well as in each of eight separate lines of business.

Human Resource Development Program Description and Delivery

Management throughout the various lines of business at CIGNA have recognized the importance of supporting newly appointed managers in the early part of their management careers. A critical part of this support has consisted of a training program designed to build the knowledge and skills necessary for success as a manager in the company.

Essentials of Management (EOM) is a three-day introduction to basic management concepts and skills that is targeted to managers with six to 18 months of experience. The corporate training function sponsors and delivers the program.

The program was developed in response to a widely felt need among the HR community to support the target population, most of whom had little or no formal training in management. EOM was first offered in January 1996 and has been run on a continual basis ever since, both in the home office in Philadelphia and at multiple field locations. The program is mandatory for managers in the target population across all lines of business as well as staff functions.

The format of the program consists of short lecture, small group discussions, skill practice, reflective writing, and question and answer segments. Following are the components of EOM:

- *The role of the manager:* This module presents the various responsibilities managers carry out in their job—coach employees, communicate relevant information, delegate effectively, accommodate employees' various personal styles, motivate employees, and manage conflict.
- *Communication skills:* This module presents fundamental communication skills of listening, paraphrasing, and asking exploratory questions in the context of the business environment. This segment includes skill practice.
- *Conflict management:* In this module, participants examine several typical responses to conflict, they identify the one that is typical of them, and they consider several protocols for dealing with conflict as it occurs within the business context of the company.
- *Feedback:* In this module, participants learn and practice a four-step model for giving information to others so that their message will be heard, understood, and acted upon.
- *Myers-Briggs Type Instrument:* In this module, the facilitator reviews the participants' MBTI results. Implications for managing the interaction of various personality types are discussed. Results are reviewed in the program and implications for management are discussed.
- *Delegation:* In this module, benefits of delegation are discussed along with personal and organizational barriers to carrying out delegation. Protocols for effective delegation are presented, and participants complete delegation guides.
- *Coaching:* In this module, participants learn coaching skills and address live issues in practicing them. The program facilitator and other participants provide feedback.
- *Motivation:* In this module, research results about what motivates employees are presented. Guided by the research findings, participants develop motivational actions they can take back to the job.

Key Evaluation Issues and Events

Evaluation of EOM in 1996 consisted of postprogram reaction evaluations and surveys of participants and their managers 10 weeks after the program. Postprogram reaction evaluations indicated that over 90 percent of the participants believed that the program "mostly met" or "fully met" its stated objectives. Participants also reported high levels of satisfaction with the program. Satisfaction levels remained high in the results of the participant surveys administered 10 weeks after the program.

Postprogram survey results indicated that over 90 percent of the participants believed that the program was a significant factor in causing them to implement the skills and knowledge addressed in the program when they returned to the job. In addition, over 90 percent of the participants' managers reported that they believed that their employees' participation in EOM was a significant factor in on-the-job implementation of knowledge and skills.

Anecdotal data from both participants and their managers were offered that supported the findings of high satisfaction and the belief that the program significantly influenced on-the-job implementation of the knowledge and skills addressed in the program.

Although the data collected were somewhat useful, analysis revealed only broad descriptions of on-the-job performance and business outcomes. During the evaluation team's examination of these questions, other critical questions surfaced, including the following:

- Is there a method to more precisely describe validated on-the-job performance?
- Is there a method that will describe validated business outcomes of the program?
- Is there an evaluation method that will allow for consideration of the effects of intervening variables, such as participant motivation, participation readiness, environmental support, additional human resource development (HRD) initiatives, and so forth.

Consideration of these sorts of questions led to the development of the critical outcome technique and to its adoption by the evaluation team to assess the effectiveness of the 1997 EOM program offerings.

Models and Techniques

The critical outcome technique (COT) is a practical evaluation system that can be applied to any performance improvement or HRD intervention (Swanson & Mattson, 1997; Mattson, 1996). Although most scholars and practitioners agree that evaluation should be an integral part of the program analysis, design, development, and delivery, in practice this is often not the case (Kirkpatrick, 1994; Swanson, 1996). The COT was developed as a means of assessing program effectiveness in a systematic, post hoc manner. As stated above, until now the primary means of predictably demonstrating the results of HRD programs has been through a systematic linkage of front-end performance analysis and systematic evaluation. Because the COT is capable of assessing results in the absence of such an analysis, it represents an important development in post hoc program evaluation.

Unlike methods of evaluation that propose categories or taxonomies of potential results of HRD programs (for example, the four levels: reaction, learning, behavior, results), the COT is a process model for assessing the outcomes of such programs. That is, it focuses less on the myriad ways to examine what might have happened as a result of a program and more on results. This is not to say that the categories of potential outcomes are invalid. On the contrary, they provide a useful way to think about results; however, they lack a practical, valid way of demonstrating whether or not those results were delivered as intended.

Critical outcomes can be thought of as either business results at the organizational, process, or individual levels or as financial results or benefits in terms of money or monetary ratios, or as both business and financial results. Business results that are monetized become financial results. For example, the business result of increasing market share by 5 percent could be converted into numbers of sales times the financial value of each sale. Another example of business results would be to increase the hourly production rate of injection molded items from 30 to 35. In each of these examples the business results can be monetized and then expressed in terms of financial results.

Financial results determine the economic value of the HRD program or intervention. In accordance with Swanson and Gradous (1988), the value of the program is equal to the performance value (financial results) minus the cost of the program. This figure can be used to produce a return-on-investment ratio (for example, Swanson & Mattson, 1997; Swanson, 1996).

It is important to note that the purpose of the COT is to provide information for decision makers. Evaluation, we believe, is an art, and, as such, every evaluation should represent an idiosyncratic effort to meet the needs of program stakeholders. Thus, although scientific or experimentally designed evaluation may meet the research standards of an investigator's peers, program evaluations need to meet the interests of the stakeholders to yield maximally useful information for decision makers.

As stated above, the COT is a process model containing five steps, or phases, as figure 1 shows.

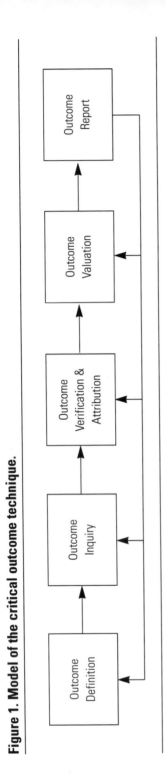

Figure 1. Model of the critical outcome technique.

In brief, to use the COT to evaluate an HRD program or intervention, an evaluator proceeds through the steps as follows:

1. The evaluator determines (post hoc) the original intended outcomes of the program.

2. The evaluator collects data from program participants regarding their attainment of the intended outcomes.

3. The evaluator validates this information through a source other than the participant (for example, the participants' supervisors).

4. The evaluator determines a performance value for each of the outcomes.

5. The evaluator produces a summary report of the evaluation findings to deliver to key stakeholders.

The steps and their use are elaborated on further in the case example below.

Implementation of the COT at CIGNA

Implementation of the COT for Essentials of Management followed the five steps of the process in order:

1. *Outcome definition:* This part of the process specifies the intended critical outcomes of the program. Put simply, the key question in this phase of the process is, "What were the intended or potential critical outcomes of the program?" It is important to note that not all programs or interventions may have been designed with business or financial outcomes as their direct objectives. In the case of EOM, the objectives of the program were to develop skills in the areas of:

• coaching employees for improved performance
• providing developmental, constructive feedback
• delegation
• motivating staff
• communicating expectations and managing results
• managing conflict
• handling difficult employee situations
• accommodating differences in individual styles.

The scope of EOM is broad in order to accommodate the diversity of needs of the targeted participants, that is, new managers with six to 18 months of experience. Thus, there was no expectation that participants would leave the program with a highly developed set of skills in each of the content areas. Rather, the overarching goals of the program were to define for the participants just what it is that managers in the company are expected to do as well as to provide baseline management skills in core management practices. Thus, the evaluation team would consider any application back on the job of a skill or set of skills acquired during the course of the program an achievement of a program objective. To define the critical outcomes for EOM, the assistant director for training and development reviewed the course objectives for the program, searching for the most specific information regarding desirable or potential outcomes. Because the application of skills learned in the program could potentially lead to a panoply of business or financial outcomes, a decision was made to make a broad inquiry of participants regarding the actual outcomes of their applied program knowledge and skills.

2. *Outcome inquiry:* The main question in this phase is, "What were the actual (as opposed to the intended) outcomes of the program?" The source of data for this phase is the program participants. Because the participants in EOM came from all areas of the company and from a variety of locations around the country, the most expedient method for collecting data was through an e-mail survey, a sample of which appears in figure 2. The use of e-mail for data collection made the process simple and relatively easy. One person was able to send surveys to 100 participants in less than two hours. Participants returned the surveys via e-mail within 72 hours. The response rate was 40 percent.

Although the ultimate intent of the COT is to ascertain a "good enough" estimate of the value of improved performance, in this case, the evaluation team decided to solicit information regarding the application of skills learned in the program. This was done to prompt respondents to think first about the application of skills and then about any effects in terms of outcomes due to such application.

3. *Outcome verification and attribution:* There are two main questions in this phase of the COT process: "Did the outcomes really occur as reported by the participant?" and "Would the outcomes have occurred without the program?" To answer the first question, we consulted the program's stakeholders. In this case, the stakeholders were the participants' managers. These managers are responsible for holding the participants accountable for how well they manage and supervise; as such they have direct motivation for observing the participants back on the job to assess the extent to which they put new skills into practice.

To collect data from participants' managers, the evaluation team developed an e-mail survey similar to the one used for the participants, and they sent it to the managers of 100 participants. A response turnaround of 72 hours was again requested; the response rate was 30 percent. A sample of this survey appears in figure 3.

To answer the second question, evaluators conducted in-person interviews with managers of groups of employees who attended the

Figure 2. Outcome inquiry: participant survey instrument.

Training Follow-up Survey
Corporate Training & Development

Essentials of Management

Corporate Training & Development is interested in knowing how well you have been able to take what you learned in this course and put it into practice back on the job. Would you please take a minute to complete this brief survey? We would appreciate your response by: _____.
Thank you for your time.

Dates of program attended: _____

1. Please check the skills or learning you have put into practice back on the job since attending this program:

   _____ Feedback   _____ Delegation   _____ Meyers-Briggs

   _____ Coaching   _____ Motivation   _____ Conflict Management

   _____ Other_____

   Please provide a specific description of how you applied this skill or learning on the job:

   _____

   _____

2. Please check the statement that best describes the outcome you have achieved by putting into practice the skills and learning you described above.

   _____ Increased productivity—please describe this result and the dollars gained by the increase.

   _____ Process improvement—greater efficiency, faster turnaround, better customer service. Please describe the improvement and specify dollars saved.

   _____ Decreased turnover—You retained an employee you were expecting to terminate or demote. Please specify dollars saved by not hiring a new employee.

   _____ Other—please describe and specify dollars saved.

   _____

   _____

program as well as HR representatives of selected business units where the participants work. The goal of the interviews was to determine what organizational dynamics may have influenced the participants' perception of the impact of EOM (for example, attendance at similar programs around the time they attended EOM, halo effect, en-

Figure 3. Outcome verification: survey instrument for manager of participant.

Training Follow-up Survey
Corporate Training & Development

Essentials of Management

Your employee(s) named below recently participated in Corporate Training & Development's Essentials of Management program. We are interested in knowing how well your employee(s) have been able to take what they learned in this course and put it into practice back on the job. Would you please take a minute to complete this brief survey? We would appreciate your response by: _____
Thank you for your time.

Name of employee(s): _____   Date(s) of program attended: _____

1. Please check the skills or learning you have put into practice back on the job since attending this program:

    _____ Feedback   _____ Delegation   _____ Meyers-Briggs

    _____ Coaching   _____ Motivation   _____ Conflict Management

    _____ Other_____

    Please provide a specific description of how you applied this skill or learning on the job:

    _____

    _____

2. Please check the statement that best describes the outcome you have achieved by putting into practice the skills and learning you described above.

    _____ Increased productivity—please describe this result and the dollars gained by the increase.

    _____ Process improvement—greater efficiency, faster turnaround, better customer service. Please describe the improvement and specify dollars saved.

    _____ Decreased turnover—You retained an employee you were expecting to terminate or demote. Please specify dollars saved by not hiring a new employee.

    _____ Other—please describe and specify dollars saved.

    _____

    _____

vironmental factors that reinforce or inhibit use of the skills addressed in the program). Results of the interviews indicated that there was no single factor that had a unilaterally significant effect on outcomes produced by the application of EOM skills.

4. *Outcome valuation.* The primary question in this phase is, "How much are these outcomes worth?" In the case of EOM, the critical outcomes are management behaviors whose effect on business outcomes are secondary, tertiary, or beyond. For instance, coaching an employee effectively may improve a specific aspect of that employee's job performance. In turn, the improved job performance may effect a chain of actions that ultimately bear upon business results. Management behaviors are part of a complex network of factors that influence business outcomes. Although there is widespread agreement that skilled managers are critical to business success, it is difficult to attribute a specific management behavior to a specific business outcome. Participants in EOM and their managers were given the option to describe business outcomes of participation in the program in terms of productivity improvement, process improvement, or decreased turnover. The surveys asked the participants to estimate the dollars saved or realized using their best judgment. Participants' managers were asked, both via survey and in-person interviews, to verify the dollar figures reported by the participants.

5. *Outcome report:* Figure 4 shows an outcome report designed for the primary stakeholders of the EOM program: senior HR management, the training team, and HR professionals who need to assess training needs of groups and individuals in their respective business units. The report summarizes the outcomes in abbreviated and narrative forms.

Results of the Implementation of COT at CIGNA

The outcome inquiry phase yielded information that strongly indicated that participants in EOM left the program and made good-faith efforts to implement the skills addressed in the program back on the job. Data addressing the level of on-the-job implementation of feedback and delegation were particularly strong: 89 percent and 62 percent, respectively. Usage percentages in the remaining skills ranged from 54 percent to 46 percent. The data from the program participants indicate that several program objectives were achieved in terms of application of learned skills on the job; however, critical outcome attainment was more difficult—although not impossible—to ascertain. Outcome verification data from participant managers provided a second perspective on the job skill applications. Their data were generally consistent with the implementation levels participants provided. The results suggested that skills that were presented in a highly structured format (feedback, delegation) were more likely to be reported as implemented than those presented more conceptually.

Figure 4. Sample critical outcome evaluation report.

CIGNA Corporation

Program: Essentials of Management
Dates: 1997
Participants: 90 Managers

Program Description:

Essentials of Management is an intensive three-day program introduction to basic management concepts and skills. It is sponsored and delivered by the corporate training function and is targeted to the new manager with six to eighteen months of experience. The program is mandatory for managers in the target population across all lines of business as well as staff functions.

Outcome Summary:

In summary, the 1997 Essentials of Management programs were very effective. See the following page for a further breakdown of these results, and contact Lawrence Quartana if you wish additional information.

OUTCOMES	OUTCOME VALUE
Performance Outcomes	
Application of Feedback Skills	89%
Application of Delegation Skills	62%
Application of Coaching Skills	54%
Application of Conflict Management Skills	46%
Application of Motivation Skills	46%
Business Outcomes	
Cost savings attributed to application of communication skills	$188,000
Cost savings attributed to turnover reduction	$20,000
Improved time utilization	Significant improvement
Improved quality of claims processing	Significant improvement
Improved production, decreased rework, backlog reduction	Significant improvement

Approval: _____ Director of Training _____ Date: _____

Stakeholder Distribution List:
- President
- Sr. V.P. of Sales & Mktg.
- V.P. of National Accounts
- V.P. of HRD

Figure 4. Sample critical outcome evaluation report (continued).

Evaluation Results: 1997 Essentials of Management Program

Program Outcomes

Source of Data: Program participants

Reported Outcomes: Participants reported active implementation of skills learned in the program back on the job. The percentage of participants who reported implementing each skill is:

Feedback—89%; Delegation—62%; Coaching—54%;
Conflict Management—46%; Motivation—46%

98% of participants reported implementing at least two skills on the job.

Verified Program Outcomes

Source of data: Participant's managers

Verified outcomes: Management gave explicit verification of $188,000 in cost savings that resulted from application of communication skills addressed in the program.

Management was rarely in a position to directly observe application of skills learned in the program. Management was able to observe the outcomes of skill implementation.

Outcomes observed include:
* Increased confidence, improved morale, reduced stress, and reduced overt conflict.
* Management was unable to verify or deny cost savings realized by reduced turnover.

Value of Program Outcomes:

MONETIZED BUSINESS RESULTS:
* A cost savings of $188,000, directly verified by management, was realized by a specific implementation of communication skills learned in the program.
* Reduced turnover resulting in approximately $10,000 in savings was reported by participants; management did not report awareness of this cost savings, but it was not denied.
* Participants and managers had difficulty assigning a dollar value to most outcomes, though most expressed confidence that some business value was realized.

NONMONETIZED BUSINESS RESULTS:
Nonmonetized business results that were reported and verified included:

Better time utilization, improved quality (claims processing), decreased backlog (claims processing), improved morale, and reduced rework.

Participants reported that, as expected, assigning dollar values to skill implementation was difficult. In some isolated cases, specific dollar savings were estimated on the basis of elimination of turnover. These dollar figures were based on standard costs associated with hiring and training a new employee. Participants identified additional outcomes, such as better morale and better time utilization, which do not have an assignable financial value, but do secondarily affect business outcomes. Other business outcomes were reported, such as backlog reductions and quality improvement, which have an assignable financial value in principle, but insufficient data were available to accurately specify a dollar figure. A dramatic exception included a significant cost savings ($188,000) that was specifically attributed to implementation of EOM skills. The participant's manager verified the attribution.

Costs

Costs involved in implementing the COT for EOM consisted of two components:
- administrative time: setting up e-mail distribution lists, sending e-mail, printing e-mail responses, sorting responses by program, and tallying data
- professional time: survey design, data analysis, report preparation.

The total hours for professional and administrative time were 14 and 20 hours, respectively. The approximate value of time required to implement the COT was $2,500, which is very low when compared with the cost of designing and developing a three-day program and paying participants to attend for three days.

Data Analysis

The analysis of data in this application of the critical outcome technique was fairly straightforward. Quantitative data were tabulated by category of outcome, as figure 4 shows.

Respondents presented qualitative data, in most cases, to further substantiate achievement of a given outcome (for example, to provide an example of the application of the skill).

In some instances, qualitative date were coded and categorized. For example, several managers observed skill implementation such as conflict management. In this case, the number of managers reporting specific examples was aggregated. Coding of responses was facilitated by the fact that categories of responses were supplied. For responses that were not assigned a category, the analyst created one post hoc. Connotatively similar responses (for example, "increased confidence" and "improved self-assurance") were counted and categorized together according to the analyst's criteria. This approach, albeit not foolproof, is desirable, as we lack procedures to differentially weight separate reports of outcomes (Weber, 1990).

Conclusions

From this pilot application of the critical outcome technique to the Essentials of Management program, we learned the following:

- The COT demonstrated that several program objectives were achieved and verified by the participants' managers.
- The COT demonstrated that business outcomes were achieved that were attributable to participation in EOM. In some cases, plausible estimates of dollar values were possible.
- This application of the COT achieved the goal of providing information that is useful to program stakeholders (rather than precise measurements of "truth").

In short, the EOM program did what it was designed to do—provide participants with baseline development in core management practices. The levels of implementation of the skills addressed in the program speak not only to the effectiveness of the program's design and delivery, but also to the presence of environmental factors that encourage the use of these skills in live circumstances.

With this application of the COT, we also have learned to refine our data-gathering techniques to get information that is more closely aligned with the COT model. In phase one, it was difficult for the evaluators to think of potential program outcomes in terms of financial and business results because of the original objective of the program. The objective of the program was not that the participants would leave with a highly developed skill set, but more that they would develop managerial skills in the areas emphasized in the program. For this reason, the internal company evaluator struggled with making the linkage between learning outcomes and organizational outcomes.

To assist in helping evaluators make the linkages between potential financial and business outcomes, a need has clearly been established for the development of a tool that shows the potential linkages between learning and critical outcomes. To this end, an outcome definition matrix has been developed and is described in a forthcoming article.

For example, in phase three, outcome attribution and verification, getting information from the participants' managers about factors mitigating the application of skills learned in EOM was a difficult process. Not surprisingly, many of these managers were not used to thinking in terms of other potential causes of behavior. To improve our ability to gather information in this phase, better data-gathering tools will be constructed. Additionally, questions regarding mitigating factors could also be asked of program participants. Therefore, an improved outcome inquiry tool would incorporate questions regarding such factors. This tool will also be described in a forthcoming article.

In sum, there are several areas that can be exploited to improve the effectiveness of the COT in ascertaining business and financial outcomes of HRD programs. Subsequent applications will employ refined data-gathering tools to better guide evaluators in using the COT. On a positive note, this application has demonstrated that it is possible to provide stakeholders with valuable information about business outcomes not garnered through rigorous, or even semi-rigorous experimentally oriented designs. The use by others of this method is encouraged and welcomed, along with suggested revisions and refinements.

Questions for Discussion

1. Why is any application of skills on the job not considered achievement of outcome?
2. Why is it important to be able to attribute and verify outcomes?
3. What are some possible factors that may help or hinder a person's ability to apply skills learned in a training program like Essentials of Management?
4. What types of information are important for stakeholders to receive?
5. Why is it difficult to place financial value on some outcomes?
6. What are some benefits of reporting nonfinancial outcomes?

The Authors

Brent W. Mattson is an organization development consultant for Norwest Mortgage, Inc., a division of Norwest Corporation. He is also a doctoral candidate in the human resource development program at the University of Minnesota and former managing editor of the *Human Resource Development Quarterly*. He has consulted with several *Fortune* 500 companies including CIGNA, Sears, Roebuck, Pentair, and West Publishing. Mattson's current research involves the validation techniques for measuring outcomes of human resource development programs. He can be contacted at the following address: 9034 Neill Lake Road, Eden Prairie, MN 55347.

Lawrence J. Quartana is assistant director, corporate training and development, for CIGNA Corporation. He is involved in training design and delivery and organizational development, and serves as the primary internal resource for outcome measurement of human resource development programs. Quartana has provided training and organizational development consultation services to Rohm & Haas, Excel Industries, Rhone-Poulenc, and Yale/New Haven Hospital. He holds an undergraduate degree in engineering from Tulane University and a Ph.D. in organizational development from Temple University.

Richard A. Swanson is professor and director of the Human Resource Development Research Center at the University of Minnesota, and is senior partner of Swanson & Associates, Incorporated. Swanson is an internationally recognized authority on organizational change and performance improvement. During Swanson's 28 years of experience, he has performed consulting work for several of the largest corporations in the world. In 1995, the American Society for Training & Development established the Richard A. Swanson Award for Excellence in Research. He is the founding editor of the *Human Resource Development Quarterly* and is past president of the Academy of Human Resource Development, the leading scholarly organization in the profession.

References

Kirkpatrick, D.L. (1994). *Evaluating Training Programs: The Four Levels.* San Francisco: Berrett-Koehler.

Mattson, B.W. (1996). "Proposal for the Development of a Model to Assess the Critical Outcomes of Human Resource Development Interventions." Unpublished manuscript.

Swanson, R.A. (1994). *Analysis for Improving Performance: Tools for Diagnosing Organizations and Documenting Workplace Expertise.* San Francisco: Berrett-Koehler.

Swanson, R.A. (1996). *Performance-Learning-Satisfaction Evaluation System: The Application of the Three Domain Evaluation Model to Performance Improvement, Human Resource Development, Organization Development, and Personnel Training and Development.* St. Paul: University of Minnesota Human Resource Development Research Center.

Swanson, R.A., and B.W. Mattson. (1997). "Development and Validation of the Critical Outcome Technique." In R. Torraco, editor, *Academy of Human Resource Development 1997 Annual Proceedings* (pp. 64–71), Atlanta.

Swanson, R. A., and D.B. Gradous. (1988). *Forecasting the Financial Benefits of Human Resource Development.* San Francisco: Jossey-Bass.

Weber, R.P. (1990). *Basic Content Analysis.* Newbury Park, CA: Sage.

Using Instrumentation to Manage the Business

Amoco Corporation

Dian K. Castle

Amoco Corporation is an organization committed to measurement. This article is an example of how it uses measurement as a tool to manage its business. The case study presents the Amoco Renewal Survey, an annual survey of Amoco employees by the Corporate Human Resource Council, as a performance scorecard for the corporation, its business groups, and departments.

Background

In 1988, Larry Fuller, CEO of Amoco Corporation, gave birth to Amoco's Renewal Process. It represents the relentless pursuit of continuous improvement in all of its business processes toward increasing performance. Strategic corporate renewal involves a continuous reassessment of the five subsystems of Amoco business performance. These subsystems include strategy, structure, processes, rewards, and people. The renewal star, illustrated in figure 1, represents this broad management model. The model reminds the members of executive management, the Strategic Planning Committee (SPC), to be conscious of every point on the star as they make changes in the organization. They communicate any changes throughout the organization with the intent of creating understanding, ownership, and commitment. They realize that the success of any strategy depends upon the capability of the people who execute it.

Since a major 1994 restructuring effort moved Amoco from three operating companies to sectors, there has been an increased emphasis

This case was prepared to serve as a basis for discussion rather than to illustrate either effective or ineffective administrative and management practices.

Figure 1. Renewal star.

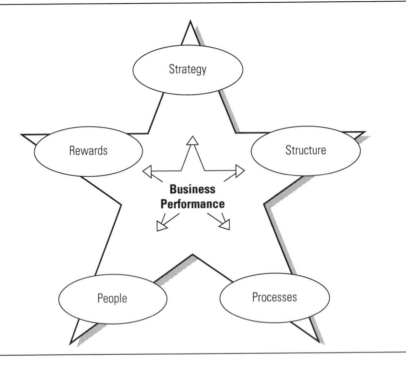

on strategic management. The reorganization eliminated a layer of management and thereby provided more flexibility to the various business sectors, including the newly formed Shared Services organization. Shared Services represents all of the common support functions for the entire corporation. This restructuring promoted an accelerated rate of enterprise transformation aimed toward preeminence in operational excellence by moving psychologically and structurally from a corporation run by command and control to one run by empowerment and autonomy of employees within the prescribed values and goals. Amoco expects a 15 percent return on capital employed (ROCE), 10 percent growth in earnings, and 10 percent growth in capital over the next five years. Renewal continues to measure Amoco's success toward that improved business performance.

The renewal process has several components, including a professional development process and survey effort. Amoco calls the professional development effort the renewal series. It is an annual education program of Amoco's top 3,500 managers worldwide emphasizing development for strategic alignment. The other component is the renewal survey. It is an instrument designed to track 12 business-related categories linked to the Amoco business model. The Amoco business model, illustrated in figure 2, depicts Amoco as a learning organization. The model highlights leadership as the driver of business results. It is imperative, then, that in the cycle of reassessment for continuous improvement the business results of growth, profitability, customer focus, cost leadership, speed, agility, and others are measured and tracked to the leadership. Leadership also examines the systems that produce those results. These systems include information and analysis, human resources (HR) development and management, and operational processes.

Most of the 12 business-related categories of the renewal survey are grouped into three indices that cover the critical dimensions of the Amoco business model. These indices and related categories measure performance in areas critical to building organizational capability and executing strategy. Therefore, these 12 categories basically make up the "people" component of a balanced scorecard; they are critical to business performance. A description of these indices follows:

- *Leadership capability index:* Reflects the ability of Amoco's leadership to build a shared mindset, set goals and direction, promote Amoco values, and encourage effective management practices throughout the corporation. *(Category: leadership capability)*
- *Employee capability index:* Reflects the ability to fully utilize people, to build human competency and commitment, and enable people to perform more effectively. *(Categories: employee commitment, empowerment, career management, and diversity)*
- *Customer focus index:* Reflects the ability of the company to direct energies of the organization and its employees toward establishing systems and processes that lead to continuous improvement and provide value for the customer. *(Categories: teamwork, customer satisfaction, measurement, improving business processes, and sharing best practices)*

Since 1991, each unit has used employee surveys to gather perspectives on business issues. In 1994, Larry Fuller decided the corporation would use the renewal survey. The SPC designates it as the tool to track business results. By the year 2000, the committee expects the corporation to reach what it calls High Performance Company's Norm. This high performance norm is presently based on 22 companies whose financial performance is first or second within their respective industries and whose practices are similar to Amoco's concerning mission, vision, and values. These companies are known for their progressive practices and some of them are candidates or recipients of the Malcolm Baldrige National Quality Award. The SPC charges HR managers with the responsibility to guide their business group leadership teams

Figure 2. Amoco business model.

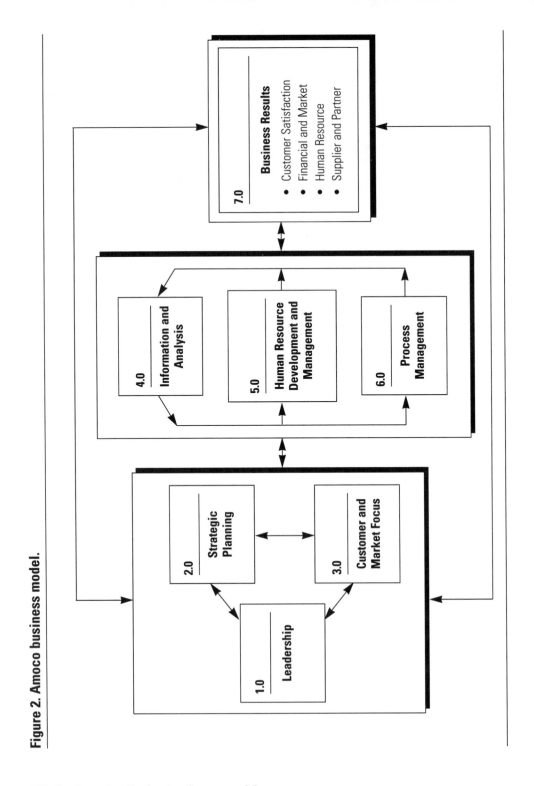

in the use of the renewal survey as a tool to manage their business-es. In addition, the SPC partners with the Organization Capability Group (OCG), one component of the Human Resources Shared Services team, to assist business units, particularly HR managers, in fulfilling this re-sponsibility. This partnership began two years ago.

Issues

During the past two years the OCG has designed a number of interventions including workshops, communications vehicles, and knowl-edge management systems to enable the HR managers to successfully discharge their duties. At the same time, Amoco continues to lag the high performance norm, even when that norm appears to be declining in some categories.

Amoco upholds measurement as a value. Amoco believes it has the measurement systems, resources, authority, and accountability nec-essary to achieve results. Therefore, the organization is committed to measuring what is important as opposed to attributing importance to only that which can be measured. Consequently, this poses a dif-ficult situation for the OCG, the SPC, and Amoco itself, especially as it relates to the renewal survey.

In the spirit of continuous improvement, the OCG reassesses its practices, processes, and projects, including those involving the re-newal survey. During the planning period prior to the analysis of the results of the renewal survey, the OCG team members discussed the outcomes of their performance concerning the renewal survey. One member of that team is an instructional designer. The team believes that its performance is reflected in the results of the survey itself. In other words, because there has been no progress toward achieve-ment of the high performance norm, then some of that accountability rests on their shoulders. Therefore, they are using evaluation design to determine causes for this next year of operation. As they have de-signed interventions to build the capability of HR managers to pre-pare business group leadership teams to use the survey as a tool to manage their businesses, they have devised an evaluation design to measure the impact of the interventions.

The OCG realizes that there are a number of variables that have an impact on the HR managers' discharge of their duty concerning the renewal survey. In fact, there are also variables that have an im-pact on the OCG's role in this process. The OCG has made every ef-fort to rule out contamination in the elements of their evaluation design. This case study presents a discussion of that evaluation design, specif-ically as it relates to the particular intervention of a workshop. In effect, it is an evaluation of the renewal survey as a tool for managing business performance. There are both training and nontraining solutions here, and there are many factors contributing to the final outcome. Therefore, neither training nor evaluation can be credited for all positive change that is expected.

Methodology
Description of Workshop and Participants

Using the Amoco Renewal Survey is the title of an eight-hour workshop designed for HR managers. The outcome of the workshop is to prepare HR managers to guide business group leadership teams in the use of the renewal survey as a tool for managing their businesses. The vice president of human resources writes a letter to HR managers informing them of their responsibility and the use of this workshop as preparation for their responsibility. He also encourages them to invite change management professionals from other parts of the Amoco organization to join them in this effort. These professionals traditionally serve as consultants to HR managers and can assist them in their efforts related to this responsibility.

The HR audience comprises varying levels of experience in the HR discipline, in Amoco, and in the use of the renewal survey. In spite of the vice president's request, not all HR managers attend, nor do all participants interface with their business group leadership teams. Some participants have a grounding in data analysis; others have no idea how to read the data, much less analyze or interpret it.

The workshop identifies 10 primary tasks critical to the participants' completion of the outcome of the workshop (that is, to prepare participants to guide their business group leadership teams to use the renewal survey as a tool to manage their businesses). A list of those tasks follows:

1. Identify "people" drivers and results of their business group performance.
2. Determine which of these people drivers and results are/should/could be measured by the renewal survey and other indicators.
3. Prioritize these people drivers and results.
4. Analyze the impact of these people drivers and results on other business initiatives affecting their business group.
5. Determine specific renewal survey categories, items, and indices that assess key "people" drivers and results for their business group.
6. Interpret renewal survey data relative to those categories, items, and indices in terms of business group performance and trends.
7. Plan follow-up action to improve performance in critical areas.

8. Prioritize follow-up action.

9. Integrate the renewal survey with other business initiatives that have an impact on their business group.

10. Create a forum for sharing learnings relevant to the renewal survey. The instruction consists of small group activities designed for business group teams of the HR managers and their consultants.

The consultants write objectives based on these tasks. A sample objective of the performance-based workshop is "Using ARS data, set targets for improvement in areas critical to the execution of the business group strategy." In addition, the consultants design learning activities that make up 70 percent of the design of the workshop, which give participants experience in working with their business group data in making applications for strategic management purposes. Two OCG consultants facilitate the workshop, and they use multiple learning methods and media.

Kirkpatrick's Model

OCG consultants follow Kirkpatrick's evaluation model. In pursuit of the measurement value, they strive to prove the value of training to a client through documentation that the training has achieved the desired outcome. Amoco's learning business depends upon demonstrating the value of the training investment. The evaluation approach emphasizes a client focus tied to business results. The four levels of Kirkpatrick's model are

- Level 1, reaction
- Level 2, learning
- Level 3, behavioral change
- Level 4, organizational impact.

Participant reaction surveys, sometimes referred to as smile sheets, are questionnaires typically distributed at the close of each workshop session. They contain items that are important to the instructional designers and assess the participants' level of satisfaction with the learning experience. In other words, they measure how well participants like a particular training program (that is, the participants' reaction to the program). Some sample items from the survey accompanying the delivery of this workshop used to assess reaction appear in figure 3.

OCG consultants develop criterion-referenced tests to assess Kirkpatrick's Level 2, learning. Items included on the pencil-paper test correspond to the objectives of the workshop. They examine the theory and concepts of the learning program in accordance with Bloom's taxonomy, as applied in the design of the workshop. They administer the test prior to the beginning of the workshop and again at the close of the workshop. They hypothesize that the training program results in a higher score at the end than at the beginning. If this is not the case, then learning did not take place as a result of the training program. Additionally, they may administer the test to HR managers who do not attend the workshop. This method allows them to compare the performance of a test group who experienced the intervention with a control group that did not participate in the learning program. To demonstrate that the training program added value, the scores of the test group should be significantly higher than those of the control group. The test group is the group that attended the learning experience. The OCG consultants also design performance-based measures. These are incorporated into the learning exercises that the HR teams perform during their attendance at the workshop. Workshop facilitators examine participant performance in accordance with criteria established for success.

Approximately 90 to 120 days after the training program, OCG consultants assess behavioral change, Level 3 of the Kirkpatrick model. Consultants examine the transference of workshop behaviors into workplace performance. OCG consultants will request, either on a random or volunteer basis, action plans from business groups who sent HR managers to the workshop. They will examine these plans to determine the application of the knowledge and skills gained during participation in the workshop. They will also examine those plans in conjunction with the group's business plan, change plan, strategy, goals, and objectives to ensure integration with the renewal survey. Throughout the year, OCG consultants will examine the communications from these business groups to note reports of progress with the renewal survey action plans. Lastly, OCG consultants will monitor the shared learning database for participation by workshop attendees.

The objectives of most learning interventions are stated in terms of the desired results. Level 4 of the Kirkpatrick model assesses the organizational impact of a training program. OCG consultants will wait until next year to conduct this level of evaluation on the workshop. At that time, they will examine the results of the 1998 renewal survey against the action plans from the 1997 renewal survey. The criterion of measure will be increased on-time attainment of business group goals and objectives. Organizational impact sometimes takes years to assess.

At this time there are no plans to assess return-on-investment (that is, to measure whether the cost of the intervention was worth the benefits yielded). Perhaps the OCG will consider this in the future.

Figure 3. Level 1 sample evaluation form.

WORKSHOP EVALUATION REPORT

Instructions: Listed in the matrix below are six skill statements. Please read each statement. In the left column, labeled COMPETENCE, rate the degree to which you feel competent demonstrating the skills you have just learned. In the right column, labeled CONFIDENCE, rate your level of confidence that you will be able to use these skills back on the job.

	COMPETENCE			SKILL STATEMENTS		CONFIDENCE		
Extremely Competent		Not at all Competent			Extremely Competent		Not at all Competent	
5	4	3	2	1	Produce a Driver-Result Map for my business group	5	4	3	2	1
5	4	3	2	1	Work with my leadership team to finalize the map and prioritize key "people" measures for my business group	5	4	3	2	1

Please answer these questions in the space provided.

1. What was the most valuable thing you learned during this workshop?

2. What feedback can you give us on improving the usefulness of the workshop? Please be specific.

3. What actions will you take as a result of your attendance at this workshop?

continued on page 238

Figure 3. Level 1 sample evaluation form (continued).

Instructions: All the items listed below are about the effectiveness and efficiency of the learning experience in which you have just participated. Your responses to the following questions are valuable to the workshop design team. Please use the scale to rate your reaction to the item, write the number corresponding to the rating in the box to the right of the item.

Strongly Agree 1	Agree 2	Neutral 3	Disagree 4	Strongly Disagree 5

No.	Item	Rating
1	The content of the learning experience was appropriate to my level of preparation and ability.	
2	I understand the objectives of the learning experience.	

For any item(s) you rated 2 or 1, please suggest how it may be improved.

Item No.	Suggestion

Evaluation Matrix

To guide their work in developing their evaluation design, the OCG consultants use the evaluation matrix appearing in figure 4. The matrix adheres to the Kirkpatrick model. The first column lists the level of evaluation according to Kirkpatrick's taxonomy. A brief description of that particular level appears in the "purpose" column. For example, because Level 2 is concerned with learning, then it follows that its purpose is, "How much did the learners learn from the training program?"

The third column contains the objectives. Here evaluators decide what criteria are important to assess for that particular level of evaluation; they determine what it is that they want to find out. For example, to assess organizational impact, OCG consultants look for improvement in 1998 renewal survey results in the categories HR managers select as critical to the success of their business unit's strategy. It is only in increases in these categories that business performance is going to improve in Amoco overall and that the corporate goals of 15 percent ROCE, 10 percent growth in earnings, and 15 percent in capital will be attained. Also, improvement is required to reach the high performance norm.

The next three columns address the methods used for data collection. Here the OCG consultants determine the questions that will provide the answers to achieve the objectives. In addition, they determine what instrument or instruments will be used to answer the questions, and from whom the information will be sought. A key adage to remember in this step is to use multiple methods to collect data from multiple sources. This approach increases the validity of the evaluation. Referring to the previously listed objectives, OCG consultants conduct document analysis. They review the work of HR managers and their leadership teams to determine the linkage between identified categories or indices and business unit strategy. They also obtain the current measures for those items. Then, in 1998, they would analyze the same items to determine the change in score. Also, OCG consultants would interview a sample of HR managers and their business group leadership teams. During these interviews, they would ask questions to determine the linkage between business performance and the items of focus. They would also want to determine from the HR managers which components of the workshop assisted them in working with their leadership teams.

Under the "data collection" column, OCG consultants list who does the data collecting, such as the interviewing and research; when it is done; and where it takes place. The consultants use this information

Figure 4. Evaluation matrix.

Levels of Evaluation	Purpose	Objectives	Questions	Methods Instrument	Sample	Who	Data Collection When	Where	Data Analysis
1 Reaction	How well did the learners like the training program?								
2 Learning	How much did the learners learn from the program?								
3 Behavior Change	To what degree was the learning transferred to the job?								
4 Organization Impact	What impact did the training program have on the organization?								

to ensure that all the tasks are completed in an effective and efficient manner. The last column, "data analysis," provides space to list the results of the data collection. Upon the analysis of the data, OCG consultants can determine whether their hypotheses are correct and the workshop intervention was successful. If the data suggest improvements, OCG consultants can incorporate them in the forthcoming year.

Results

Results of the 1997 renewal survey have been distributed throughout the organization and workshops were scheduled to begin in the first quarter of 1998. Action plans should be formulated and communicated throughout business groups by the close of the second quarter of 1998. At this point, it is too early to tell what effect the evaluation design will have on business performance and Amoco's bottom line. However, OCG consultants are confident that they will obtain a rich database from which to draw in their continuous improvement efforts.

Conclusion

The OCG is intent in its focus on value creation (that is, adding value to Amoco by helping to build capabilities through a variety of current and new projects). The OCG recognizes that there is much to do to enhance its ability to create even more value by providing high-quality products and seamless services to its clients. Meeting this challenge is the OCG's primary objective. Therefore, evaluation is, and will continue to be, a core process of its operations, and emphasis will be on its systemic and methodical practice. Barriers and obstacles will loom large as opportunities for an even more successful consulting practice.

Evaluation is a process fully integrated into the design, development, and implementation of a number of learning and organization development interventions. It focuses on the Kirkpatrick model; it is not sporadic or haphazard. Certainly, this attitude fosters measurement as a critical element in the Amoco culture.

Questions for Discussion

1. What is the impact of the issues on the evaluation design?
2. How does the design attempt to ensure that real learning takes place as a result of the training intervention?
3. List the different methods used in this evaluation design. What are the advantages and disadvantages to each method within the context of this evaluation design?

4. Why is this evaluation design important to the OCG? to the SPC? to the business groups? to the participants?

5. In the Level 3 evaluation, how can the design account for a systematic appraisal of on-the-job performance on a before-and-after basis?

6. How is this evaluation linked to strategic business goals?

7. What are the contaminating factors contributing to the Level 4 evaluation of this workshop?

8. Should Level 4 evaluation be pursued in light of its complexity? Why does evaluation become more difficult, complicated, expensive, important, and meaningful as it moves from Level 1 through Level 4?

The Author

Dian K. Castle is an OCG consultant at Amoco Corporation. While serving as lead consultant for Purchasing and Materials Management Services, she designed learning and organization development interventions to provide her clients with solutions targeted toward improving business results. The OCG exists to ensure that Amoco has the capabilities to execute its strategies. It provides a wide range of organization capability assessment and development services to meet the specific demands of each of Amoco's business groups and departments. Castle also serves on the training and development graduate adjunct faculty of Roosevelt University, Chicago and is currently teaching methods of research for training. Castle earned her doctorate in human resource development. She can be contacted at Amoco Corporation, Organization Capability Group, Chicago, IL 60601.

Transfer of Training

Nordisk Kellog

Nils Asmussen

This evaluation design shows how learning evaluation can be extended to measure the transfer of training. Furthermore, it demonstrates that the extent to which trainees forget what they have learned at a course is an indicator that the course is irrelevant to them and represents an imprecise needs analysis.

Background

Nordisk Kellog is a medium-sized company with 400 employees. A large part of its production is exported.

For many years the firm has supported a wide range of internal courses, a number of which have been regularly evaluated using Kirkpatrick's model with four evaluation levels. These evaluations have involved all four levels, so the firm has a tradition of measuring the effects of its courses. However, the firm decided to focus on a particular part of the training process, namely the transfer of training from course to job.

The course selected for measurement was Fault Finding. Particular importance was attached to learning measurements (Kirkpatrick's Level 2), the aim of which was to determine the effect of learning in practice. Electricians, smiths, and other technicians have participated in the course.

The aim of the training, which is made up of several offerings of the course, is to eliminate the demarcation lines between differ-

This case was prepared to serve as a basis for discussion rather than to illustrate either effective or ineffective administrative and management practices.

ent groups of skilled workers. Electricians should be able to do smiths' work, smiths to do electricians' work, and so forth. A technical college developed these courses, where they are also held. The course in question is one of a series of standard publicly financed courses offered to Danish companies. The first course in the series is Fault Finding, which has been chosen as a model. Our evaluation design has been based on this course in order to show how we have measured the effect of learning and transfer of training. The course consists of three subject areas in equal parts: electricity, pneumatics, and hydraulics.

This design is based on the assumption that we can follow the transfer of training from course to job because we presume that participants will remember what they have learned during the course if the subsequent practical training in the firm is relevant to their everyday work. The aim here is to discover the extent to which one of the conditions for the transfer of training, namely, relevance of training, has been met.

Learning

Learning has been followed by three measurements: at the start of the course, A measurement; at the end of the course, B measurement; and after practical training in the firm, C measurement. The three measurements use the same 61 multiple-choice questions, which are designed to discover participants' knowledge of the main areas of the course.

By measuring participants' learning after the course, when they have been back at their jobs for a while, it is possible to show whether what they have learned in the period between course and practice has been of relevance to their jobs, as figure 1 shows. Participants are much more likely to retain what they learned during the course if they are given the opportunity to use this new knowledge in their jobs (transfer of training).

Our hypothesis is that knowledge and skills (learning) are dynamic elements, which, to be maintained, must be used regularly. If acquired knowledge is not used, then it is gradually lost or forgotten. Only by ensuring that participants apply their new knowledge can this loss be reduced. The reduction in loss of learning is, thus, closely related to its degree of job relevance. The greater the relevance to everyday work, the more learning is likely to lead to an actual increase in knowledge and skills after the end of the course.

Figure 1. Evaluation design.

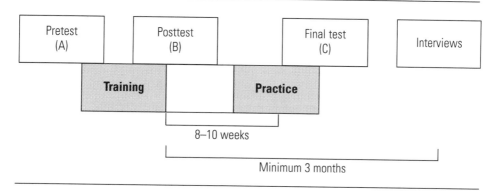

Effect of the Course

Table 1 shows the percentage of questions participants could answer correctly before and after the course. The difference between these two measurements is the learning effect.

Note that the standard deviation falls from before to after (from 24.2 to 16.3). We know from other measurements that, ideally, the standard deviation of a learning measurement after the course should be under 10.0.

The before level should lie between 20 percent and 30 percent. A before level that is too high shows that participants already know a relatively large part of the course material and will therefore get less out of the course; a before level that is too low can mean that participants will have problems in following the course. A high before level and a high standard deviation (here 24.2) indicate that the need for training should have been evaluated more carefully.

Table 2 shows the learning effect for different subject areas.

The high overall before average (63.8 percent) is due to electricians' prior knowledge of the electricity part of the course, but this was expected when the firm selected the three groups to participate in the same course. The reason for mixing the groups was to give them the possibility of learning from one another by strengthening their understanding of and sense of community with one another.

There was an effect for all groups from the pneumatics and hydraulics part of the course, with an increase in knowledge between 40.0 percent and 56.7 percent. The more modest effect from the electricity part was due to the electricians' high before level.

Table 1. Learning average, Fault Finding.

		Pre	Post	Effect
Electricity questions	n=36	47.5%	78.7%	31.2%
Pneumatics questions	n=14	43.0%	86.7%	43.7%
Hydraulics questions	n=11	26.7%	70.1%	43.4%
All	n=61	42.4% std. dev. 24.2	78.7% std. dev. 16.3	36.3%

n=44 (participants)

Regression Analysis

As previously mentioned, participants' knowledge of the course content limits the size of the learning effect. In other words, the learning effect always has an upper limit, which is proportional to participants' prior knowledge of the course content.

In the regression diagram in figure 2, the before percentages and learning effect are plotted in a coordinate system for each of the 61 questions in the test. A regression curve is then calculated and drawn. The regression curve expresses a tendency for correlation between participants' prior knowledge and realized effect during the course. The steeper the tendency curve, the greater the correlation between the before level and the learning effect. Each point in the regression diagram thus represents a question, given by its before level (the x axis) and its effect (the y axis).

The regression curve is therefore a function of the relationship between prior knowledge and realized effect per question, and can thus be used to predict what effect a result on the one axis is likely to produce on the other axis if participants' level of knowledge is the same. Thus, if a new fault finding course were held, and if an average of 50 percent of participants answer correctly in the pretest (x axis), then the course would have a tendency to give an overall effect of about 32 percent.

If the aim of future courses in fault finding is to produce a learning effect of, say, 45 percent, then given the same conditions, this will be possible if an average 26 percent of participants answered correctly at the start of the course (B).

Table 2. Subject average, Fault Finding.

	Electricians n=9			Smiths n=30			Others		
	Pre	Post	Effect	Pre	Post	Effect	Pre	Post	Effect
Electricity questions	82.7%	96.0%	13.3%	38.4%	73.6%	35.2%	38.3%	77.8%	39.4%
Pneumatics questions	41.9%	94.0%	52.1%	44.1%	84.1%	40.0%	38.5%	89.2%	50.8%
Hydraulics questions	30.6%	74.1%	43.5%	26.7%	67.8%	41.1%	20.0%	76.7%	56.7%
All	63.8%	91.3%	27.5%	37.3%	74.7%	37.4%	34.8%	80.0%	45.3%

Figure 2. Regression diagram, Fault Finding.

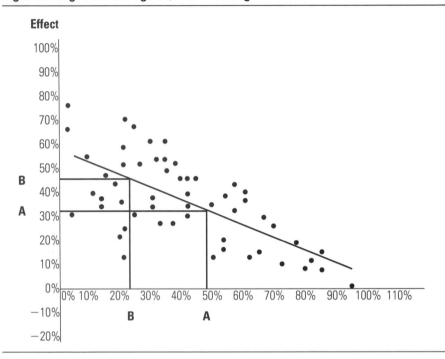

Learning and Practice

Some time after the end of the course, a third learning measurement was carried out to investigate the transfer of knowledge from course to job. This measurement was partly in relation to participants' return to work in the firm and partly in relation to the solving of various practical problems. The practical training was carried out at Nordisk Kellog, most of it about eight weeks after the end of the course. This training covered main areas of the course curriculum and confronted participants with a number of practical, job-relevant problems.

Measuring participants' knowledge and learning after they have applied it on the job makes it possible to identify any changes in learning from course to workplace. What and how much knowledge is used or remembered from the course after the participant has returned to work? Have participants been able to retain their knowledge, and to what extent? Participants are expected to retain their newly acquired knowledge to the extent that they have been able to use it in their jobs.

A loss or limited increase in knowledge after the practice measurement reflects the extent to which the course content is relevant to the participants' job. The learning and practice diagrams contain six different types of results, as table 3 shows.

1. Column "pre A" shows participants' knowledge at the start of the course.
2. Column "post B" shows participants' knowledge at the end of the course.
3. Column "practice C" shows participants' knowledge measured after the practical training in the firm.
4. Column "learning effect B-A" shows the learning effect of the actual course (that is, the difference between columns 1 and 2).
5. Column "job effect C-B" shows any change in participants' level of knowledge from the end of the course to the measurement of practical training (that is, the difference between columns 2 and 3).
6. Column "job index c-b/b-a" shows the percentage changes in participants' knowledge.

Learning and Practice, Fault Finding

The practice measurement for Fault Finding shows that 69.5 percent of participants answered all the questions correctly (table 3, bottom of column C). At the end of the course, an average of 78.7 percent answered correctly (bottom of column B). This gives a job effect, or a change in the average correct answers, of −9.2 percent. In other words, 9.2 percent fewer participants answered the questions correctly after the job and practical training period. Although 9.2 percent might not seem much, it should be remembered that in order to estimate the relative loss of knowledge compared with what is learned, the job effect must be related to the learning effect. Naturally, participants do not forget what they knew before they started the course, so this knowledge is not included as part of what can be lost.

The job index shows how much participants have lost of the knowledge they acquired during the course. The total percentage loss of knowledge for the whole Fault Finding course was thus 25.3 percent (table 3, bottom right). This means that about one-fourth of what participants learned at the course was lost again during the job or practice period. In other words, a transfer loss for the whole course was about 25 percent from course to job. The transfer loss for hydraulics was especially high, almost 41 percent, because the firm hardly ever uses hydraulic equipment. This has therefore made transfer difficult, and the relevance criterion is not met to the same extent for this subject as for the other.

The opposite is also true: The more extensive use of electrical and pneumatic equipment has resulted in a transfer loss here of only about 20 percent, half that of hydraulics.

Table 3. Practice average, Fault Finding.

Column:		1	2	3	4	5	6
		Pre A	Post B	Practice C	Learning Effect B-A	Job Effect C-B	Job Index c-b/b-a
Electricity questions	n=36	47.5%	78.7%	72.1%	31.2%	−6.6%	−21.2%
Pneumatics questions	n=14	43.0%	86.7%	78.0%	43.7%	−8.7%	−19.9%
Hydraulics questions	n=11	26.7%	70.1%	52.5%	43.4%	−17.6%	−40.6%
All	n=61	42.4%	78.7%	69.5%	36.3%	−9.2%	−25.3%

The results of the third learning measurement can be seen in figure 3. The points in the figure show the position of each question in the learning test. The results constitute the difference in participants' scores in the B and C measurements.

Figure 3 shows which parts of the course have higher scores in the third learning test (the points above the horizontal 5 percent curve) and which parts have lower scores (the points below the 0 percent curve). What is most remarkable is that participants' level of knowledge in some parts of the course increased after the course had ended. The increase occurred during the practical training period, which was planned as a period in which participants could practice the skills

Figure 3. Transfer of learning, Fault Finding.

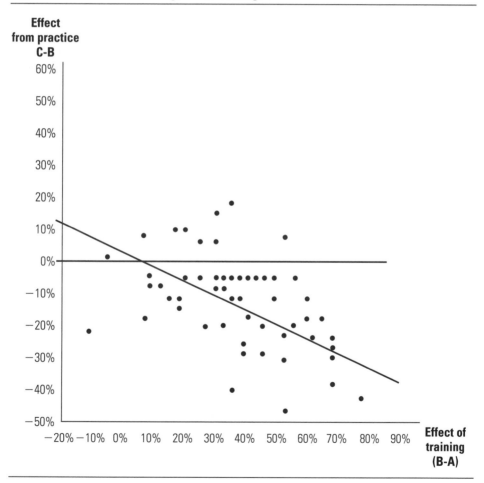

they learned in theory during the course. Learning is enhanced when participants have the opportunity to try out in practice what they have learned during the course. This makes it even more important to ensure that the course content is highly relevant to participants. The higher the relevance, the lower the loss.

The interviews with the participants showed that the loss was greatest in those parts of the course that were not included in subsequent practical training. Where the level of knowledge could be maintained or even increased, there was a merging of course and practice.

By repeating the third learning measurement, therefore, it is possible to ascertain which parts of the course have been useful in participants' everyday work (those areas with no effect or a positive effect in the C measurement) and which parts were irrelevant (those areas that show a loss in the learning level after the C measurement). When the loss exceeds 10 percent, the course content should be reevaluated because a loss of this size is a sign of lack of relevance.

The third learning measurement (C measurement) can be used to determine whether the assessment of training needs before the course has been accurate enough. The greater the fall in level of knowledge from the B to the C measurement, the more inaccurate the assessment has been and the greater the transfer loss that must be expected. A loss of knowledge after a course is thus not always due to a natural forgetfulness, as is so often assumed, but rather to the fact that the course has included subjects that have little or no relevance to participants' jobs.

As mentioned at the beginning, the study design is based on the hypothesis that there will be no loss of knowledge from the second (B) to the third (C) measurement if what is learned during the course has the necessary relevance to the participants' job.

It has been shown that what people learn during a course tends to be forgotten as the course recedes further into the background. The speed with which this newly acquired knowledge is lost can be illustrated by the typical course of a retention curve, as shown in figure 4.

The curve in the figure, however, is from a study in which participants were required to learn meaningless words or random numbers, which naturally were of no relevance to them at all. Nevertheless, that finding has fostered the myth that it is only natural for knowledge to be forgotten after a period of time, although something will always remain. This myth is based on the fact that forgotten knowledge—numbers, words, and the like—have no relevance or particular meaning for the person concerned.

Figure 4. Retention curve.

Reproduction

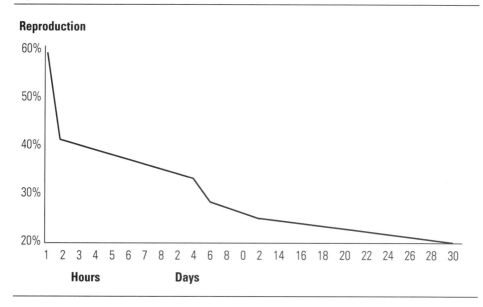

Notwithstanding, learning—and forgetfulness—in connection with the further training of employees, especially further training that aims to provide job-relevant knowledge, is another matter. The message to all those responsible for training should therefore be that forgetfulness is not a natural phenomenon connected with learning. Forgetfulness in connection with courses reflects the fact that the course content has not been sufficiently relevant to participants because knowledge would hardly be forgotten after a course if participants continued to use it in their jobs. If this is the case, they will be able to maintain—or even increase—the level of knowledge they had at the end of the course.

Put simply, if course material is later forgotten, it is because it has not been sufficiently relevant to participants, and is therefore more an expression of the inaccuracy in the way that training needs have been defined.

In conclusion, it should be mentioned that we also carried out analyses of a possible relationship between reaction and learning. We found negative correlation between these levels in several courses, which means that most satisfied participants were those with the lowest learning effect, and the least satisfied participants were those with the highest learning effect. This result shows that reaction measurements alone are an insufficient evaluation basis for the choice between relevant and irrelevant training.

Questions for Discussion

1. What problems arise from using training as a means of breaking down professional boundaries? Discuss and evaluate.

2. How would you go about involving electricians more in the process?

3. What do you think could be done to lessen the loss of transfer of training?

4. What are some possible explanations for the difference in learning effect for the various occupational groups in the course? Discuss and evaluate.

5. Evaluate these differences in relation to the participating occupational groups. What could the reason be?

The Author

Nils Asmussen is manager of CUE Consult A/S, a consultant for the evaluation of training. A former training manager in a Danish bank, Nils Asmussen has been a consultant for more than 20 years, with extensive experience with both Danish and foreign firms. He has specialized in and carried out evaluations of training in a large number of countries and has also written a number of articles and books on evaluation. He can be contacted at CUE Consult A/S, Science Park Arhus, Gustav Wieds Vej 10, DK 8000 Arhus C, Denmark; asmussen @cue.dk.

References

Asmussen, N. (1992). *Transformation af uddannelse. Intern uddannelse og jobadfaerd* (Transfer of Training. Internal Training and Job Behavior). Arhus.

Asmussen, N. (1994). *Effektundersogelse af efteruddannelse for plejepersonalet I Ringkobing Amt* (A Study of the Effect of Further Training for Care Personnel in Ringkobing County). Arhus.

Asmussen, N. (1996). *Uddannelse, udvikling og Evaluering* (Training, Development and Evaluation). Arhus.

Kirkpatrick, D.L. (1994). *The Four Levels.* San Francisco: Berrett-Koehler.

Phillips, J.J., editor. *Measuring Return on Investment.* Alexandria, VA: American Society for Training & Development.

Wexley, K.N., and T.T. Baldwin. (1986). "Posttraining Strategies for Facilitating Positive Transfer: An Empirical Exploration," *Academy of Management Journal, (29)*3.

Nova Means New: One University's Evaluation for Reinvention

Nova State University

Heidi Henson

This case explores the issue of measuring the overall effectiveness of diversity training and programs at an educational institution. Although diversity programs are in effect at many organizations, both public and private, there is little evaluation of whether they produce affective or behavioral outcomes. Practitioners not only need to develop broader methods of evaluation, but also to consider if the ones in place provide the kind of data that best answers what results have been achieved.

The research for this case was conducted using qualitative methods, specifically on-site interviews with 30 respondents (16 faculty, 13 administrators, and one student). The author has also conducted document analysis of the results of various quantitative and qualitative student interviews that the university conducted. Therefore, this case explores both older and newer data as well as internal and external evaluations. It also provides an overview of the numerous efforts the institution has made to evaluate its programs, how it may fall short in this endeavor, and where it might head for the future.

Background

Nova State University is located in a rural state in the northwestern United States. There are over 20,000 students enrolled in undergraduate, graduate, continuing education, and certification programs. Most of these students are from the state, although due to its strong pharmacy and health science programs, it draws applicants from throughout the country. There are also approximately 3,000 international students.

Roughly 75 percent of these students are enrolled in the graduate programs. In-state undergraduate tuition plus room and board is approximately $6,000 for one academic year.

Nova State has more than 7,000 faculty and staff. Most of the faculty are originally from other states and countries, although Nova State has recently considered hiring its own graduates as faculty in order to build its minority population. As the university receives the bulk of its operating funds from the state (42 percent), Nova State must follow the mandates of the State Board of Regents. This governing body determines the university's strategic directions in terms of research, staff and student populations, and administrative governance. Although the amount fluctuates from year to year, Nova State receives approximately $150 million annually in funds and grants for educational programs.

The Players

In the winter of 1996–1997, I interviewed 30 members of the Nova State community, all of whom served or serve on the Diversity Council. This group was formed in 1991 and comprised faculty and staff selected by the president of the university, Robert Jaffari. Two students served on the committee as well, at the request of a participating faculty member. Committee members were chosen to be representatives of their school or office, although in my interviews with committee members, all stated that they were not sure why they personally had been selected. In addition, I talked to three members who were no longer on the committee because Jaffari asked them to step down. They were no surer of the reason for this than were the people who serve on the committee.

As previously stated, I set out to measure the outcomes of diversity efforts at Nova State. This committee is my primary and purposive sample. Yet I soon found one of the main problems in assessing the success of the committee was in the nebulous purpose of the committee itself. In my interviews, I determined a definite conflict over what the mission of the committee was. In the course of 30 interviews, I heard numerous responses to what the committee was focused on. Some of the more pronounced were "We were in simply an advisory role, we weren't supposed to be making policy." This was stated by John Burke, the director of the Faculty and Staff Support Center. According to Elizabeth McDonald, women's studies professor, "President Jaffari met with us early on to clarify just that issue. Our role was to evaluate how the diversity plan was being enacted. We were supposed to be auditors, not advisors." The third central response was best articulated by Dennis Pitkowski, director of student affairs: "I have no idea what the committee was supposed to be about. I don't think Jaffari knew. We were just told to meet, and we tried to figure out the rest from there." All other responses were a variation of these statements. All indicate a common barrier to assessing any training or development method: If the purpose and objectives weren't clear, how can the evaluation be?

Climate Surveys

One of the more prominent and arguably more comprehensive means of evaluation undertaken by Nova State were the 1993 Climate for Diversity surveys of faculty, staff, and students. These surveys were facilitated by the Diversity Council and were used to form the diversity plan for the university as well as the university-wide strategic plan. Effort and expense were invested in the evaluation of the present state of the university prior to the council's exploring what needed to be implemented to bring Nova State to its desired future.

There were three separate questionnaires—for faculty, staff, and student—although all covered similar issues. All questionnaires had 45 questions, structured by responses on a 1-5 Likert scale, agree-disagree statements, or a range from poor to excellent concerning satisfaction level with various elements of academic and community experiences. There were also questions that required respondents to write longer responses, such as "What do you think can be done at Nova State to strengthen and improve the climate for diversity?" and "What other comments do you have about this issue?"

The results of the faculty survey were stated in 47 pages. Overall, most faculty (61 percent) felt that the climate for diversity was not positive. The responses from women faculty members were more negative than those from male professors. Women tended to see the campus as sexist about females, homophobic, and unsupportive. When asked to rate the university's efforts to encourage diversity, over 50 percent of all women reported that the university was not doing enough to foster mentoring relationships between junior and senior faculty. More than 60 percent of women also indicated that recruitment and faculty development funds for women were not sufficient and not equal to those provided to men. Approximately 25 percent of all faculty stated that they had been discriminated against, with over twice as many women (34 percent) than men (15 percent) reporting this. More than 37 percent of the ethnic minority faculty, and over 75 percent of the

African American faculty, indicated they had experienced discrimination, compared to 21 percent of the total nonminority faculty.

The staff questionnaire elicited similar results. In general, women staff members felt they were limited by the glass ceiling at Nova State and that they were not given the opportunities to develop skills and expertise that male staff members were. They also indicated, by a landslide of 89 percent, that there were not as many women in key administrative roles as there should be. As with the faculty, women staff members were more supportive of efforts to enhance diversity on campus overall than their male counterparts (82 percent to 31 percent). In response to a question concerning whether attention to diversity created harmony or divisiveness, far more men than women chose the latter (74 percent men to 26 percent women).

The student questionnaire centered around students' experiences at Nova State and their assessment of their comfort level with faculty and staff. Included were questions about whether staff and faculty were responsive to diverse populations. Most (63 percent) felt that staff and faculty were open to women's issues, but far fewer indicated that they were sensitive to the needs of ethnic and racial minorities (36 percent), people with disabilities (32 percent), and gay, lesbian, and bisexual students (21 percent). On a 1-5 Likert scale, on a question about whether Nova State was nonhomophobic or homophobic, all groups reporting (men, women, ethnic, and racial minorities) indicated that the climate was slightly homophobic. The student questionnaire, like those for the faculty and staff, also asked if the individual had been sexually harassed. Some 66 percent of women students said they had, compared with only 18 percent of male students.

In addition to breaking down each questionnaire separately, the Council decided to compile the results of the entire responding population. The comprehensive results provided several important conclusions. When asked to indicate how satisfied they were with their situation at Nova State, 58 percent were fairly or very satisfied and 27 percent indicated they were not satisfied. Regarding the climate for diversity issues at Nova State, the average of the responses from male respondents was good. Ethnic minority and female faculty responses averaged at fair. This was applicable across the board—from faculty, staff, and student populations. It was also the case in response to every question: Men overall tended not to see the climate as unaccepting of diversity; they did not indicate having been discriminated against; and they tended to see diversity as creating divisiveness. In all, 92 percent of all those reporting said that they believed diversity was good for Nova State and that it should be supported. Only 34 percent felt that Nova State had already achieved a positive climate for diversity.

The write-in responses from the faculty, staff, and students regarding their considerations for improving the climate for diversity issues yielded few responses. Two items listed that were considered likely to hurt the climate more than help it were the hiring of its own minority graduates into faculty and staff positions and the counting of diversity service work toward tenure and promotion. Ironically, numerous respondents in my study stated these two items when I asked them, "What could Nova State do to make diversity work?"

The Happy Sheet

Since 1991, Nova State has undoubtedly stepped up its efforts to promote diversity. Again, whether it is producing positive outcomes from these efforts is unclear. However, in the fall of 1991, the public relations office issued *Diversity: What We've Done,* a sheet that measures approximately 18 inches by 5 inches and lists all the diversity programs and efforts that Nova State has undertaken over the past six years. The programs are listed under the college responsible and list such varied items as the committees to discuss various diversity-related issues on campus and in the community and the amounts of funding that have been provided to departments, offices, and minority groups for diversity-related programs. An item mentioned several ways and times, in different categories, is the new diversity requirement passed in 1996 by the provost's office. It goes into effect in fall 1997 and stipulates that to graduate, each undergraduate student must take six credit hours of course work in diversity issues: three with an international focus, three on domestic issues.

The target audience of this publication is not clear—the regents, parents, the media, or internal audiences. It became obvious to me, however, that it was accomplishing part of its intended public relations message when several administrators referred to it as a source of pride. "If you read it," said Maria Sanchez, assistant to the provost, "you can see that really a lot has been done. There are always people who are going to say that it hasn't. But you can't please [everyone]. That's just not possible." Several "not pleased" people responded negatively to the items listed. In response to my holding up the sheet during the interview, one professor replied, "If you read that [sheet], you'll see that much of that stuff was done a long time ago. And much of it was not Jaffari's doing. It was insisted upon by the regents or provided for with outside funds." Yet another pointed out that it was more a statement of everything that would seem slightly related, not just items that were really having an impact. I was struck by this when I examined it. Many of the items were very small in scope, and the sheet didn't provide a solid means of evaluating whether the listed programs would contribute to the overall effort for diversity at Nova State. There were no data on how many people took advantage of the programs and funding opportunities or if the committees accomplished certain goals. Possibly the lack of such information indicates the difficulty in trying to devise a method for evaluating such results.

Focus Groups

In the fall of 1995, two years after the climate surveys, 20 diversity focus groups were formed, made up of various constituents of the Nova State population. Two education professors serving on the Diversity Council suggested these meetings to bring a broader level of evaluation and a qualitative focus to the issue. The sense from the committee at that time, according to the chair, was that they needed richer data and would get it by allowing people to air concerns in a more complete and relational fashion.

The composition of the separate focus groups was as follows:
- 1 senior level administrator
- 1 lower level administrator
- 1 junior faculty, male
- 1 junior faculty, female
- 1 senior faculty, female
- 1 senior faculty, male
- 1 Native American faculty, staff and students
- 3 Hispanic faculty, staff and students
- 3 African American faculty, staff and students
- 2 gay and lesbian faculty, staff and students
- 2 Asian American faculty, staff and students
- 3 international students.

The Diversity Council hired two sociology doctoral candidates as central facilitators for the groups. The graduate students and the Human Resource office chose respondents by approaching people and asking if they would like to participate. Arguably, those who agreed were those who were concerned with and interested in the topic. The sessions, lasting two to three hours each, were driven by the group's responses to four open-ended questions:
- Did you feel welcome when you came to Nova State?
- Do you feel welcome now?

- What do you like about the climate at Nova State?
- What do you not like?

The facilitators asked clarifying and probing questions for each one.

I was not able to read transcripts of these focus groups as they were not created. One graduate student was responsible for listening to the tapes and developing themes from what the respondents said. This student then passed the themes on to the council, who used it to develop the diversity plan discussed later in this case. I interviewed this student, and he reported the central themes to me. Overall, he said, the respondents were negative about the climate at Nova State. They discussed specific experiences they had had. The general tenor of the focus groups centered around what was wrong with Nova State's approach to diversity. Women in both staff and faculty positions indicated that Nova State was not family-friendly. Women faculty talked about how family responsibilities had affected their ability to gain tenure. Staff stated that it had limited their ability to move into positions of more authority and compensation. Older workers also felt that their advancement had been limited by age discrimination. The senior-level administrators stated that Jaffari "micromanaged"; he did not share control and authority with them, rather asked for their input with no intention of using it. Both of these sentiments were echoed throughout my interviews. The faculty of both genders and levels said that research was valued far more than teaching, and that grant money and notoriety coming into the university was the primary focus in their departments and schools. Thus, there were no incentives for them to incorporate diversity into their teaching or service work because there was too much pressure to conduct research and publish.

Strategic Plan

In 1994, Jaffari released the university's strategic plan for the years 1995–2000. The 30-page document detailed more than 15 items. The goal related to diversity stated five key areas for the university to focus on in the years ahead. It was to do the following:

- increase the diversity of the undergraduate and graduate student body through aggressive recruitment and retention programs
- increase the diversity of university employees through aggressive faculty and staff recruitment and retention programs and through visiting scholar programs
- foster an environment where differences among people are respected and mutual understanding is enhanced

- provide a diverse curriculum that values the contributions of all people, prepares students to meet the challenges of a diverse world, and takes a meaningful step toward the elimination of injustices in our society
- expand programs for faculty and staff development related to diversity.

The plan listed specific strategies from these objectives as well as numerous suggestions for offering programs and incentives for faculty, staff, and students to engage in activities related to diversity. The plan also briefly outlined proposed evaluation measures for such programs. The measures for increasing populations included gauging enrollment, retention, and graduation rates as well as conducting exit interviews. All of these activities have taken place without favorable results. At present, retention rates are down from three years ago (from 74 percent to 65 percent), and attraction and climate continue to be areas of concern. Almost all areas of evaluation center on numbers, not only of populations, but also of lectures, participation in programs, and other quantitative indicators of Nova State's cooperation with minority populations. The only item that contains a suggestion of qualitative measures is the fourth strategy. This would be evaluated by "outcomes assessment measures related to diversity in the curriculum," to quote from the plan. What exactly these measures would be is not clear, and to the extent of my research, they have not yet been implemented.

Diversity Plan

After distribution of the data from the climate surveys and focus groups, the Diversity Council examined the results and began to draft a diversity plan for the entire university. The final draft was 21 pages long and centered around the key point that the university must strive to make itself more diverse by recruiting underrepresented groups for faculty and staff positions as well as in the student body. Once these groups had been recruited, the council urged, there must be a university-wide focus on retaining them because retention of faculty and staff had also declined in recent years. The council also called for extensive development of programs that targeted creating an understanding of diversity issues for university constituents. These included training, monetary recognition for diversity efforts, offering new curriculum, and redesigning appraisal and evaluation policies for faculty and staff. The council also outlined five specific goals for Nova State. These were to:
- clarify university standards and expectations on all levels
- promote a sense of multicultural diversity and its benefits

- establish ways the university can create a positive climate
- identify individual responsibilities in maintaining a supportive climate
- emphasize the benefits to be had from a supportive climate.

The final 10 pages of this plan provide concrete objectives and accountability determinations for all the suggestions they had made. It was specifically stated who should carry out each objective and by what date. It is a very auspicious document. When I reviewed it, I realized that since 1994, many of these items have come to fruition. Some new minority hires have been made, though some have been lost. One training course, *Discussing Diversity,* has been offered, a 12-hour course open to all faculty and staff. It began in fall 1996 and, thus far, 75 people have participated. It is not mandatory.

I have also observed a definite emphasis on incorporating multicultural curricula. Grants have been made available for this purpose, and two people I interviewed said they were working on this issue for their courses. I also discovered that so far only the liberal arts and social sciences programs are making these efforts. Overall, in my interviews I sensed that most of the respondents felt that this plan was not utilized in any systematic way and thus had been a waste of their time. In addition, as this plan is now three years old, everything in it was slated to come to fruition by 1996. Arguably, it has not.

The Problems

Throughout this case study, I have outlined numerous issues about the diversity plan at Nova State. Here I would like to synthesize the past research with the findings of my recent study. In this way, the problems may be examined as a whole to determine solutions.

First, the climate surveys, focus groups, and my interviews all indicate that there is a disparity between different groups' perspectives on the importance of creating a diverse institution and how far Nova State is from that goal. Women and minority group members tend to see the climate as less positive and the issue of diversity as more vital to Nova State's success.

There is also a sense of cynicism about the mission of the committee and the implementation of the diversity plan. The council has not been meeting regularly this year, and many of the people I spoke with indicated that they felt Nova State had done about all it was going to do for diversity. Some even felt the positive efforts were having no impact.

One of the other difficulties that Nova State faces, which arguably most institutions do, is that nonmandatory diversity programs and research are only addressing those people who are interested in these issues anyway. When many people are missing from training or program efforts, there is not only a barrier to broad dispensation of the content, there is also a bias created by those who are present. There becomes a lack of diversity in discussions about diversity.

In several interviews, I was also told about how the majority student population at Nova State was a large cause of their problems with diversity. Many of the respondents cited white students from rural areas as the creators of the uncomfortable climate. According to Len Travnot, an assistant professor of pharmacy, many students at Nova State have never even seen people of color and are not prepared to positively interact with them. "They can do all they want around here for [diversity]," he said. "But it's a white campus, and a white state. You can't change that."

Another issue that has had an impact on the university's landscape of diversity issues is the naming of a building that houses administrative offices in honor of William Blakemore, the fifth president of Nova State. The decision to name the building for him had reportedly been under discussion for a decade, but it was not until the fall of 1996 that it was officially dedicated. Most of the funds for the building came from prominent members of the alumni association. When the decision was first announced to the public, there was a substantial protest about some of the remarks Blakemore made about women and African Americans. First and foremost, he believed that women should not be sharing space with men in the classroom. His remarks may be summed up by the following quote, "[Women] have a role in this society—not to take an education, but to create life. Aside from that, there is nothing on this earth more vital for them." He was even less open to African Americans, whom he considered "of such a poor ability to learn and read that there will never be a place for them in a university of such stature, or any other I suspect." Many of his speeches and writings offered similar views, and many students and faculty lobbied to have the building's name changed to that of someone who was more respectful of women and minorities. Others argued, however, that the university should not judge people apart from their historical context, and that if they did, there would not be buildings named after anyone. This debate raged on the campus for months, to the extent that it received some national attention when it was picked up by the Associated Press and written about in publications like *USA Today,* the *New York Times,* and the *Chronicle of Higher Education.*

To date, no real resolution has been found to this issue. In January 1997, Jaffari finally refused protesters' demands for the name change, though a small movement to press for this remains. This issue is worth noting in that in every interview I conducted when I asked respondents about their impression of the climate for diversity issues at Nova State, Blakemore Hall would inevitably come up. There were many opinions as to whether people felt the name should be changed—some did, some didn't, some weren't sure—but many people said Jaffari did not do all he could to honor the students' and faculty's protests. Overall, everyone felt the situation could have been handled differently in order to promote a better understanding of diversity issues.

My interviews also revealed disparate views about whether Jaffari is truly committed to creating a diverse and accepting institution. As much of the literature on diversity attests, efforts are only able to be successful when the management or administrator is completely and visibly committed to them. There is still skepticism as to whether this is the case for Jaffari. "He needs to put his money where his mouth is. He's so top-down though he could never release control," said Mia Carter, one of the two students who chose to serve on the Diversity Council. "You have to be willing to try to implement what people say. Don't ask if you don't want to do something about it. "

Several people who shared Carter's opinion of Jaffari still felt that when there was a big problem with diversity on campus, something was done about it. "It was reactionary, though. And like throwing money at it," said James Dodd, a minority student counselor. Those who were in power positions—the director of university publications, the dean of the law school, the director of corporate gifts—felt that these efforts were more streamlined and that they were done as part of a larger, cohesive effort by the president to meet these needs. "I really think he's doing what he can. And despite what people say, I think he really cares about these [diversity] issues," said Norma Marsden, the dean of the law school. This sentiment is echoed by Doug Parillo of the university publications office: "I think he's passionate about diversity. There is no doubt that he has put a lot of money into it." If money equals commitment, then this statement would appear to be true. Though I was unable to get a monetary figure on how much has been allocated for the implementation of the diversity plan, there have been two "diversity hire" faculty positions allocated each for the 1996–1997 and the 1997–1998 academic years. The funds for this have come from the provost's office and were given to the ethnic and racial studies departments (African American, American Indian, and Latina and Latino studies programs). Even critics of Jaffari's stance on diversity have been supportive of this.

In our interview, Debra Kimbrel, coordinator of the School of Social Work, was positive about the faculty development grants that Jaffari has made available to different departments for developing courses to integrate multicultural perspectives as well as to meet the new diversity requirements. A colleague in her department recently received $25,000 to further her work with training faculty to use inclusive teaching methods. "That is a step in the right direction," says Kimbrel, "something positive that has actually gone through. But there are many other steps." She was also very critical of Jaffari's approach to diversity overall. She thinks that in his eight years at the institution, it has turned from "a university into a corporation," to use her words. She elaborated: "The emphasis from him is not on 'are students learning and is change being affected?' It's on 'are we making money?'"

Another component that Nova State must address is how the success of these initiatives will be measured. When asked about the efforts to bring in minority faculty, Anika Blake, an associate professor of sociology, said, "They can get faculty here if they try hard enough. That isn't the hard part—they've made money available; they are conducting searches as we speak. The hard part is measuring if it's making a difference. So far, I haven't seen them do that." I then asked her how the administration could measure these effects, and rather than offer a means of evaluation, she countered with a more macro than micro answer. "It's not just about evaluating that one thing. Because diversity is not working is not just that there aren't many people of color here. It goes deeper than that. It's about whether Nova State really wants to change. Is it going to be willing to change [its] whole system, to really try to understand the minority experience here? And then to try to change that? Not that I've seen. They can't even keep people here, and they can't understand why."

Another comment to this effect came from Jake Johnson, the director of admissions. Johnson had been in his current position for four years, and he also attended Nova State for his undergraduate and graduate degrees. "I was an activist about all this stuff back in the 1960s. So we've been talking about this stuff a long time," he said. "What I'm not seeing now though, that concerns me, is any unification of diversity efforts across the campus. We've got offices for this and that, departments are doing their own things for diversity, but no one is trying to bring it all together. It's like 30 years ago, like we have to start from scratch."

Through the course of my research, I came to see evidence of Johnson's point. Nova State does have many offices and programs that pay attention, at least on the surface, to diversity concerns. There is a Minority Student Affairs office, an Affirmative Action office, a Women's Center, an Office of Women in Health Professions, a Center for Women in Government, a Black Entrepreneurial Center, a Black Cultural Center, a Hispanic Student Center, an International Student Center, a Teaching Development Center (which focuses a fair percentage of its efforts on addressing multicultural teaching methods), a Multicultural Education Program, and a Training and Development program that sponsors the *Discussing Diversity* course. There are also academic programs that center around the diverse populations: African American Studies, Women's Studies, American Indian Studies, and Latina-Latino Studies. There is the Diversity Council, and there are also numerous mentoring programs that specifically target racial and ethnic minorities. There are also numerous scholarships specifically for attracting and retaining underrepresented populations. The plethora of programs, without unification, reminded me of a comment someone made when I conducted a similar study at a corporation: "All this attention is maybe a step in the right direction," she said. "But I can't help but think that having everyone all over the place, separating into little camps, creates more divisiveness than unity."

A large part of what keeps Nova State's diversity efforts from being as systematic and effective as they could be is that the issue of diversity at a major land-grant institution, or any large institution, is so broad and hard to contain. There are many issues that fall under the heading "diversity," compounded by how many perspectives there are in a population of over 27,000 people. For an institution that must please not only its faculty, staff, and students but also the alumni, parents, and state government, it becomes even more complex.

The Solutions

Many potential solutions to these problems emerged in my interviews. Most respondents felt that the new diversity requirements for students were going to make a difference. Most also said training would help, and although many said they think it's impossible to require it of faculty because of academic freedom, many said it could be strongly encouraged. Certainly staff and administrators could have this exposure required as part of their job. Several people suggested more rewards be given for diversity efforts, possibly grants or counting service more toward tenure and not requiring as much research. Johnson said simply that the university should make it a priority: "Put as much money into it as they do into athletics. You start putting that money out there, you're going to get results." Parillo and Marsden concurred, stating that offering small grants or other incentives to faculty who try to incorporate diversity into their classes would be successful. Some people said to totally restructure. A few respondents said making diversity work was just a matter of getting more minorities to attend Nova State.

Tony del Toya, one of Nova State's legal advisors, suggested that people switch roles in order to become more understanding of their differences. "A white with a black, a straight with a gay, nonhandicapped with handicapped." He went on to tell of the experiences he has had as a black man on campus. People often assume he isn't a professional. They think he's a student, and in one case, a maintenance worker. "I was in on a Saturday, was wearing jeans and a sweatshirt, and this group of community leaders [who were using the building] came up to me in the hall and asked me to mop up something they had spilt . . . It was awful. Things like that used to happen a lot. Sometimes they still do."

This example seems appropriate to show how we understand each other. If each person's experience is unique and pertinent to this issue, then we have to spend more time understanding the small story. This is not found on a survey; it comes from talking to people, getting them to articulate their experiences. Nova State would seemingly need more forums for people to do this. Maybe groups can be meeting regularly in small groups in their departments and sharing their ideas on the progress being made at the university.

Through the course of the three months I spent at Nova State, I have come to think they missed the mark on the Blakemore Hall issue. Despite the noting of other people being racist in the past and that alumni money had been slated for the hall, Jaffari was presented this opportunity to show constituents that he really cared about how they felt and about integrating their perspective into the university culture. The one action of renaming the building would have sent a clear, positive statement. Although some may argue this would be giving in to pressure, one must also acknowledge that pressure is always exerted in some way.

Several people suggested that the university create a position to oversee and evaluate the entire diversity effort. Although there are numerous offices and departments addressing diversity, there is little evaluation at present.

If this position could not be created, then a committee—possibly the Diversity Council—could be assigned this role. The committee might be more productive if broken into smaller groups, and each school or office could choose its own representative. In this way, the people on the committee would want to be there and would have a vision of their role. Then, the committee might also set up a reporting system so that its work and results would be known throughout the university and people would know whom to turn to when they had questions or information.

Conclusions

Nova State must put as much expense and effort into evaluating the efforts in the present as it did just trying to get a baseline. Although gathering preprogram data was important, it is now time to focus on evaluating the present and planning for the future. Some progress has been made: the six credits of diversity requirements, funds for multicultural studies faculty to come in, grants to faculty, and a one-credit diversity course. However, so far they are only, as expressed in one interviewee's words, "preaching to the choir." The people who take advantage of these programs are those who are interested in diversity anyway. There is a vast majority out there that is not being touched. Public perception is still a big issue, and even those people who care about these issues—the majority of those I spoke to—don't feel enough progress has been made. There have to be more programs and more visible commitment to the issue, university-wide. Many people seemed to indicate that if people in administration start visibly taking diversity seriously, then other people will as well.

Overall, there is a real need to evaluate what people are saying about diversity on campus and what is actually being accomplished. Broader levels of assessment are missing, and as one respondent said, "It [seems] like they are throwing a lot of money at it—like scattering seeds to the wind. But they're not stopping to see if anything is growing."

Questions for Discussion

1. What can Nova State do to synthesize its diversity evaluation programs?
2. How can it reach beyond "the choir" and get more people participating in diversity programs?
3. Should Nova State provide incentives to faculty and staff to meet diversity objectives? How would this work?
4. How does Nova State measure what students are learning through the new diversity requirements?
5. What other types of measurement would you suggest to determine affective and behavioral outcomes?

The Author

Heidi Henson is an educator and consultant in the areas of diversity, business communication, and adult learning. She holds a B.A. from Boston College, an M.A. from Harvard University, and an Ed.D. from Drake University. She teaches graduate courses in managing diversity, facilitation, and adult development, and her training programs address a variety of organizational development issues. Henson can be contacted at 515.244.3544.

Notes

This case is timely for students and educators because it provides an overview of measurement efforts in an often unevaluated arena. It offers both older quantitative and qualitative data as well as data recently obtained through on-site interviewing and document analysis. This case raises the question of how best to tackle a tough evaluation issue—a comprehensive subject that is sensitive, multifaceted, and ultimately subjective. Participants who work with this case will be able to assess the effectiveness of the methods of evaluation outlined here and try to structure future efforts for gauging affective and behavioral outcomes.

A Survey of Supervisors' and Managers' Perceptions of HRD Training Effectiveness

Texas Instruments' Defense Systems and Electronics Group

Monica Luketich

In industrial training, a major evaluation issue is whether training is transferred back to the job. Supervisors and managers evaluate the effectiveness of their employees' training and have many opportunities to encourage or discourage training. A survey instrument questioning supervisors' and managers' perceptions of training effectiveness, transference, and their own methods of positive reinforcement of training was developed and validated. A random sample of supervisors and managers (165 people from the Defense Systems and Electronics Group) was selected for completing this 24-question phone survey. The results indicated that the managers' and supervisors' perceptions were more positive than had been anticipated. The data were to be used to provide a baseline for future human resource development course evaluations.

Background

In 1990, the management of Texas Instruments' Defense Systems and Electronics Group (DSEG) decided to complete an application for the Malcolm Baldrige National Quality Award. One section of the application (4.3.b) dealt with supervisor reinforcement of training. The training group for DSEG, referred to as Human Resources Development (HRD), did not have Level 3 evaluation data for their courses. Management decided that these data needed to be collected and reported for the application. The research coordinator had one month to plan how to collect the data, create instruments, complete the surveys, analyze the data, and write the final report. Specifics from the

This case was prepared to serve as a basis for discussion rather than to illustrate either effective or ineffective administrative and management practices.

research do not appear in this case study in order to protect Texas Instruments' internal data. This case study documents the process of creating the instrument and conducting the research.

DSEG's Business

The Defense Systems and Electronics Group was one of the major business groups within Texas Instruments. Others included Semiconductor, Corporate, and Commercial Products. Texas Instruments (TI) had a hierarchical management system. Just as TI was broken into business units, so was DSEG. Each of these units within DSEG was called an entity, and this survey had nine entities. The main products of DSEG were guided missiles and radar units. A large percentage of the employees were engineers and technicians who needed highly technical training to upgrade their skills. The terms *supervisor* and *manager* are not interchangeable: Supervisors are the immediate level of supervision above individual contributors; managers have responsibility for several supervisors beneath them and are usually responsible for running a department or project.

HRD History

The HRD group had been in existence for about 10 years. At this time, the department had four groups: software training, engineering training, leadership development training, and clerical support. Although the groups were located under one roof, there was little interaction among them. The other DSEG units viewed all of HRD as a separate group, not tied into the technical projects. This separation was accentuated because HRD was on a separate physical campus from the technical projects. Most of HRD's interaction with the projects were through steering committees made up of representatives from the technical disciplines, such as electrical engineering. Those committees were one of HRD's customers.

Evaluation of Courses

Evaluation is a necessary element of curriculum and instructional design. Depending on the instructional design model used and the location of the designer within the model at a given time, various types of evaluation are feasible. HRD used Kirkpatrick's four levels of evaluation (1959), as shown in table 1.

There also seem to be sublevels of evaluation, depending on the degree of scientific sophistication that the evaluator requires or can tolerate. The sublevels range from simple methods that are not very

Table 1. Description of levels of evaluation.

Level of Evaluation	What Is Evaluated?	Evaluation Questions	How Can Data Be Collected?
1	Trainee reaction	How do the learners evaluate the course?	End-of-course rating form
2	Achievement of learning objectives	Did the learners achieve the course objectives?	Tests, simulations, supervised practice
3	Behavior (transfer of skills to job)	Are the skills or knowledge being used on the job?	Productivity measures, supervisor perceptions, trainees' surveys
4	Company results	How has the company's productivity improved?	Profits, customer satisfaction

expensive to implement to expensive and difficult procedures that can be experimentally accurate. Table 2 summarizes the sublevels and shows various activities for evaluation at each level.

To find out what supervisors thought of HRD training, a Level 3 evaluation was needed. Although Level 1 evaluations (smile sheets) were used in all courses, and Level 2 tests were used in some courses, no large-scale Level 3 evaluation had been implemented. One person was given the assignment to plan, implement, analyze, and report on a Level 3 evaluation in one month.

Methodology of Survey

After being told of the assignment, the research coordinator interviewed a supervisor and TI's resident Malcolm Baldrige expert to clarify the goals of the research project and the data needed for the award application. The research would answer the question, "What are the current benefits of employee training as perceived by DSEG supervisors and managers?" The research would fulfill three purposes:
1. Construct an evaluation instrument for Level 3 evaluations.
2. Collect baseline data concerning course evaluation as seen from supervisors' and managers' perceptions.
3. Compare the results of the data for various entities within DSEG.

Members of management agreed on requirements for the instrument. These requirements were:
1. The instrument was geared toward supervisor and management perceptions. Because of possible bias of trainees in self-evaluation, supervisors and managers were thought to be less biased. Also, supervisors are considered to be one of HRD's customers.
2. The instrument had to be easy to answer and to tabulate.
3. It needed to be a short form, taking little of the supervisors' time to respond.
4. Identification of the responses would be by entities only, not individuals' names.
5. The method would allow for meeting the short project deadline of one month.
6. The data from the instrument would show supervisors' and managers' attitudes toward HRD training, as the Malcolm Baldrige application required.
7. The data would show the supervisors' and managers' perception of transference of employee training to the job (Level 3 evaluation).

Knowing these requirements, the research coordinator searched for available instruments. Several instruments have been created for

Table 2. Sublevels of evaluation.

Increasing cost and difficulty →

Increasing degree of scientific sophistication →

Levels	Informal Observation	Posttraining Measurement	Pre- and Posttraining Measurements
1 Student Reaction	• Informal comments by students • Teacher's observation of students' reaction	• Smile Sheets	• Attitude inventories before and after class
2 Learning Objectives	• Observation of student exercises or behavior • Ask questions to test knowledge without recording results	• Checklists • Written tests • Performance tests with specific criteria	• Pre- and postvalidated and reliable tests
3 Behavior (Transfer of Skills)	• Survey of students' or supervisors' perceptions (type of usage on job or if skills are used on job)	• Count number of mistakes • Document amount of rework • Quantify number of times information or skills were used on job	• Compare two groups: test and control • Compare one group before and after training
4 Company Results	• Survey of perceptions • Informal comments from supervisors or students	• Amount of rework prevented • Estimate savings contributed to new skills or knowledge	• Compare bottom line of company before and after specific training

Level 3 evaluation of specific training or courses. Phillips (1983) gives good directions as to how to evaluate training, but the only instrument shown is a self-evaluation questionnaire for new supervisors. Friedman and Yarbrough (1985) give a summary evaluation form that is intended to provide information for the organization sponsoring the training, such as cost-benefit ratio, efficiency, and utility of the training. The questions do not reflect these aims. Another Friedman form gathers co-workers' reactions to training by comparing before and after behaviors for specific training, after the worker has returned to the job. The specific questions were not given, and the responses would be difficult to tabulate. Therefore, a generic Level 3 evaluation instrument did not seem to exist that met the requirements.

The Instrument

The first step was to create a valid instrument that met the requirements. After talking to the TI Baldrige expert, the research coordinator developed an initial set of questions. The following groups discussed and reviewed these questions with the expert:

1. Statisticians were asked for options in answering the questions that would provide usable statistical results. The goal was to make answering the questions as easy as possible to encourage survey returns. Ranges of percentage application were used instead of specific percentages in answers. In other words, people would be asked if something happened never (less than 25 percent of the time), sometimes (25-50 percent), usually (50-75 percent), or all the time (75-100 percent).

2. A committee of departmental trainers and instructional designers verified the instrument's construct validity. (Did it measure what we thought it would measure?) They validated the behaviors indicating supervisors' reinforcement of training and transference of training by employees.

3. Managers within HRD reviewed the questions for applicability and appropriateness.

Management decided that supervisors and managers with fewer than five people would not be given the entire survey, only question 24 (from the following list). The survey was revised and pretested through the HRD department, whose members suggested very few changes. Following is the list of 24 questions that were used for the survey. Additional demographics were collected and considered separately from these 24 questions.

1. Are you told when an employee is attending an HRD course?

2. As a result of training, are your employees better able to verbalize (talk about) their needs or requirements?

3. When you see a course certificate in an office, do you make a positive comment about it?

4. Do you discuss with employees ideas or skills they learned in class that are directly related to their jobs?

5. Do you publicly recognize employees who go to classes, for instance, by mentioning them at department meetings or putting it into weekly reports?

6. Do you consider training part of the promotability of your employees?

7. Do you discuss training needs with your employees two or more times per year?

8. Do you have to explain to employees that what they learned in class is not how the task is done in your area?

9. Do you check training records to see who has taken part?

10. Do you use TEMS or TEPS (internal tracking systems) to research training questions?

11. When giving a new assignment, do you discuss training needs with the employee?

12. Do you review training histories when doing performance reviews?

13. While your employees are in class, do you delegate their workload to their peers?

14. To what extent do you think TI training is a good investment of your employees' time?

15. Do you think TI adequately trains your employees for their jobs?

16. Do you see an improvement in employee productivity after training?

17. Are your employees applying their newly learned skills and knowledge on the job?

18. As the result of training, are your employees communicating more effectively through writing and documentation?

19. Do you refer employees to their peers when they have questions concerning courses you cannot answer?

20. To what extent do you help your employees remain technically current, even when it is not directly related to their job?

(The following questions were open ended.)

21. Do you have direct control over an employee's training?

22. Over the past year, have the numbers of redesigns changed?

23. Over the past year, have the number of electronic change notices (ECNs) designs changed?

24. How do you provide your employees with on-the-job reinforcement of skills learned in training?

Who Got the Survey and How?

The target population was all DSEG supervisors and managers. The company's database for employees had a special code for supervisors and managers, therefore those names from DSEG could be pulled separately. A systematic sample of 500 names was drawn from the list. These names, phone numbers, and entity numbers were then printed.

At the time of the survey, upper management decided that the survey would be conducted by phone instead of by electronic mail, as originally planned. This change was made because the timing of this survey coincided with the annual corporate attitude survey. If the managers and supervisors received both written surveys, they might be less likely to answer this one. A phone survey was seen as taking less response time.

The research coordinator wrote, read, and timed the phone script. Changes in the wording were made to take into account transmission over the phone. Complex or unpronounceable words were changed to words that were easier to understand over the phone. Explanations to the questions and answers to possible questions about the survey were written into the script. HRD management and the vice president of personnel then reviewed and approved the script.

All phone calls and data collection had to be completed within a seven-day period because of the project completion date. Numerous volunteers from HRD were needed. A memo containing an explanation of the purpose of the survey, a copy of the survey, and the coordinator's expectations of the volunteers was distributed to all HRD personnel. This was followed by individual discussions with each person within the department to answer their questions concerning the survey and to increase the number of volunteers. Most people wanted to know how to answer certain questions on the criticality of the survey. Managers, instructors from all three groups, instructional designers, and clerical support were called, and 30 people volunteered to make phone calls to the sample population.

Each volunteer received a packet containing a cover letter, the phone script, and a list of names and computerized answer forms. The cover letter gave information about labor charging (DSEG is a Department of Defense contractor, and all employees must charge their labor time to the correct contract charge number) and referrals for questions they could not answer. The answer forms were marked using a pencil and could be scanned into the computer file. The file could then be manipulated and analyzed quickly. The forms allowed for quick data collection and compilation because the questions and answer ranges were preprinted on the generic forms. The only identification in the forms was the entity number.

During the seven-day calling period, the surveys were turned in to the research coordinator as completed so that a running total could be kept. If callers could not get one name on the list, they tried the next name. A graph was constructed and placed in a prominent location to help motivate and notify employees of the progress toward the number set as the goal of completed surveys. After seven days, 165 surveys were completed; 40 of these were from supervisors and managers with fewer than five direct reporting employees. Although this degraded the sample, management decided that the degradation was not severe. The survey was ended.

Results

The callers recorded the interview answers on the computer forms, and the forms were scanned into the computer file. The answers received were tabulated, and percentages and means for each answer were calculated using a standard statistical program. The statistics were calculated for both the individual entities within DSEG and the total for all answers. Simple analysis of variance was run for each question, comparing the four entities that returned the largest number of surveys. (There were nine entities, but five of them returned fewer than five surveys.) Significant differences between the entities were tested using t tests. The analysis of variance indicated that for only two survey questions did the entities differ significantly. A correlation matrix was created for the entire survey. Comments made during the interviews were written down as given and appeared as a 15-page list in the original report's appendix.

The breakdown of the number of entities represented in the survey was shown as a pie chart. All other data were shown as bar charts. The two answer categories of >75 percent and 50–75 percent were combined for the data into one category labeled "greater than 50 percent of the time." Likewise, the two lower categories of <25 percent and 25–50 percent were combined into one category labeled "less than 50 percent of the time." The graph length showed the percentage of respondents that answered that statement as applying either less than or more than 50 percent of the time. A sample chart is shown in figure 1.

Figure 1. Sample graph.

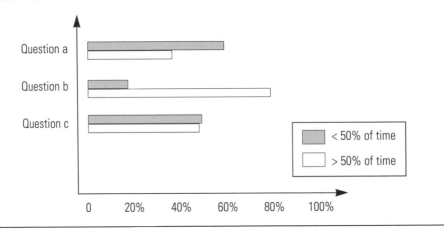

Conclusions

The following conclusions were drawn for the data collected.

1. Supervisors' and managers' perceptions are more positive toward HRD training than originally anticipated.

2. In general, some measurements, such as the number of ECN changes, cannot be tied directly to training because of many other factors. Measurements such as these need to be formally made before and after specific courses in order to show causes and effects of the training.

3. Supervisors and managers are thinking about and discussing training with their employees.

4. Supervisors and managers were more willing to take time and discuss training with the caller than anticipated. Only five people did not want to participate in the survey because they were too busy. Most people asked if they could be called again at a later time, after meetings.

5. Entities perceived aspects of training differently from one another. No conclusions as to cause can be made from the available data; too many factors are involved.

Recommendations

The research coordinator made the following recommendations to HRD concerning this survey:

• The survey instrument should be refined. Some questions did not provide any information about the transfer of skills to the job because of the number of other factors that could influence those numbers.

• The survey, in a revised form, should be repeated periodically to:
  —Provide feedback to HRD concerning training and its perceived value.

—Give HRD the opportunity to talk to the customers. Many people were delighted to get the chance to talk to HRD about problems, frustrations, and ideas they had.
- Give ideas to supervisors and managers as to behavior they should be exhibiting concerning training. As one person said when asked how he reinforces skills learned in class, he replied, "I don't. I will now!"
- The data collected from this survey should be compared with information from other types of evaluation data in order to see patterns and trends concerning training. In this way, instructors can find conflicting data and attempt to resolve the conflicts and differences in perceptions between students and supervisors.

Costs of Research

The number of people and time involved was large. The people included:

- One research coordinator who spent one month in panic.
- One Malcolm Baldrige expert who helped define the application requirements for that section.
- Two statisticians to help decide on tests for the data and to calculate the required number of people to call (sample size).
- One software programmer to set up the scannable answer sheets.
- One data interpreter who could read what the statistical program printed out.
- Two database experts who generated the random sample of supervisors' and managers' names.
- Five instrument reviewers.
- Thirty phone callers—each survey took about 30 minutes to conduct once the caller got the supervisor or manager on the phone. Many times the callers had to set up appointments to call back and conduct the interview.
- HRD managers who gave input and answered questions about procedure as needed.

Labor costs, both for conducting the research and work that was done on overtime because of the interviews, varied depending on the pay scale of the individuals involved.

After the Research

This research was the basis for one paragraph in the Baldrige application for that year. DSEG did win the Malcolm Baldrige National Quality Award in 1992, two years after the survey detailed in this chapter.

An online Level 3 instrument was created and used, starting in 1995.

This particular questionnaire was never repeated. The online system has only five generic questions.

Questions for Discussion

1. How would you have collected information and data in a short period of time?
2. Do you think people in your organization would give complete and honest answers to a survey? Would it help to keep respondents anonymous as TI did?
3. Who was the audience for the results of this survey? Who would be the audience in your organization?
4. Is an ongoing Level 3 evaluation needed, or is a periodic evaluation sufficient?
5. This survey resulted in one paragraph in a report. Do you think the effort involved was justified for that one paragraph?
6. Because this survey did not measure use of learning, only reported on perceptions, some people say that it was not valid or scientific enough. How scientific do data need to be in your organization?
7. What questions would you ask on a Level 3 evaluation survey? Would you use those in the case study or modify them?

The Author

Monica Luketich is an instructional designer for Barrios Technology, where she assists trainers in creating lessons for the astronauts. Prior to Barrios, she was an instructional designer for Texas Instruments, where she provided instructional design support to various training organizations. She conducted needs and job analyses, developed courses and training materials, facilitated joint application designs (JADs), and conducted research into evaluation techniques. She received her Ed.D. from West Virginia University in curriculum and instruction in adult and science education. Luketich has taught classes to students from sixth grade to university level in topics such as sciences, remedial math, computer science, and karate for over 20 years. She can be contacted at 16460 Highway 3, Apartment 1216, Webster, Texas 77598.

References

Brinkerhoff, R.O. (1987). *Achieving Results for Training.* San Francisco: Jossey-Bass.

Craig, R., editor. (1987). *Training and Development Handbook* (3d edition). New York: McGraw-Hill.

Friedman, P., and E. Yarbrough. (1985). *Training Strategies from Start to Finish.* Englewood Cliffs, NJ: Prentice-Hall.

Kirkpatrick, D. (1959, December). "Techniques for Evaluating Training Programs—Part 2: Learning." *Journal of the American Society of Training Directors,* 21–26.

Lusterman, S. (1975). *Education in Industry.* New York: Conference Board.

Nitko, A.J. (1983). *Educational Test and Measurement: An Introduction.* New York: Harcourt Brace Jovanovich.

Phillips, J.J. (1983). *Handbook of Training Evaluation and Measurement Methods.* Houston: Gulf.

Romiszowski, A.J. (1984). *Producing Instructional Systems.* New York: Nichols.

Scriven, M. (1967). "Goals of Evaluation Versus Roles of Evaluation: Formative and Summative Evaluation." In R.M.W. Tyler, R.M. Gagne, and M. Scrivens (editors), *Perspectives of Curriculum Evaluation.* Chicago: Rand McNally.

Zemke, R., and T. Kramlinger. (1982). *Figuring Things Out: A Trainer's Guide to Needs and Task Analysis.* New York: Addison-Wesley.

From Puzzles to Problems: Assessing the Value of Education in a Business Context With Concept Mapping and Pattern Matching

Andersen Consulting

Daniel J. McLinden and William M.K. Trochim

Determining the value of an investment in education is a critical issue in business today. Perhaps equally important is the need to apply sound methodology to assess the value of programs designed to effect a change in people and their organizations. Although a variety of social science research methods are currently in use in efforts to determine the value of education, there is a need to expand the evaluation tool kit. In addition to assessing program results, this case illustrates and recommends a method of rigorously conceptualizing program impact. We have used this methodology—concept mapping and pattern matching—to conceptualize program impact and to then provide a framework for determining the impact of a program on expected results. Results from this case showed that the program studied successfully achieved the performance expected from training, although the outcome diminished slightly over time. In addition to this overall assessment of effectiveness, the method provided detailed diagnostic information about which topics were being conveyed well (linkage) and which were failing to meet the expected outcome (disconnect). This information was especially valuable for development teams that needed to know how best to redesign training programs as part of a continual improvement effort.

Background

What value does business derive from its investment in education? Business executives base decisions about the operation of a business on the answer to that question, and at the same, training executives

This case was prepared to serve as a basis for discussion rather than to illustrate either effective or ineffective administrative and management practices.

attempt to provide the answer. Although the need to assess and communicate the value of education seems clear, a comprehensive response to this need has not been forthcoming. The level of evaluation in the field of training seems small compared with the need. The scope, at least for the investment in training in the United States, is estimated in excess of $50 billion. Obviously the figure is larger if we take an international view. Clearly, the value of this level of investment needs to be substantiated to be maintained, and quite possibly this level even needs to be increased. However, neither action will occur or endure for long without compelling evidence of value, and efforts to demonstrate the value of training need to grow.

When compelling evidence of training value is required, often the quick reaction is to calculate the costs of training and the financial benefits that result from the investment in training. This approach to evaluation applies in educational programs the analytical techniques that are similar to those used to evaluate stocks, bonds, and other financial variables. For example, placing money in various financial instruments clearly leads to some measurable outcome. Through judicious insight, an investor may have a return that is both positive and in excess of other competing alternatives for the same investment dollars. By applying various formulas, the investor can clearly see the outcome of an investment strategy. This evaluation approach is compelling because it holds promise for determining the monetary value of an investment in education. To be sure, when feasible, the capability to apply the same techniques to training provides strong estimates of the relationship between training costs and training value. However, the difficulty that arises is in the level of proof necessary to claim the benefit (or loss) that can be attributed to training. The variables involved in a financial transaction are straightforward, and the action of investing in specific instruments is linked unequivocally to the outcome. However, education involves a series of human transactions that introduce ambiguity. Disentangling the variables that introduce ambiguity to achieve a level of scientific proof is difficult in most cases and arguably not cost-effective in others. As a result, some programs may be able to demonstrate economic gains. Other programs may be unable to demonstrate gains, not because the program is at fault but because the unique features that make the proof of a financial result possible are not present. Such features include control over the implementation of the program, access to financial measures of outcomes, and a clear relationship between the training program and any changes in business activity. Therefore, what of situations where the cost of experimental methods is too high relative to the benefit or where it is simply not possible to implement a financial analysis or where other evidence would suffice? In part, the difficulty of addressing the question may be that the definition of educational value has become synonymous with the analysis of work hours, profits, and so forth. To be sure, these variables are important, but this view may be detrimental if it stymies evaluation based on other models of how the educational process unfolds in and adds value to an organization. Equally compelling methods to demonstrate value are necessary.

What are the alternatives? Adding to the evaluation tool set may first involve a shift in assumptions about the nature of training evaluation.[1] Specifically, evaluating training should be viewed not as a puzzle but as a complex problem. Consider the difference between solving a puzzle and solving a problem. Completing a puzzle requires one to fit all the pieces to complete the picture or in terms of a financial model, to calculate all the financial formulas to determine value. Although solving a puzzle can indeed be complex, the process assumes that all the pieces are given and ultimately a single clear and unambiguous answer exists. In other words, costs can be specified, revenues to training determined, and a clear formulaic relationship exists between the two variables. Contrast puzzle solving with the problem solving typical of work environments. Multiple "right" answers generally exist for business problems, establishing "truth" may involve making trade-offs between competing alternatives, and less-than-ideal "solutions" are sometimes selected due to a lack of resources or a host of other constraints. The domain of education is no less complex.

Rather than completing a puzzle, assessing educational value is an effort in solving problems in which the training professional must, in effect, create some of the pieces of the puzzle, act without knowing how the final picture will look, and be satisfied when the final picture contains some ambiguity. This view of educational value is in contrast to a view of training evaluation as solving a puzzle or, in other words, as applying measurement tools. Viewing the determination of training value as a measurement exercise is problematic because training value is not an objective entity existing somewhere out there and waiting to be measured. Rather, value represents a constructed reality that depends on the views of individuals or stakeholder groups associated with the process. Consequently, the construction of the meaning of value cannot come solely from an analysis of business activities but must include the constructed interpretations of value from multiple stakeholders. Over the course of several projects designed to answer the question, "What is the value of this program?" it became apparent that educational evaluation must encompass methods that can deal with the psychological and sociological complexity of the educational enterprise. Such methods need to be able both to measure value in the development and delivery of a complex service and communicate clearly the results to business people not necessarily interested in the fine points of complex statistics and research design.

Stakeholder Transactions in Educational Evaluation

Much of the effort in determining value seems devoted to addressing the question, "To what extent did the N days spent at the XYZ program lead to increased sales?" This is a focus on the educational event as a cause of a specific economic result. A different premise and one that forms the basis for an alternative approach to evaluation is to focus not on the educational event per se, but on the human transactions involved in the educational cycle. Figure 1 provides a generic view of those transactions, some of which correspond to the educational event whereas others precede and follow. There are two key aspects portrayed in this figure.

First, assessing program effects (see the far right side of the second row in figure 1) represents one link in a chain of events. The chain begins with the individuals who have decided to fund an educational response to some business need. The distance between the strategic business decision and the ultimate effects for the client or customer is populated with other stakeholder groups. It would be overly idealistic to assume that developers develop what they are directed to build, learners learn what they are told are the objectives, and supervisors in the field support the use of skills that executives thought were necessary. Most organizations are loosely coupled, and each stakeholder group will bring a different set of concerns to the educational process and will, in turn, influence that process in different ways.

For example, business executives are typically concerned with developing and implementing strategies to be responsive to the marketplace; they may conclude that training is one way to develop or support a response to market forces. The instructional development team, although not unconcerned with the marketplace, focuses its decision making on techniques for delivering instructional content. It is not that an instructional development team will work at cross-purposes to the strategic intents of an executive team, but its focus will be different. The developers' mental model of the program will

Figure 1. A transactional model of educational value.

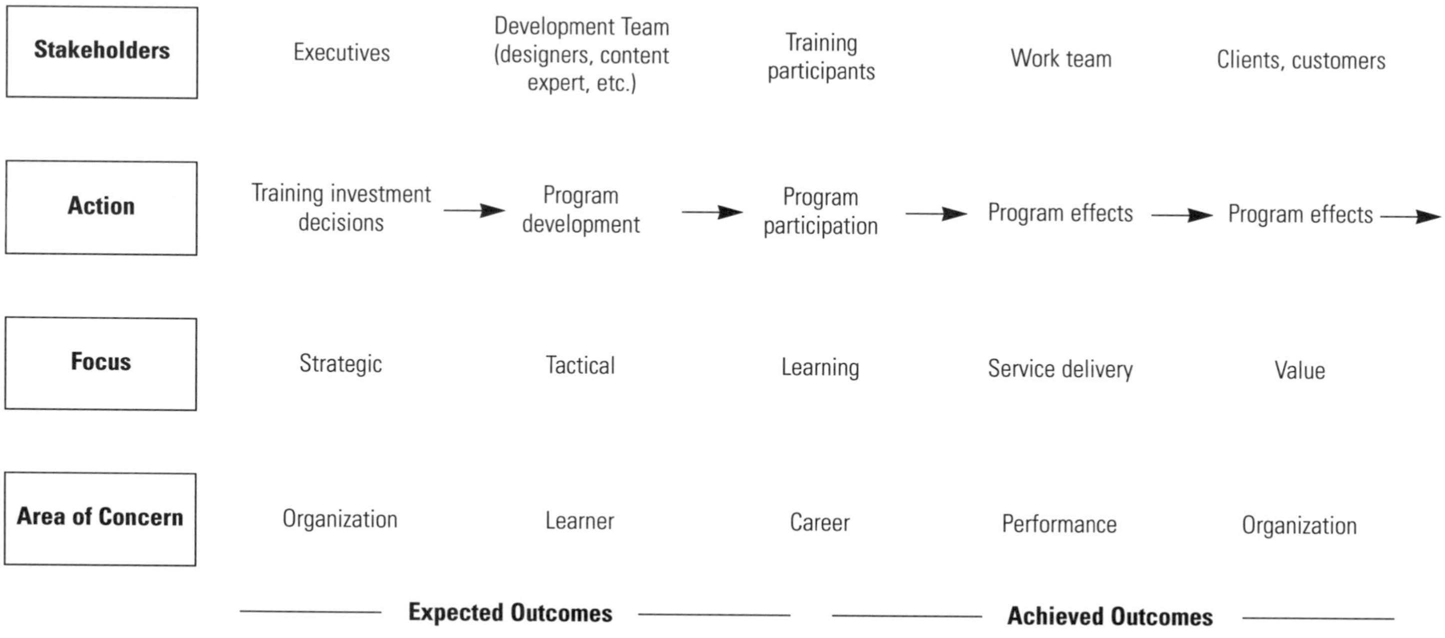

Stakeholders	Executives	Development Team (designers, content expert, etc.)	Training participants	Work team	Clients, customers
Action	Training investment decisions →	Program development →	Program participation →	Program effects →	Program effects →
Focus	Strategic	Tactical	Learning	Service delivery	Value
Area of Concern	Organization	Learner	Career	Performance	Organization

Expected Outcomes — **Achieved Outcomes**

drive day-to-day decisions about building a product. That focus may not be an exact replica of the executives' strategically focused mental model of the final product. Similarly, although the executive team's primary concern is strategy, its members have at least implicit tactical beliefs about the program, such as how it will be delivered and the types of activities. The result is that the arrows in figure 1 can portray either a potential linkage or a disconnect between stakeholders' groups. That is, the implicit mental models concerning strategy and tactics that any stakeholder group may hold vary between being quite similar (a linkage) to quite dissimilar (a disconnect) when compared to those of another stakeholder group. If stakeholders do not agree on a rigorous and explicit definition of the basis for evaluating the program, it is likely that the program cannot be evaluated, regardless of the methods used. Consequently, a basic premise of determining value should be that, the *evaluation effort must not only encompass post-training evaluation but also begin prior to the development of training. Further, the evaluation must be concerned with making explicit and then integrating the expectations of stakeholders across the lifecycle.*

Second, there is a dichotomy in figure 1 between those who play a dominant role in setting expectations and those who are the recipients of programs designed on the basis of those expectations. Mentally divide figure 1 in half vertically so that "executives" and "development team" appear on the left and the remaining stakeholder groups are on the right. On the left side, the strategic and tactical stakeholders will make decisions on the basis of what they want to accomplish, in other words, they will set the expectations for the program. On the right side are the stakeholders who will experience the effects of the program. Using an algebraic equation as a metaphor, the outcomes from a program ought to equal the intents of the program. In cases in which intents and outcomes do not match, an inequality exists. This inequality can be remedied by working to change one side of the equation or the other. In other words, modify the intents of the program or modify the program to achieve the intended outcomes. Therefore, a second premise is that *the value of a program ought to be judged on the basis of the degree of linkage between expected and achieved outcomes.*

In light of this view of the educational process, the methodological process becomes one of evaluating the linkages between the human transactions. Although the training event is certainly part of the transactions, the focus has to be on the human transactions involved in program development and delivery. The question then becomes, "How can these transactions be evaluated to determine the level of training value?" The methodology of concept mapping and pattern matching holds promise for addressing this need to value the return on the investment in education on the basis of this transactional model of the educational process.

An Example of a Concept Mapping and Pattern Matching Application
Procedures

The authors began implementation of this evaluation methodology with a school designed to develop new programming skills for experienced programmers. The school was one week long and relied extensively on a team-based approach to learning. Concept mapping was accomplished in four steps: (1) generate expectations, (2) sort the expectations, (3) rate the expectations, and (4) analyze the results and facilitate dialogue. Readers seeking a more detailed explanation of the methodology of concept mapping and pattern matching should read the articles by William Trochim listed at the conclusion of this chapter.

The training development team generated 66 statements that described the outcomes of the training program. These were detailed and specific statements of what a training participant will know or be able to do as a result of successful completion of the program. Next, developers, managers, and content experts were asked to complete a process that made explicit their mental model of the program and intended effects. Individuals worked alone and completed two tasks.

First, they sorted or organized each of the 66 outcomes into concepts. For the sorting task, statements were printed on individual cards[2] along with an identifying number. Nine participants were instructed to work individually and group the 66 statement cards into groups "in a way that makes sense to you." The only restrictions in this sorting task were that there could not be (a) 66 groups of one item each, (b) one group consisting of all 66 items, or (c) a "miscellaneous" group with multiple items (any item thought to be unique was to be put in its own separate group). After sorting the statements, each participant recorded the contents of each group by listing the statement identifying numbers along with a short label describing the contents of the group. In effect each stakeholder was describing his or her unique view of the structure of these training outcomes.

Second, individuals rated the degree of impact each outcome should have in the program. In the rating task, the statements were listed in questionnaire form, and each stakeholder was asked to rate each statement on a 5-point Likert-type response scale in terms of how important the statement is to the training program (1=relatively unimportant, and 5=extremely important). All of the statements had some degree of importance with respect to the program. Therefore, it was stressed that the rating should be considered a relative judgment of the importance of each item to all the other items brainstormed. As a consequence, a rating of one or relatively unimportant did not mean that an item was not important but was simply relatively less important than other items that represented other aspects of the training program. In this step each stakeholder was able to provide his or her unique perspective on the value associated with various aspects of the training program.

Analysis

The analytical task combined the unique and individually generated data from sorting and rating to create a group perspective of the training program. Aggregating the data generated in this process requires use of sophisticated statistical algorithms, multidimensional scaling, and cluster analysis as well as unique graphic portrayals of the results. Our use of an integrated software program[3] kept the statistical aspects of this process transparent to the participants in this process. However, we include some of the details here to provide the reader with a sense of the underlying rigor in this process. The concept mapping analysis begins with construction from the sort information of an NxN binary, symmetric matrix of similarities, X_{ij}. For any two items i and j, a 1 was placed in X_{ij} if the participant placed the two items in the same group; otherwise a 0 was entered. The total NxN similarity matrix, T_{ij}, was obtained by summing across the individual X_{ij} matrices. Thus, any cell in this matrix could take integer values between 0 and 9 (that is, the nine people who sorted the statements); the value indicates the number of people who placed the i,j pair in the same group. The total similarity matrix T_{ij} was analyzed using nonmetric multidimensional scaling (MDS) analysis with a two-dimensional solution. The analysis yielded a two-dimensional (x,y) configuration of the set of statements based on the criterion that statements grouped together most often are located more proximately in two-dimensional space, whereas those grouped together less frequently are further apart.

The x and y coordinates for each item were the input for hierarchical cluster analysis.[4] Using the x and y coordinates as input to the cluster analysis in effect forces the cluster analysis to partition the items into nonoverlapping clusters. There is no simple mathe-matical criterion by which a final number of clusters can be select-ed. The procedure followed here was to examine an initial cluster solution that, on average, placed five statements in each cluster. Then, successively lower and higher cluster solutions were examined, with a judgment made at each level about whether the merger or split of clusters seemed substantively reasonable. In this case, the seven-clus-ter solution preserved the most detail and yielded substantively in-terpretable clusters of statements.

Concept Mapping Results

The x and y coordinates of the 66 points were graphed in two dimensions. This point map displayed the location of all the train-ing outcomes on the basis of the stakeholders' perspectives. Outcomes closer to each other indicated that stakeholders' meanings were sim-ilar, whereas those that were far apart were quite different.

A "cluster map" was also generated, which partitioned the orig-inal 66 points enclosed by boundaries of seven clusters, or concepts. Finally, the rating data were averaged across persons for each item and each cluster. This rating information was depicted graphically in a cluster rating map, which showed the cluster average rating us-ing the third dimension (higher = more important). The evaluators then presented these results to the participant group and worked with them to identify a short text label indicative of the content for each of the seven clusters.

The result of the effort to set expectations was a map of the sev-en clusters of outcomes, as shown in figure 2. The concepts that emerged (for example, teamwork, prototype development, analysis[5]) repre-sented the interpretation of the specific ideas in each of these clus-ters. The location of each of the 66 separate outcomes (that is, the point map) is not shown because that level of detail is beyond the scope of this paper. However, as an example, the specific outcomes that clustered into a concept termed prototyping are shown. A sim-ilar level of detail exists within each of the clusters. Finally, the rel-ative importance of each of the concepts is indicated by the height (higher = more important). The height of each cluster results from the average importance value of each of the items contained in a cluster. These values resulted from the relative ratings of each stake-holder involved in this task. In effect, this concept map portrays the intent of this school as expressed by the combined expectations from multiple stakeholders.

Figure 2. Concept map of expected outcomes.

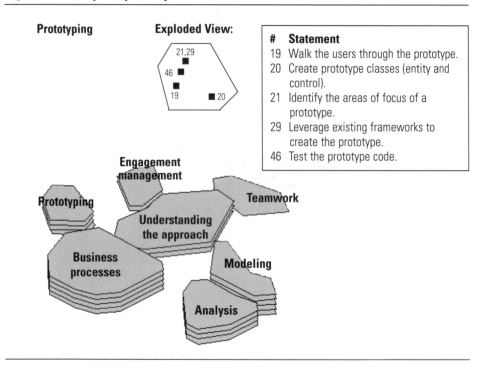

Prototyping

Exploded View:

#	Statement
19	Walk the users through the prototype.
20	Create prototype classes (entity and control).
21	Identify the areas of focus of a prototype.
29	Leverage existing frameworks to create the prototype.
46	Test the prototype code.

Pattern Matching Results

Assuming that the program's participants ought to be affected in a way that is consistent with the intent of the school (that is, the importance of each component), we obtained participant data on each of the 66 outcomes at the educational events. Although data could have been obtained in a variety of ways, we decided to directly ask each of the participants to indicate their level of learning on each of the 66 outcomes. At the initial test of the program (alpha test), five participants assessed their competence at the beginning and at the conclusion of the school.

Pattern matching assumes that a correspondence ought to exist between the intended emphases of the program and the observed gains. If the design of the program had the intended effects, the greatest gains in learning ought to be in those areas that were most emphasized (that is, most important) in the program (see figure 3). A visual comparison of the map in figure 2 (expectations based on program design) with the map in figure 3 (outcomes based on learning) shows that for the most part the patterns do match. Concepts that were more important (that is, had greater height) in the educational design (expectations) showed greater gains (that is, had greater height) in learning on the outcome map. The match suggests that the program was effective in achieving its aims. However, the match also showed several areas were not as closely aligned as desired. Analysis showed a decline and understanding the approach showed a gain. This information provided the development team with direction for work prior to additional testing.

In addition to the quick visual comparison of figures 2 and 3, a more exacting comparison was also used. In figure 4 the average value of each concept was plotted along an axis for expectations and along an axis for outcomes. These two axes were then placed in parallel and lines were drawn to connect corresponding clusters. In cases where relative outcomes matched expectations (linkage), the connecting lines were horizontal or nearly so. If all concepts were in alignment, the graph would resemble a ladder; we have coined the term *ladder graph* to describe these graphs. Likewise, lines crossing at steep angles portray a lack of linkage or relative disconnect between concepts. For example, two characteristics of the pattern in figure 4 are apparent. The outcome area understanding the approach had a stronger gain than was expected, and although analysis was an important area in

Figure 3. Impact of the program on learning outcomes.

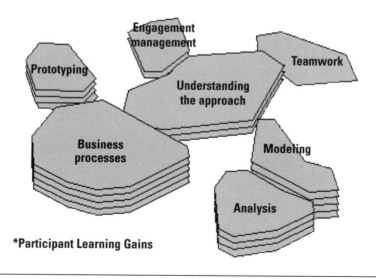

the design, this concept did not show a commensurate gain on the outcome side. Rather than a summary grade on performance, this type of analysis is more diagnostic and offers the development team a focus for dialogue about needed continuous improvements.

Subsequent evaluation efforts were aimed at obtaining feedback from participants three to six months after training, as shown in figure 5. Again we elected to ask past program participants (n=23) about their experience. These results showed that although program was generally effective, the match declined in several areas. Former participants did not feel as competent in the key technical skills that were desired from the course. Interviews suggested that the increased disconnects resulted from a lack of opportunities to apply newly learned skills. Additionally, the most notable change was the teamwork cluster, which suggests that this concept or skill area may be more important to job performance than expected at the outset of the program.

Implications of This Example for Program Development and Evaluation

There are several immediately apparent advantages to using the concept mapping and pattern matching approach to assessing the effects of a training program. First, the process involves all of the relevant stakeholder groups (for example, initiating executives, program developers, managers) in contributing input relevant to their perspectives. Second, because concept mapping is done when the training effort is just beginning, and is followed (through pattern matching) all the way through to outcome assessment, the process assures that there will be continuity from conception to outcome and consensus over time across the various stakeholder groups. Third, because the major products of the process are visual, they are readily understandable by the various stakeholder groups. Developers and initiators are more easily able to recall the important emphases in the training and how these are interrelated. They can easily summarize how the training is affecting outcomes, in specific topical areas as well as for the training program as a whole. Fourth, because the process is based on state-of-the-art statistical methods (although these are transparent to the participating stakeholders), there is a high degree of rigor and credibility in the results. Fifth, the results are useful both for providing detailed diagnostic feedback that suggests to development teams where improvements might be made and providing an assessment of the overall strength of the program effect. For example, it was clear from the initial concept mapping that although analysis was

Figure 4. Pattern match of expectations to learning outcomes.

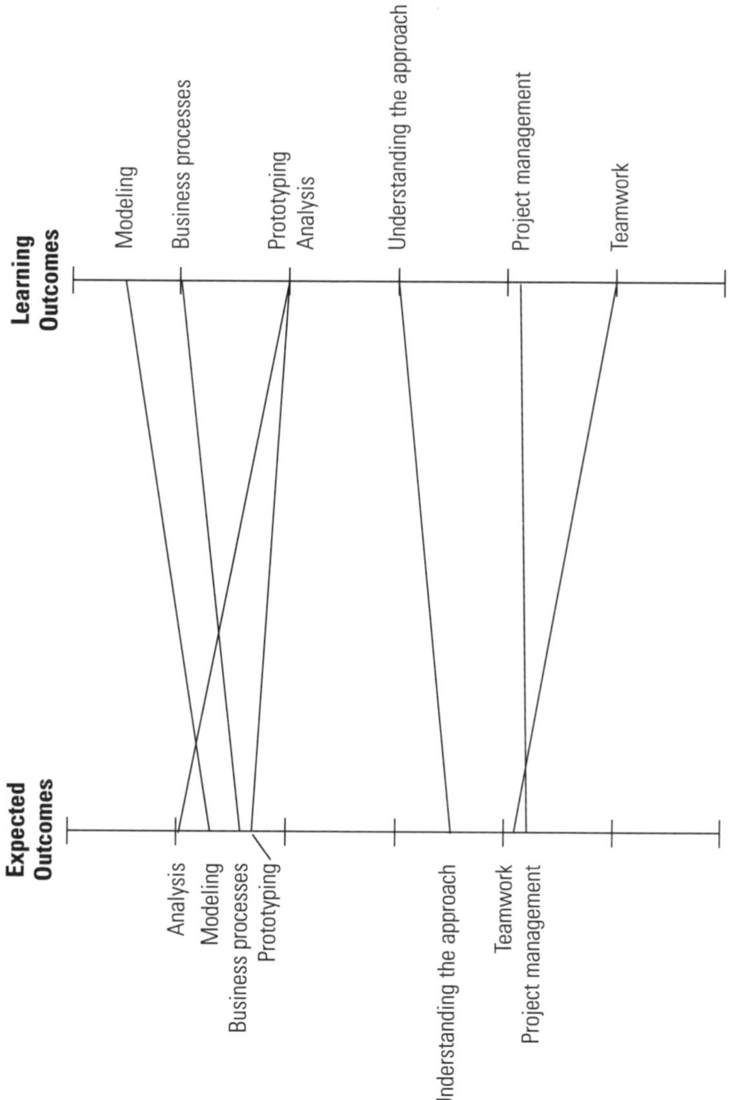

Figure 5. Pattern match of program design to job-related outcomes.

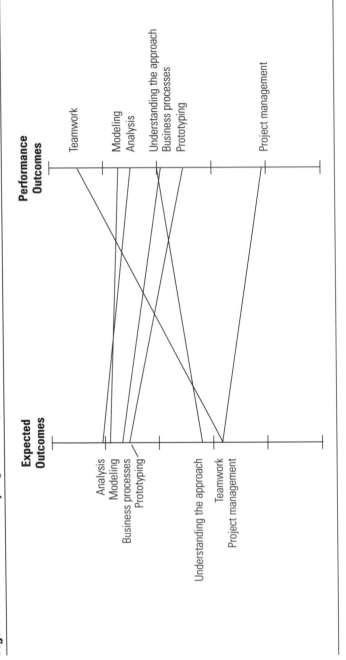

deemed the most important expectation for training, it ranked only fourth in importance in terms of observed gains. This suggested to the development team that they revisit how they were presenting material related to that topic, with the possibility that they might make it more salient in the next session of the training. Conversely, the evidence in the follow-up data indicated that the greatest long-term gains were in the area of teamwork. Although teamwork was rated next to last in importance, developers suggested that the current emphasis on teamwork in the course could be softened (while simultaneously adding emphasis in other more important areas) without any significant loss of desired outcome. At a more macro level, the linkages between the expected and observed outcomes suggest that on the whole the training was getting across the desired material.

Implications of This Methodology for Evaluating the Value of Educational Programs

The seminal points on evaluating the effects of training programs were made by Kirkpatrick, who introduced the concept of levels of evaluation. Kirkpatrick defined four levels: reaction, the degree to which a student liked a program; learning, the degree to which a student gained knowledge, skills, or changed attitudes; behavior, the individual's application of skills on the job; and results, improvement or decreasing problems for the organization. To say that Kirkpatrick's concept of levels resonated with the training community would be an understatement. Discussion of evaluative activities in training is often framed in terms of specific levels. In spite of the fact that many authors recommend moderate use of experimental methods, there is a strong interest in the field in demonstrating value by scientifically proving the economic return from training programs. However, not all programs are amenable to achieving the level of proof implied by experimental approaches. Now may be an opportune time to reconsider the definition of training value along with the utility of all levels, including Level 1.

First, the implicit meaning in levels is that higher levels of evaluation produce a more substantive conclusion than do lower levels. This implication has helped move the training community and our stakeholders away from quick reactions by students as a measure of value. However, it may have also moved the community away from gaining the proper perspective of those involved in the educational enterprise. In some cases, gaining the personal perspective of training participants can have more value than other measures. For example, in the transactional model, our concern is seeking input from training participants on their specific learning experiences. This is unlike asking students to react to features of the training event (for example, overall quality, timing, instructional materials) about which they would certainly have opinions but would lack the appropriate context to make a properly informed judgment. Training participants are not aware of the management decisions made during the development of the program. Some of these decisions may reflect trade-offs between the desire for optimization and the need to develop and deliver a product within a specified time at a specified cost. Further, a rigorous testing program could have been instituted to establish more valid measures of learning than self-report. However, the time and effort required would be high, and the additional value, as compared to self-report, low. As a result, students' self-assessment of their learning at the conclusion of the event was sufficient evidence to credibly demonstrate the value of the program.

Second, the need for Level 4 evaluation may be driving the field of training toward a focus on assessment strategies that assume that value can be proved through a measurement exercise. Evaluation methods must be responsive to a broad range of issues caused by the increasing complexity of the educational process. In business and industry, education is undergoing substantial change. For example, development teams that used to choose between lectures and self-study now must consider interactive multimedia, team-based learning, integrated performance support, and so on as well as the traditional approaches. Likewise, the business environment is undergoing radical change. *Customer-driven, reengineering, downsizing,* and *teaming* are just a few of the terms describing organizational changes businesses are using to respond to the marketplace. Within this complex and turbulent environment, the traditional approaches to evaluating the value of training also need to undergo some transformation. The methodology of concept mapping and pattern matching seems to have addressed the need to be responsive to the complexity of education in a business environment in a way that portrays evidence (or lack thereof) in a compelling manner. Furthermore, our experience is that this process has the potential to include other types of measures and rely on financial or other measures of organizational productivity to assess outcomes. That is, if the outcomes for concepts could be operationalized as objective measures (money, time, and so on), the pattern match between these outcomes and the expected impact of the program could be evaluated. Likewise, the use of the participants' reactions to a program also ought to be considered a valid assessment of the educational program. However, as we have demonstrated here, their reactions and those of other stakeholders' groups (for example, supervisors) should be given serious consideration if the goal is a compelling portrayal of value.

Conclusion

Although much of the effort in development and delivery of training programs seems justified and effective on an intuitive level, evidence to substantiate this intuition is, at best, sparse. And with the annual cost of training estimated at tens of billions of dollars, it should come as no surprise that the term *return-on-investment* has become the current hot topic in training. More surprising is the fact that the field has come this far without substantial evidence of what occurs as a result of an investment in education. Although this trend seems to be changing, much of the effort seems aimed at expanding the application of traditional research solutions such as experimentation. Although these traditional evaluation approaches will continue to have value for specific reasons on specific programs, addressing the scope of a multibillion-dollar figure or the value of multiple educational programs across a diverse organization will require more expansive thinking about the techniques of evaluation. In our work at Andersen Consulting Education we believe we have begun the process of redefinition and have successfully expanded methods to address training value. Perhaps most important, the concept mapping and pattern matching approach moves us away from the mentality of solving precut puzzles and toward the idea of viewing the training endeavor as a complex problem involving multiple stakeholder groups who bring different perspectives to the educational effort. Although not abandoning the goal of understanding how training affects the bottom line, the concept mapping and pattern matching approach rightly focuses our attention on achieving the return on our expectations that we had in mind when originally undertaking training development.

Questions for Discussion

1. The case suggests that evaluation of training programs requires both measures and the collaboration of stakeholders. In what situations, other than training, does this model seem appropriate?
2. If the evaluation specialists had been required to draw return-on-investment conclusions, how could the methodology used in this case have been utilized to encompass that need?

3. The results in this case are portrayed graphically. Although the graphs are data driven, tables of figures are not presented. How is this similar or different from other results you have seen? What benefits can you see in this approach to reporting?

4. The case emphasizes conceptualizing program impact through concept mapping. How does this differ from other evaluation efforts with which you are familiar?

The Authors

Daniel J. McLinden is director of evaluation and performance measurement for Andersen Consulting at the Center for Professional Education in St. Charles, Illinois. Over the course of his career in human resource development in business, his consulting efforts have included program evaluation, needs assessment, testing, and organizational assessment. His current focus is on conceptualizing program impact and the evaluation of investments in the development of human resources. Much of his current work in writing and presentations has focused on the importance of linking program conceptualization and evaluation. McLinden holds a doctorate in educational psychology from Northern Illinois University. He can be contacted at the following address: Andersen Consulting, Center for Professional Education, 1405 North Fifth Avenue, St. Charles, IL 60174-1264; e-mail: daniel.j.mclinden@ac.com.

William M. K. Trochim is a Professor at Cornell University and the creator of the concept mapping and pattern matching methods, the programmer of The Concept System computer program, and a co-founder of Concept Systems, Inc. He received his Ph.D. in methodology and evaluation research from the Department of Psychology at Northwestern University. He specializes in program evaluation and planning at Cornell, is a faculty member in the Department of Human Service Studies, and is a member of the graduate fields of education, epidemiology, and human development and family studies. Trochim has published widely on evaluation and social research methods, and is an internationally recognized expert in evaluation methods, including conceptualization approaches, causal assessment, experimental design, and the theory of validity in research.

Resources and References
Statistics and Research Methodology

Everitt, B. (1980). *Cluster Analysis*. New York: Halsted Press.

Kruskal, J.B., and M. Wish. (1978). *Multidimensional Scaling*. Beverly Hills, CA: Sage.

Rosenberg, S., and M.P. Kim. (1975). "The Method of Sorting as a Data Gathering Procedure in Multivariate Research." *Multivariate Behavioral Research, 10,* 489–502.

Weller, S.C., and A.K. Romney. (1988). *Systematic Data Collection.* Newbury Park, CA: Sage.

Training Evaluation and Impact Assessment

Kirkpatrick, D.L. (1987). "Evaluation." In R.L. Craig and L.R. Bittell (editors), *Training and Development Handbook* (pp. 301–319). New York: McGraw-Hill.

McLinden, D.J. (1995). "Proof, Evidence, and Complexity: Understanding the Impact of Training and Development in Business." *Performance Improvement Quarterly, 8*(3), 3–18.

McLinden, D.J., M.J. Davis, and D.E. Sheriff. (1993). "Impact on Financial Productivity: A Study of Training Effects on Consulting Services." *Human Resource Development Quarterly. 4*(4), 367–375.

Phillips, J.J. (1994). *Return on Investment in Human Resource Development: Cases on the Economic Benefits of HRD.* Alexandria, VA: American Society for Training & Development.

Phillips, J.J. (1997). *Return on Investment in Training and Performance Improvement Programs.* Houston: Gulf.

Levels of Training Investments

Training Budgets. (1995). "1995 Industry Report." *Training, 32*(10) 41–48.

Training Budgets. (1996). "1996 Industry Report." *Training, 33*(10) 41–49.

Concept Mapping and Pattern Matching

Concept mapping software: Concept Systems, Inc. 118 Prospect Street, Suite 309, Ithaca, NY 14850; 607.272.1206.

Trochim, W.M.K. (1989a). "An Introduction to Concept Mapping for Planning and Evaluation." *Evaluation and Program Planning, 12,* 1–16.

Trochim, W.M.K. (1989b). "Outcome Pattern Matching and Program Theory." *Evaluation and Program Planning, 12,* 355–366.

Notes

[1] Readers interested in additional research methods should consult Phillips (1997) for methods of estimating financial variables.

[2] At the time this project was conducted, we used the paper version of the process described here. Subsequently, we have used the Windows version of Concept Systems© Inc. software for other evaluation projects and have, for the most part, utilized an online version of the sorting and rating tasks contained in the software.

[3]Results reported here used concept mapping software by Concept Systems© Inc. Readers interested in additional information on the software should contact the software company. Readers interested in the statistical processes should consult the suggested readings at the end of this chapter.

[4]Concept Systems© software uses Ward's method as the basis for defining a cluster

[5]Due to the proprietary nature of the content, the specific technical skill areas are not described completely.

About the Series Editor

Jack J. Phillips has more than 27 years of professional experience in human resources and management and has served as training and development manager at two Fortune 500 firms, been president of a regional federal savings bank, and was management professor at a major state university.

In 1992, Phillips founded Performance Resources Organization, an international consulting firm specializing in human resources accountability programs. Phillips consults with clients in the United States, Canada, England, Belgium, Germany, Sweden, Italy, South Africa, Mexico, Venezuela, Malaysia, Indonesia, Hong Kong, Australia, and Singapore. His clients include Motorola, Andersen Consulting, State Street Bank, UPS, Nortel, Canadian Imperial Bank of Commerce, DHL Worldwide Express, Singapore Airlines, Caltex Pacific, First Union National Bank, Exxon, and Federal Express. He has also consulted with several state and federal government agencies in the United States, Canada, Europe, and Asia.

A frequent contributor to management literature, Phillips has authored or edited 20 books including *Return on Investment in Training and Performance Improvement* (1997), *Accountability in Human Resource Management* (1996), *Handbook of Training Evaluation and Measurement Methods* (3d edition, 1997), *Measuring Return on Investment* (vol. 1, 1994; vol. 2, 1997), *Conducting Needs Assessment* (1995), *The Development of a Human Resource Effectiveness Index* (1988), *Recruiting, Training and Retaining New Employees* (1987), and *Improving Supervisors' Effectiveness* (1985), which won an award from the Society for Human Resource Management. Phillips has written more than 100 articles for professional, business, and trade publications.

Phillips has earned undergraduate degrees in electrical engineering, physics, and mathematics from Southern Polytechnic State University and Ogelthorpe University; a master's in decision sciences from Georgia State University; and a Ph.D. in human resource management from the University of Alabama. In 1987, he won the Yoder-Heneman

Personnel Creative Application Award from the Society for Human Resource Management. He is an active member of several professional organizations.

Jack Phillips can be reached at Performance Resources Organization, P.O. Box 380637, Birmingham, AL 35238-0637; phone: 205. 678.9700; fax: 205.678.8070.